# The Substance of Play

## Principles of Pre-primary Teaching

K.T. Margaret

Orient BlackSwan

THE SUBSTANCE OF PLAY: PRINCIPLES OF PRE-PRIMARY TEACHING

**ORIENT BLACKSWAN PRIVATE LIMITED**

*Registered Office*
3-6-752 Himayatnagar, Hyderabad 500 029, Telangana, India
e-mail: centraloffice@orientblackswan.com

*Other Offices*
Bengaluru, Bhopal, Chennai, Guwahati, Hyderabad, Jaipur, Kolkata, Lucknow, Mumbai, New Delhi, Noida, Patna, Vijayawada


First published 2018

026582
05122017

ISBN 978-93-5287-139-1

*Typeset in*
Adobe Garamond Pro 11.5/13.5
by Shine Graphics, Delhi

*Printed at*
Yash Printographics, Noida

*Published by*
Orient BlackSwan Private Limited
3-6-752, Himayatnagar,
Hyderabad 500 029, Telangana, India
Email: info@orientblackswan.com

I believe there are those who consider teaching and learning to not only be the art of sharing knowledge but also an act of love which encourages a freedom of spirit. This book is dedicated to them and to those who value their call to be teachers.

# Publisher's Acknowledgements

*69 Bank Street Publications*, vol. 3, no. 5, 1937. "Meeting Reality", by Terry Spitalny.

*69 Bank Street Publications*, vol. 1, no. 3, 1934. "A Dream for the Nursery Years", by Barbara Biber.

*69 Bank Street Publications*, vol. 2, no. 8, 1936. "Nursery School as the Beginning of Education", by Barbara Biber.

A. S. Neill, *Summerhill* (pages 11, 92), published in 1980 by Penguin Books. Worldwide copyright rests with Zoë Neill Readhead.

Though the author has tried to recreate events, locales and conversations from her memories, the names of individuals have been changed in order to maintain their anonymity.

# Contents

# Acknowledgements

Nadya Ornstein Pant

The basis of my work was given to me by Ms Nadya Ornstein Pant, a pioneer in the field of education for young children. I owe my gratitude to her for making me who I am today as a teacher.

Mr Prakash Patil, the managing trustee of Vidya Mytri Trust, offered his complete support in helping me finish this book. The team from Wipro helped to form the Vidya Mytri Trust and located the reliable Ms Lavanya Murali, who aided with the documentation of this manual. They also provided invaluable financial support. I thank Prakash Patil, Lavanya Murali and the Wipro team for their generous help.

I also thank the members of Jo Mythri Trust, whose encouragement and support helped me to continue and complete this work.

Finally, when I approached Orient BlackSwan for publication, I received a very positive response from Ms Padmaja Anant. This gave me the confidence to go ahead with this work. I am also grateful to the reviewer commissioned by the publisher for suggestions for improving the book; it helped me see things clearly.

The spirit of the Almighty moves through all of us involved in this work to bring a transformation in the hearts and minds of young learners.

# Introduction

Modern psychology has enabled parents and teachers to recognise the importance of the type of education that pre-primary children should receive. Besides this, many educators have contributed insightful works on the development of young children and their patterns of learning. This has benefitted many teachers working with young children.

I have acquired a degree of clarity from such works and also from my visits to playschool centres during the early 1970s. Here, I briefly examine some of the more common and established methods of education for pre-primary children.

## Maria Montessori (1870–1952)

The Montessori method of education is a popular method used worldwide for teaching young children.

The nursery school where I taught in the 1970s used Montessori equipment but not the Montessori method. The materials were colourful, attractive, precise and orderly arranged. The children enjoyed playing with them.

This approach focuses on three basic phases. Phase one involves a series of exercises on practical life (everyday living) which are precisely worked out and demonstrated. For example, the teacher and the children might discuss interesting things which happened the previous day. Or, the children might clean and dust the rooms, polish their shoes, practice buttoning clothes. The idea is to have the children perform a simple, daily task. Phase two involves sensory-motor learning, where students have to complete exercises on sensory discrimination using Montessori equipment. No sense is neglected, and materials may focus on more than just one sense. 'The third phase develops manual dexterity into writing; visual and auditory integrations into reading; and, most elaborated of all, a complex of relationships into physical and mathematical concepts' (*Montessori in Perspective* 70).

This method of education can lead to advanced academic achievements; by the age of 5 or 6, these children are learning to read, write and solve mathematical problems which students of another method of education only learn when older.

The Montessori method introduces concepts and symbols which are basic components of any educational experience. Activities are repeated every day, and due to the self-corrective aspect of Montessori material—which involves only *one* correct way or sequence to solve an exercise—children gain great satisfaction from successfully completing their tasks. The environment allows children to freely interact with their learning materials, while the focus is largely on cognitive development.

The children work in a non-competitive atmosphere. There are no rewards, no grades, no reprimands and no praises. The necessity for caring for each individual child is stressed. Children learn with interest, joy and eagerness.

The educational philosophy preached by Johann Heinrich Pestalozzi, Friedrich Fröbel and Jean Jacques Rousseau—that children learn through experience, through seeing and feeling real objects—and the revolutionary concept developed by John Dewey's 'learning by doing', strongly influenced modern educational thoughts and practices. Maria Montessori applied these philosophies to her system of education with a focus on the importance of sensory-motor learning. The primary aim of Montessori education is to foster a child's competence and personality.

This method of education may provide invaluable material and experience for the earnest teacher. In my case, it created a satisfactory atmosphere of learning in my classes, though I always felt something was missing.

## Margaret McMillan (1860–1931)

McMillan was influential in setting in motion the American Nursery School movement in the 1900s. Her years of experience working with young children in a slum district of London convinced her that a poor learning environment resulted in a lack of cognitive growth in children. She observed that those children who were deprived of healthy emotional stimuli displayed a remarkable mental apathy. This mental apathy exhibited itself through poor drawings, poor vocabulary, a general lack of interest, an inability to think clearly, a lack of clear mental images and a lot of confused experiences.

McMillan stressed the importance of a child's emotional development. She integrated emotional and sensory-motor development into her curriculum and believed children benefitted from working in groups—sharing material and completing activities together. It was her opinion that providing children with a healthy environment and allowing them to express their thoughts and feelings through external media—via drawings, interacting in a group or talking to a teacher—would enrich cognitive growth. She also emphasised the importance of working with the children's families and visiting their homes to help reverse any negative effects of social deprivation. Through such work, teachers could encourage a dialogue between parents and children where they discussed their family history, perhaps by talking about grandparents or great grandparents and trying to recall as many details about them and their lives. This would help children treasure relationships, learn that they belonged to people worth remembering and realise that life is not trivial.

During my time as a teacher, I noticed that children from a poor economic background often suffered from not experiencing the rich and healthy bonds of a nurturing relationship. This, in turn, negatively affected their mental, intellectual, emotional and social growth. I found a sense of belonging to a place or family was vital to the positive development of a child's personality. One can only learn in an atmosphere of love, and love involves a relationship.

## The American Nursery School

Around 1921, only five nursery schools were operating in America. One of them was Bank Street School, and another was Teachers

College of Columbia University. The Walden School (1914) and Play School (1914) were two others I have heard of and read about. These nursery schools made important contributions to the education of young children.

It was also around this time, between 1920 to 1930, that Freud's writings became popular and influenced the field of education, resulting in teachers and educators gaining an awareness of the importance of emotional and social development in young children. It was given more attention and grew to become a clearly defined goal of nursery schools.

> Probably the most challenging and at least temporarily disrupting and explosive concept about young children were the psychoanalytic contribution that children have feelings. Freud's treatment of psychotic adults convinced him that powerful feelings of anger, anxiety and fear are present in early childhood, even in infancy. These are potential influences of the child's ability to learn and to be his most effective self. (*Montessori in Perspective* 52)

Freud's concept, however, was not unanimously accepted. There were sharply varying responses: 'Some reacted by total acceptance and a consequent gearing of goals and curriculum to the recognition of the dynamic nature of children's responses and learning. Others reacted by total rejection and denial; still others with the entire uneasy and partially understood acceptance' (52).

Those who accepted this concept did not consider themselves to be both teacher and therapist. They were aware that children's learning, influenced by feelings, needed limits. Young children needed direction and guidance from adults in order to understand and manage their feelings. This did not mean the elimination of frustrating experiences by substituting them with only gratifying experiences. With this clarity, children were permitted to play freely without being disturbed and were allowed to express their fantasy life though play. The teacher was an observer attentive to what the child did and said, and who, when needed, guided the child. 'Even the view of play material changed. Mixing water and sand, modelling with clay and pasting paper cutouts together become important activities for the mastery of anal instincts' (21).

What I understood from the Bank Street approach was that thoughts and emotions are interconnected and are interacting spheres of development. Reading some of the publications by *69 Bank Street* about education during the 1930s and 1940s helped clarify the importance of emotional development in young children and its effect on their personality development.

I was impressed by this passage in an article from the third volume of *69 Bank Street*:

> In this social situation we are allowed to see the bad as well as the good, the negative as well as the positive. And we as teachers feel that we cannot damn the bad and the negative as irretrievably unsocial, because in group after group, year after year, all the behavior that has been called bad or negative invariably manifests itself. It must be a natural part of growth. Now we recognize an instinctual need in the child to express what has been called by some evil and ugly, by others unsociable. It seems to me there can be no better time than now, at two and three and four and five, to express this evil and ugly and negative; so that perhaps at twenty or thirty the individual will not be ostracized as unsocial because of behavior which is infantile and childish. He had the chance to be a four-year-old—he was one—and then he was through. (Spitalny)

These and other findings from across the globe contributed to the realisation that a child's pre-primary school years were vital and formative. An urgent need for preschool education developed around the 1990s, perhaps due to the social and economic changes of the time. The demand for nursery schools was driven by the preschool movement, which in turn was influenced by Freud's hypothesis on childhood. The education of young children changed from being subject-centric to child-centric, and from there to the development of various aspects of a child, from sensory-motor development to emotional development, and then from there to the inclusion of family and parents as part of the personality development process.

## Play Activities

In India, during the latter half of the twentieth century, the importance of preschool education was recognised and influenced by the thoughts and works of Gijubhai Badheka—who wrote *Divaswapna*—and Tarabai Modak, among others, who were considered to be pioneers of the preschool movement. 'Preschool' was formally documented as Early Childhood Care and Education (ECCE). The ECCE framework included two components: Early Childhood Development (ECD), which dealt with the all-round development of a child, and Early Childhood Education (ECE), which focused on preschool education for children between the ages of three to six. Maria Montessori's visit to India in 1936 had a notable influence on preschool education in the country as it led to the establishment of preschool education centres in Gujarat. A request made by Mahatma Gandhi, when Maria Montessori visited him in 1937, to 'Indianise' her method and make it more easily available and accessible to rural India, resulted in free basic-education centres in rural parts of the country.

The National Curriculum Framework (NCF 2005), in its position paper on ECE, described the early childhood stage as a critical period during which lifelong foundations are laid for a child's all-round development. A preschool curriculum was thus formed based on the insights and philosophies of Western thinkers and practitioners like Rousseau, Fröbel, Dewey, Montessori, and Indian thinkers like Gandhi, Tagore, Badheka and Modak. It also incorporated ideas taken from scholars in development psychology like Jean Piaget, Jerome Bruner and Lev Vygotsky.

They emphasised play as a child's natural mode of learning. Based on this, elaborate activities were listed and classified according to different domains of development. These domains were all interrelated. Development and learning were integrated.

The curriculum includes play activities, group activities, sensory training, hand work, artistic activities, personal hygiene, music, learning activities and informal activities. It is an activity-oriented, play-way curriculum, and its aim is the appropriate practice of activities which cover all areas of development—physical, social, emotional and cognitive.

Assessments are purely qualitative and based on observations recorded by a teacher. The ECCE curriculum has 'play' as a basis for learning. The day begins with songs, group movements and physical exercises. The daily schedule helps put into action all these activities, and there are specific timings for different activities.

Preschool education is also provided by voluntary and non-governmental organisations. They play a vital role in providing preschool education for children from socially and economically backward communities. I have observed that children who have attended these centres before moving on to primary school have performed better than those who did not. Most of these alternative programmes function effectively. There are many voluntary and NGO programmes, including Ruchika, Self Employed Women's Association (SEWA) and Pratham, to mention a few. Some universities also have laboratory nursery schools attached to them, particularly those with a Department of Child Development.

I visited two playschools in the late 1970s. One was the playschool of the educational consultant Indira Swaminathan, which was located in Bangalore and which I still fondly remember. In those days this playschool used most of the play activities mentioned above. It was a centre where children moved about freely and worked happily. The school had a pleasant atmosphere.

In a good playschool, children happily move from one activity to another, free of tension and involved in their tasks. The teacher carefully guides them, offering assistance in a friendly manner when they need help. No doubt children take in a lot, learn a lot and are equipped for primary-school education.

But in such play centres, does an individual child get the time and space he needs to sort out problems relevant to his age group, or reconcile himself with his feelings and reflect on his actions to gain self-confidence? For example, let us imagine a child's inner urge compels her to draw, and to work on her drawing for as long as she needs to, however many days that may be. During that time she reflects on her work but does not participate in any other activities.

Will we, as teachers, be able to respect the child's instincts—trust her and give her the time and space she needs to reflect on her work—or will we be upset that the child is wasting her time doing nothing? Will we feel that she hasn't learnt anything by choosing not to participate in any of the developmental learning activities which we adults have provided? Here I share an incident which happened in the nursery class where I used to teach.

Shankar and Navin, two four-year-olds, had a fight while they were playing with wooden building blocks. A group of twenty-five children of this age were involved in different activities in different parts of the building. I helped them both see their mistake and moved on to another group. The principal of our school came to visit the nursery section. She saw Shankar sitting in the dolls' corner, doing nothing. She said, 'One little boy is sitting in the dolls' corner. He is not taking part in any of the activities. He is wasting his time. Why is he not interested?'

I told her, 'I do not know, will you kindly ask him why he is wasting his time? I cannot leave this group right now.'

She hurried to speak with Shankar. When she returned, she said, 'I am surprised. The child told me he had a fight with another boy. He is sitting and thinking about it. He felt he was at fault and he wants to apologise to his friend.'

So, in this instance, the child was not actually wasting his time but was going through a very important learning process.

In our country, Freudian insight on the behaviour of children has not yet been used or applied in early childhood education centres. Instead, the activities and experiments focus exclusively on external or structural characteristics.

Every educational endeavour seeks to answer a few questions:

- What is it that we want from education?
- What should education do for our children?
- What are our dreams, ambitions, hopes, values, and attitudes in life for our children?
- Where will these expectations of ours take us and our children?

When we are unable to master powerful emotions like fear, jealousy, anger and hatred, these emotions threaten to overwhelm us and our societies in devastating and destructive forms. That is when we hear: 'It's mine—just for me, for my family, for my country.' How do we learn to share possessions and love? How do we learn to share ourselves? How do we help ourselves and our children do this difficult and necessary job? How do we help them grow up emotionally healthy in increasingly acquisitive societies which value possessions more than people? How will we form a society for mutual aid? For it is only through mutual cooperation that we will be able to continue to live on this planet and continue to develop and expand our children's spirits. If we believe in this and if this is what we want for our children, then this book may offer satisfactory solutions.

The methodology in this book was developed from what I learnt and understood from Nadya's teaching classes, from her suggestions and guidance, and also from her direct involvement during my time spent teaching. A lot of the material has been obtained from my experiences teaching three- to six-year-old children from different backgrounds, listening to their conversations and observing them while they engage with different activities.

The syllabus and contents of this manual may appear similar to what is given in any other teaching manual, handbook or guide. It may appear too simple—lacking in challenge or competition. In this book, however, I seek to arrive at methods and techniques that help fulfil teaching objectives some of us have developed for future generations. This book is thus an attempt at compiling these teaching-learning techniques, syllabuses, and lesson plans to help provide educators with guidelines on how to observe and record certain aspects of a child's growth and how to evaluate a child's development.

These methods are suitable for three- to five-year-old children and have been divided into the following age groups:

- 3 to 3+ years
- 4 to 4+ years
- 5 to 5+ years

The methods suggested in this book, however, are not instant recipes or magical formulae that can be applied to a group of children with immediate results. The teacher has to internalise the whole concept by going through the process herself. She has to discover the child in her—recognise, understand and accept its needs and patiently live with it. Only then will the adult know how to deal with the children in her care, how to apply these techniques in her classroom, and will enjoy seeing the beautiful growth process of each individual child she is teaching.

I have written two books: *The Open Classroom: A Journey through Education*, and *Learning for Life*. I believe readers would benefit from reading both books. In *The Open Classroom: A Journey through Education*, I describe my journey which led to me developing various teaching methodologies. It provides a complete picture of my explorations in education and how my notion of education developed and changed. *Learning for Life* describes the application of a methodology for children from slums and also offers an introspection of the limitations I faced in my work as a teacher.

I felt it important and necessary to share my learnings with a wider audience. I also recognised the limitation of communicating these learnings through a book, which does not give much scope for a dialogue. I would be glad to get in touch with and learn from interested readers.

I have so far not come across any material which provides detailed practical guidance on this aspect of education. I believe there are many young teachers who are searching for a deeper understanding of the processes of education, and through this book I hope to share with them the methodologies I have developed.

# 1

# The Aim of Education

Any process of education has a definite aim that it seeks to accomplish. This chapter outlines what I consider to be the primary aim of education. The methodology which I developed and put into practice, and which I elaborate on in this book, was created with the intention of fulfilling this aim.

For me, the aim of education is to make a great effort to develop a human being who is at peace with himself and his fellow human beings in his community and society. It should develop someone who is able to positively and generously share his skills with others. This, I believe, is the meaning of personality development, which is the aim of education.

What needs to be developed in order for a person to acquire such a positive personality?

A person must gain the ability to look at themselves honestly and with humility. They must recognise their negative and positive traits and accept themselves for who they are. They should patiently bear with and try to reduce their negative traits while working hard to build on their positive traits. Such a person experiences a freedom of spirit.

This involves discovering one's true self. Who am I? What am I? What are my inherent skills and talents which make me unique? What is the purpose of my life? How do I develop these skills constructively and how do I share them generously? What are my personal hindrances and obstacles? How do I work on them? What are the values which I need to develop in order to fulfil my purpose in life?

This may all sound very idealistic. Yes, logically it appears so, but in reality these are the questions we face in life and they directly affect our aspirations. For a child, this aim of education appeals to their life and soul, what they are searching for, and they willingly respond to it. Each one makes as great an effort as possible. My responsibility as a teacher and as an adult is to provide an environment to positively develop their personality.

The reader may be wondering how this aim of education fits in a manual for teaching children between the ages of 3 to 5. Is it possible to achieve this aim with such a young group of children? Isn't it too ambitious and impractical?

While it is not my intention to achieve this aim within such a short period of time, I think it is important, when we take up the responsibility to teach young children, to ask ourselves these types of questions. What is it that I want to teach these young children? Why do I want to teach them this? What is my aim? If we want to build a house, don't we have dreams and plans first? We want the house to be a beautiful one, a comfortable one, a sturdy one, and one that is built on a solid foundation. Shouldn't we have a vision about what we want our children to be when they grow up? Without such foresight, planning and teaching becomes meaningless, and I dare say the work is a waste of time for both the teacher and the child.

Our vision should be that our children are as true to themselves as possible, behaving with a freedom of spirit. Keeping this in mind, we must carefully prepare activities and lay a strong, deep foundation for our children's future. So nursery years are the period during which we lay this foundation which will help us accomplish this aim of education.

To lay a good foundation we need to know the nature of these children. Who are they? How does their growth and development take place? What are their needs and experiences during this process? What are their satisfactions, pleasures and achievements? What are their frustrations, tensions, fears and anxieties? What makes them feel guilty? What are the hurdles they face in their growth process? What kind of freedom should we give them for their personality development? When and how do we give them guidance, support, encouragement and the discipline they need for their development and growth? If we know all this—and have an understanding of our own childhood experiences of growing up—then we will be able to lay a good foundation. That is, we will be able to provide a rich and meaningful environment for our children to healthily grow.

The foremost requirement of such a rich and healthy environment is something I mentioned in *The Open Classroom*:

> First, children need honest, warm, affectionate, protective relationships with people who are close and important to them. They need to associate with people who will allow them to grow up to become their own true selves. They need reliable adults who will stand by them, accept and guide them in their growth process. This means that they need understanding and support from adults, while learning to control their impulses and express their emotions. This in turn will help them develop healthy attitudes and values in life, towards themselves and towards others. (11)

Our belief in the character of a child is necessary to help the child develop their freedom of spirit. The child should believe they are accepted, loved and valued as a person. This should be so even if the teacher rejects any undesirable behaviour in order to help the child develop a positive manner of behaviour. The following situation occurred when I was a teacher: Little Moksha, who was four-and-a-half years old, told her friends, 'Miss M loves us, but she doesn't like what we do.' When her friends discussed this in their group, the child told her friends that 'Miss M is a big bad wolf.' A lot of wisdom and understanding in that expression. Yes, we should love the children, but dislike their undesirable behaviour.

A. S. Neill said, 'Education should produce children who are at once individuals and community persons' (11). 'Children should be given a chance to grow in freedom. The bestowal of freedom is the bestowal of love. And only love can save the world' (92). Freedom is not letting loose. It is an inner discipline which enables a person to make responsible choices which they live with. Freedom is not doing whatever I want, whenever I want, according to my whims and fancies. It is not an attitude of 'I know everything, I am the master of my life.' This attitude is destructive to one's self and society.

As I mentioned in *The Open Classroom*, 'Children need to be given opportunities to explore, discover and develop their inner selves. They need time and space to explore their environment, discover their potential and develop a creative relationship with it. In the process they will learn to value and respect other people in society' (11).

Reading the experiences and experiments of teachers and educators, and books on the education of young children, I realised that all of them have expressed similar concerns about the importance of the nursery years and nursery education. All of them agree that it is through play that a child learns and develops his or her personality. Play is the most pivotal of all aspects of development of a child.

From these readings I gathered a lot of valuable material about teaching young children and how children learn. I have used this knowledge generously while writing this manual. But it is Nadya's insight into young children's behaviour and learning that I have imbibed and adopted in my methodology and in my teaching. The reason for this could be that I had a personal learning interaction with Nadya.

In the chapters which follow I try to explain the methodology and selection of teaching activities; how such activities are presented and what is their effect on the children—that is, the joy and surprise the child experiences, and the child's gradual blossoming into a beautiful person. I also discuss the limitations, frustrations and knowledge I gained from both the positive and negative experiences of this process. As I stated in *The Open Classroom*:

> The larger aim of this work is to help children build a strong base by involving the mind, heart, body and spirit during the four or five years of their early schooling. This, I believe, will help them to develop their whole personality and enable them to learn with minimum dependence on the teacher. At the same time, it will help develop their ability to interact spontaneously with the adult teacher, share the learning experience, and think and act creatively and constructively. (9)

Education is not an impersonal 'me' teaching an impersonal 'you,' but a process of evolution taking place within both the teacher and [the student]. Three factors—relationships, spirituality and work—form a complex whole in the process of education. By evolution I mean a gradual process of opening up, through which a child's inner self builds a relationship with the outer world. (13)

# 2

# The Basis of My Methodology

The basis of my methodology comes from *Outline*, by Nadya, which is an unpublished record of observations of young children's behaviour from a psychoanalytic point of view.

I realise that if this manual is to make sense to its reader, and be of help to teachers and parents of young children, then I need to provide the reason why I chose this material as the basis of my work.

For this I start with the questions: Who is Nadya? How did she come to so greatly influence my work?

Nadya Ornstein Pant was a Russian Jew who settled in America. She was born on 22 February 1900. She taught at the Walden School, New York, in the 1920s and 1930s. She was a teacher with a lot of experience in understanding the behaviour of young children and how they learn. One could say she was a researcher who tried to discover the child in every person. And, though unknown to the world, she was a pioneer in the field of education for young children. Unfortunately, her work was not published. She married an Indian scientist, Dr Bola Pant, from Uttar Pradesh. They lived in Bangalore and she was an educational consultant at a nursery school which I joined in 1970. She left Bangalore in 1984 and relocated to Uttar Pradesh, where Bola was living at the time. She died there, in 1989.

Nadya was my guide and mentor and she helped me understand myself and the nature and behaviour of young children. This enriched my teaching and learning skills. My relationship with her played a big role in my teaching career as she offered a unique approach to education and gave me the courage to implement that approach in my classes.

She believed in Freudian psychology and psychoanalysis, and she herself underwent psychoanalysis. In *The Open Classroom* I discuss how:

> The extraordinary insights of Freudian psychoanalysis in the West at the turn of the century brought about some radical changes in formal education. Sigmund Freud's theory of psychoanalysis and above all his recognition of the sexuality of children sent shock waves through Europe before being taken seriously. A few groups of teachers in Western schools courageously adapted psychoanalytical concepts in their teaching. (x)

Nadya and her team of teachers at the Walden School was one such group who courageously adapted the psychoanalytic concepts of Freud in their teaching, especially for students between the ages of three to six. I learnt these concepts from Nadya.

'They paid great attention to the emotional needs of the child, and stressed the importance of mental health for healthy personality development [. . .] They brought out valuable materials on education especially pertaining to the behaviour patterns and modes of learning among young children' (x).

Before she left for Uttar Pradesh in 1984, Nadya gave me a copy of her *Outline*. Since it is unpublished material she developed with regards to observing and recording aspects of growth in children, I thought it best to share with the readers a sample page as well as some important notes. See page 47, Figure 1 for the sample page, and see page 285 for her notes.

There are valuable teaching materials here which should be of use to readers who are serious about learning and discovering the behaviour patterns of young children, and the effect certain methodologies have on children's learning and personality development.

This material has been lying idle on my bookshelf for years, used only by me as a reference for my work. After going through a reviewer's feedback, it suddenly dawned on me that her material should not lie idle—Nadya had a purpose for giving it to me. I remember her telling me, in her teaching sessions, that what she was giving me was not just for me but had to be shared with other teachers. Perhaps it could be used by research workers in this field of education to develop valuable materials which Nadya was unable to complete. I feel the time is ripe to share her work as we are in a period in the history of education when we adults—both teachers and parents—are struggling to cope with the emotional problems of children and feel helpless, frustrated and at a loss over what to do.

I thought an extract from one of Nadya's letters to me would help shed some light on her hypothesis.

> The recording has been an independent venture. I came to feel that the material gathered might have some implications for the education of children as they matured to adulthood. Behind this recording lies twelve years of observation, modified by the psychoanalytic point of view.
>
> I cannot help but view the behaviour of children from this angle. As a way of looking at human behaviour it answers my own questions most satisfactorily. In fact, it was due to my anthropologic and psychoanalytic interest that I also become aware of a possible relationship between the behaviour of the primitive adult, the modern pre-school child and the civilised neurotic adult. It is in these early pre-school years the child's behaviour is primarily naïve and instinctual.
>
> My impression is that the story of growth is duplicated with almost startling exactness in each group, so that it has often been possible to anticipate which forms or types of behaviour would next make their appearance. The impression is that emotional growth follows a rather definite pattern, and that Freud's hypothesis about the drives of childhood contain certain verbatim reports of the behaviour of the children, myself and the other adults.
>
> I also feel that after further study, it should be possible to gather important data by some such method of observation as I have recorded in the 'Outline'.
>
> In a laboratory set-up favourable to more fruitful study, it should be possible to gather data significant to anthropology as well as education. This data might then supplement the quantity of material already obtained from child analyses. I am not yet convinced that,

in these early years at least, psychoanalysis and education are in any way opposed to each other.

Unfortunately, I don't have all the records and materials which Nadya refers to in her letter. Only a fragment of her work is available. But even this fragment contains rich and valuable material for anyone who is interested in the field of education.

After carefully going through Nadya's work, conducting an intensive study of her material and then applying it to myself and children from different backgrounds, I found her claims about the growth patterns in young children to be strikingly valid.

Children who went through this process, even for a short period—with my limited experience and understanding of the method then—were able to competently cope with problems during their adolescent and adult life.

When I met Nadya I was already a trained teacher with some experience and success in teaching high-school students and teacher trainees. I could never forget my first meeting with her. It was electrifying. Her look was piercing but also warm and compassionate. I felt I had to be very honest with her.

When I took up the job of teaching young children between the ages of three to five, I did not know much about their behaviour and growth processes. I allowed them to do their classroom activities without interfering with their learning. When Nadya went through my work, she said mine was an honest work with children compared to the other classes. She felt I needed guidance and offered to help me understand the behaviour patterns and learning processes of young children.

In the beginning I couldn't accept her theories about young children's behaviour and the reasons for it, especially with regards to sexuality. I even argued that what she was talking about came from an American culture and was not applicable to our Indian culture. Nadya did not get angry with me, nor did she argue about it, but smilingly nodded and was silent, letting me speak my mind. This helped her understand my fears, inhibitions and thoughts related to this topic. She used this understanding in her classes with me to help me gain an in-depth understanding of the child in me, thereby allowing me to understand the children in my care.

Initially, with much hesitation and fear, I applied Nadya's theory in my class. I was surprised to see the result. I realised her theory on children's growth and their behaviour did not depend on any particular culture or any particular period of time. The growth process is the same for any human child. The more I observed the similarity in the behaviour and growth processes of children from different backgrounds in my classrooms, the more I was able to see how teaching in a realistic, impactful way was different from what I was trying to do earlier as a trained and successful teacher. This brought about a change in me. I experienced peace, the ability to face the truth without fear, gained self-confidence and the joy of freedom of spirit. What I learnt is very little compared to what this method offered because I had my own limitations.

What I would like to share with every earnest teacher who is sincerely engaged in working with young children is the joy and satisfaction I experienced as a result of applying Nadya's theory. It led to me discovering the beautiful person hidden in each and every child I encountered in my classroom. I hope this manual might serve as a lighthouse for those teachers seeking to understand little children.

# 3

# What is Play Content?

Play content is different from play-based activities. As I understand it, play-based activities are activities like painting, drawing, singing, storytelling, playing with puzzles, beads, dolls, etc., which are chosen by adults with some expectation of the results. Through these activities we expect certain learning outcomes in the different domains of development in children. Whereas play content is the fundamental—the most important—subject of play. It is the substance of play. We, as teachers, discover this substance by allowing children to play with certain materials of their choice and observing them in action—listening to what they say and noticing how they use the materials. When we observe children at play we can notice a set of subjects or themes that recur, since children follow similar phases of emotional development, with similar worries, anxieties and fears exhibited in every phase. *The recurring behaviour children manifest through specific materials is called play content.*

Play content is common for children from different social, economic and cultural contexts, and even from different time periods, because the growth and development process of a human being follows a very specific pattern. Their feelings however, manifest in their play in different ways depending on the background of the child.

This is a very important chapter for a teacher in order to help him understand the behaviour of children and its implications, and thereby understand the nature of children's learning.

I thought it would be useful to first reflect on play. In the modern world of education, 'play' has become an important slogan. Educators, philosophers and thinkers unanimously accept the fact that play is the centralising factor in young children's learning.

All of a child's domains of development are geared to play in order to develop their personality.

Today, more and more teachers and educators recognise and believe in the importance of play in their classrooms. The old belief that play is a waste of time is diminishing. Even learning centres for young children are called 'play schools', stressing the importance of play in a child's life.

The reason for this realisation is the understanding that play is natural, enjoyable, rewarding and not imposed but self-initiated.

Lending importance to this fact is that modern pre-school curriculums have developed a number of play activities which help develop children's cognitive, sensory-motor, social, emotional, physical and language skills.

A lot of hard work and serious thinking went into the planning and preparation of these curriculums, including seminars, discussions, group meetings involving educators, thinkers and teachers.

If we are not cautious, then there is a danger that play could become an end in itself. We should not be satisfied with the feeling that children enjoy playing and have learnt a lot, and that there is a happy, pleasant atmosphere in our classrooms. We should critically examine what they played with and why. What are they trying to tell us through play? What should be our response?

What is our criterion, our basis, for selecting specific play activities for children's learning?

I had used a similar sort of play activity curriculum in our nursery section many years ago and I found that children enjoyed learning. The atmosphere of the nursery was pleasant. Children's learning improved and there were many smart boys and girls. I was not satisfied, however, with this sort of success. Deep inside of me I experienced an uncomfortable feeling. I felt that something was not okay, that something was missing, but I could not pinpoint what exactly it was. No doubt the children's learning had improved, but I was constantly asking myself uncomfortable questions: Who are they? What are they? What is hidden in them? Back then, I did not know the most important substance of children's play.

My concentration then was on the children's learning outcomes rather than observing what the children played with and what they expressed in their play with specific materials. I did not ask myself why they repeated the same play every day. I did not ask myself when did they stop that play and what did they do next?

It was during the course of my sessions with Nadya that I shared with her what I taught in my class and how. From her observations of my teaching, from our long discussions about the behaviour of young children and their learning process, and from our discussions about me and my behaviour with children, I began to understand and recognise the meaning and value of 'play content'.

Nadya's *Outline* made no sense to me when I first read it in the early 1970s. I was working as a teacher then, and was also in charge of the nursery section of a good school in Bangalore. I found it difficult to grasp all of her material and couldn't connect it with my teaching or with the play-activity methodology. I couldn't understand it intellectually, though it was appealing to my spirit.

After gaining insight on this material on play, I was hesitant to use it in my class. There were fears and doubts in my mind, but with courage I plunged into the unknown. The result was like a miracle: a breakthrough in teaching and learning. I experienced a freedom of spirit, like a burden had been lifted from my shoulders, and I also experienced a sense of calm, peace and joy. The same spirit was reflected in the children in my class.

This experience also brought about a change in my way of looking at children. Previously, I was looking at them through play activities and their expected learning outcomes. But now I began to see them as persons of value; when I looked at their faces I could see they were longing to tell me something—asking for a chance to explore and express themselves without fear so they could discover what was in them and come to terms with their feelings.

I also learnt another truth in teaching and learning: that it was not my job to change and shape children but my job to provide a *chance* for them to do so. It was the children's job to change and shape themselves. What a relief!

Play content is something real and natural which offers insight into a child's behaviour and life. Play activities, however, are only the means used to achieve this.

A sample play content has been provided in Nadya's record of observations of young children's behaviour. From this sample, I chose play content for my methodology.

Why did I choose play content in my teaching? The reason I preferred play content to a play-based activity curriculum was because of the change I experienced in my teaching when I implemented play content, and also because of the authenticity of the work.

Nadya's outline for play content was prepared by her for a particular purpose—it was an independent venture to satisfy her own intense wish to better understand and be aware of the behaviour of young children as they matured into adults.

I was a teacher in a formal set-up and had to work within a rigid structure. I couldn't use Nadya's complete outline in any of my teaching groups because, firstly, I was not Nadya, and secondly, I could use only what I was able to work with and was bound by certain limitations. But I was able to acquire some freedom within that structure to try out a few things in my classroom from her *Outline*.

In the next chapter I will share with you what I was able to take from Nadya's work and, in the subsequent chapters, how I used that content.

# 4

# Selected Play Content for this Manual

Play content is the recurring behaviour children manifest through specific play materials found in their natural surroundings. This recurring behaviour expresses their needs, worries, fears, and anxieties. It also gives us a clue to the nature of learning in young children, so it is important for a teacher who is concerned about the education of young children to carefully observe and learn to understand the behaviour of children in her care.

Preschool years are important because in these years a child's behaviour is naïve and instinctual. Young children reveal themselves in the presence of teachers. The teachers must be compassionate and uncritical, and must also learn to understand what the children are trying to express through their behaviour.

If adults do not place any restrictions and give children the freedom to play, the children—no matter their background—will spontaneously choose water and sand for their play. It is an instinctive choice. They do not mind getting wet or dirty rolling in the sand. In fact, they enjoy this and play to their heart's content. They also enjoy roaming about and collecting curiosities like sticks, flowers, stones, broken pieces of bangles, feathers, etc. They make their own creative, imaginative things with what they collect. For example, they may create dolls, bangles, rings, earrings, chains, simple balance scales, etc. Next, they use what they have collected and created to play different roles: family members, cooks, teachers, shoppers, thieves or policemen, soldiers who shoot at enemies, circus performers and judges to mention a few.

If we recollect our childhood days and the games we played with our friends, brothers, sisters and cousins, we notice that we have all played similar games. If we observe children playing in a field in a village or on a street in a slum or city, we find there are a lot of similarities in their play. In all these situations, what is predominant is not the materials children use but the content of their play. Children do not need expensive, sophisticated toys. For them, the emotions they experience through play is important and is what matters.

Once, while I was walking through a path in a village field, I saw a small hut made by children. I looked at it carefully. The hut was made of coconut leaves and the branches of trees. Inside, the floor was cleaned and smeared with cow dung. There were small pots and an oven made from three pieces of stones. A small basket hung from the roof of the hut. There was a collections of leaves, flowers, stones, feathers, used matchsticks, bangle pieces, lids, cotton reels, old cycle tyres, pieces of cloth, iron wires, etc. Outside, by the hut, was a small tree. A piece of an old saree was tied to a branch and a small, old doll was hanging from it in such a way that it appeared to be sleeping within its folds.

There were no children in the hut when I was there. After their play they might have gone out, perhaps to collect more things or to look after the sheep in the fields or to help their parents with work. This type of play, which involves such make-believe houses, is common for children from any background or location.

We needn't break our heads trying to find out what kind of play materials need to be given to our children. If we have eyes to see, a mind to observe and are interested in *what* children play with and *how* they play, then we will know what play materials should be given to them. From our observations of children's play we can list their major play activities and the materials required.

Major play activities include the following: doll play, kitchen play, role play, smearing clay, painting and drawing, playing with wooden building blocks, outdoor play, nature study, music and conversations. Materials required for these play activities are discussed in detail in Chapter 13.

Play activities are not given in order to measure a child's intelligence based on their performance, nor are they given to have the child complete a prescribed syllabus in a prescribed time. The aim in giving the children these play activities is to try and understand each child's behaviour so that we can help each child develop a healthy personality.

## Play Activities and Their Play Contents

Listed below are major play activities and my thoughts or observations that make up their corresponding play contents. What I have understood from my observations was that in a secure environment, free of judgment, children spontaneously express themselves—their thoughts and feelings—through these selected play activities.

### DOLL PLAY AND KITCHEN PLAY

Children's play is largely based on the realities of their lives. During the different forms of play that children engage in, it is common to find them reproducing everyday incidents and interactions that they witnessed at home or experienced with their families. This is commonly found in doll play, where children imitate their parents cooking, going to work, putting the child to sleep and so on.

The incidents which the children act out and the way in which they express their emotions are influenced by the culture and environment found in their homes. For instance, while working at the nursery school in Bangalore, I observed children from affluent families acting out scenes such as this one: The mother would care for the child, cook food and look after the house. The father would go out to work and telephone from his office to find out if everything was alright. The mother would often tell him about a sick child. The father would immediately ring up a doctor and bring him home.

The emotions expressed by these children during their role-play were always subdued.

While working with children living in a slum, I observed that the family situations acted out were different: The father would come home, drunk and abusive, and would fight and beat the wife.

During such enactments these children expressed their emotions spontaneously. They would loudly cry, fight and scream.

It was not only in doll play but also in other activities such as playing with clay, daubing paint, drawing and painting that children reproduced family situations which disturbed them.

## ROLE PLAY

This involves children performing the part of a person or character and involves fantasy, myths, symbols, magic, birth and death, questions, curiosities and interests, dreams, daydreaming, oral gratification, thumb sucking.

This is a scene I witnessed at a nursery school while teaching: One day, girls were playing 'farmer in the den' in the playground. They were walking on all four and making noises like wild animals. The boys watched the game for a while and then joined in. They became the ringmasters. They took the 'animals' around and put them in cages. Then they took them out of the cages and gave them food to eat. The animals were put in a jeep but one animal was ill and fell out of the jeep. The ringmaster gave it some medicine. The animal got up and was sent back into the cage. There she lay down flat and said, 'Now I am wounded and bleeding a lot. Okay?' After a while she got up and went out. The animals did not complain when they were beaten by the ringmaster.

This is an example where children created and lived for a while in the fantasy world of a circus. Fantasy and myth are integral parts of childhood. Fantasy is not a departure from reality. It encourages an imagination among children that helps project familiar objects and experiences into an imaginative world and, more importantly, project their anxieties and wishes. Magic, myth and death were all topics that fascinated the children I worked with.

## POTTERS CLAY

Playing with potters clay or daubing paint helps children experience the sensations of squeezing, smearing, mushing or splashing. This enables them to overcome frustrations and inhibitions they face when trying to play with urine and faeces.

Certain materials are used more frequently by three-year-olds, who later tend to supplemented these materials with others. For example, liquids to semi-solids to solids: from water and urine games to mushing a mixture of water and clay to manual activity requiring mastery and skill.

It is important to observe the development of individual patterns and the use of symbols. Do these change or become elaborate? What is the meaning of these symbols for children?

## PAINTING AND DRAWING

Painting and drawing allows the children to express their inhibitions, frustrations and anger. Questions I have asked myself while observing the children at play include: Does colour have a symbolic meaning for children? Is the development of form typical for all children? Is there a development of individual patterns in the form of elaborations and displacements. What do these patterns mean to the child?

## WOODEN BUILDING BLOCKS

Playing with wooden building blocks is a form of constructive play which helps muscular development and physical growth. This play also develops children's powers of observation, cooperation, organisation, accuracy and ability to arrange materials. It is always interesting to observe the problems in construction which the child faces or creates.

## OUTDOOR PLAY

Children are active by nature and enjoy running, jumping, climbing and other vigorous activities. The joy of motion that comes from strenuous activity gives them a feeling of accomplishment and releases in-built tension. The children use their entire body for physical activity. They therefore need space.

During outdoor play there is an element of identification and projection. They may pretend to be adults at home, adopt symbolic roles like soldiers, robbers, police officers, doctors, drivers, etc. The children may also act like wild animals, enjoying the fantasy of belonging to a circus or living in a jungle.

## NATURE STUDY

This type of play satisfies the children's curiosity for the natural world. They learn about planting and the cycle of growth. They learn about animals from dogs and cats to frogs and lizards.

## MUSIC

Singing and dancing together help to develop among the children a feeling of belonging to a group or community. They enjoy chanting and through action songs and stories indulge their imagination.

## CONVERSATIONS

This is another activity through which the children are able to satisfy their curiosity by asking questions about life. Topics which are frequently discussed, amongst themselves or with the teacher, include issues of identification and growing 'big', fearing one's father, birth and the question of where one comes from, death and the question of where things go, sexual curiosity in terms of differences between boys and girls, and feelings of power and inadequacy.

It is important to note that children often use these play activities to not only reproduce work-day situations but also to satisfy their sexual curiosity or interest in genitals.

Children often express a curiosity about the differences between the male and female sex, and male and female genitals. Their play also shows evidence of curiosity over how children are conceived and born. Once these curiosities are satisfied—without being curbed—children move on to explore other topics. If not, these curiosities resurface as they grow older and may manifest in negative forms.

## Subjective to Objective

Originally, the play content manifests itself as subjective and instinctual, which indicates the emotional level of the child. The content is about the child, their emotions, their relationships and their thoughts. As Charles Skinner discusses in his book *Educational Psychology*, over time the child interacts with other children and, while acting in accordance with the idea of what is mine is mine, also comes to appreciate the idea of what is yours is yours. Skinner claims that children are known to be generous with their possessions during this period, but it is only at the end of their third year that the children engage in cooperative play (296). In my case, I noticed that this occurred not at the end of their third year, but at the end of their fifth year.

This leads to sublimation, that is, modifying the natural expression of an impulse or instinct, to one that is socially acceptable—a process which is normal for all children.

Through the different mediums provided, children express their emotional level and gradually grow from a *subjective instinctual phase* to an *objective instinctual phase* to an *objective factual reality*. The next chapter explores this idea in further detail.

Being subjective and human, we cannot assume that we will understand and know everything about this process. We should be aware of our limitations. Then, with sincerity and humility, we can make an effort to make our children's lives happy.

# 5

# How to Use Play Content

In the beginning I found play content and Nadya's tentative hypothesis difficult to understand and assimilate. Over the course of time, with Nadya's guidance, I came to realise the depth and value of such material. This made me read related educational material, especially books by Freud.

It was not very comfortable or pleasant to read Freud's books. His work targets the deep and hidden core of one's *self*, and compels one to unmask and honestly face their inner self. To do so is very frightening, but if one has the courage to face and overcome this fear, they experience a freedom of spirit.

The practical application of Freud's theory of psychosexual development of children in my classroom teaching did help me see the validity of the concept. Additionally, I witnessed a change in the atmosphere of the classroom, which grew relaxed, natural, loving and happy.

Instead of straight away going through the practical application of play content in a classroom, I thought it would be useful to understand the meanings of a few terms used, and to offer some explanation of the tentative hypothesis used in this methodology.

According to Freudian psychosexual development, a child progresses through five stages of early childhood development and are influenced by their *personality structure* (which consists of the *Id*, *Ego*, and *Superego*). The five stages of childhood development are:

1. the oral stage, from birth to age one.
2. the anal stage, from ages two to three.
3. the phallic stage, from ages four to five.

4. the latency stage, from age six till puberty.
5. the genital stage, from puberty through adulthood.

In this manual, I deal with the first three stages of development.

We all believe that the first six years of a child's life is a crucial period for shaping his personality. What is in his personality that has to be shaped? What are the challenges he has to face in the different stages of development? What helps him do this successfully? What hindrances will he face in the process, and how does he deal with them? What is our responsibility as a teacher, or as a parent, in supporting the child in this life process?

What is this personality? Freud conceptualised three separate but interactive psychic parts called the Id, Ego, and Superego. The development of a child's personality depends upon the interaction of these three mental structures, and the result of such interaction manifests itself in the form of behaviour.

According to Freud, a human being is a storehouse of genetically inherent energy which dynamically and creatively empowers life instincts (basic survival instincts). He called this energy, particularly the energy of the sexual drive, *Libido*. Freud used the term *sexual* in a very general way to mean all pleasurable actions and thoughts.

This energy continuously seeks a means of discharge, and in turn needs to be refilled. Pleasure is experienced when this energy is set free from the Libido, and tension is experienced when this energy accumulates.

An instinctual urge to release this energy, and the desire for immediate gratification, is called a *need*. Needs drive this process of seeking pleasure and avoiding pain—a process which Freud termed the *pleasure principle*. Needs create tension. Behaviour is directed towards the reduction of this tension. Behaviour does not happen by chance. All actions and thoughts are motivated by this urge. This urge has to be released in a reasonable way for, if totally repressed, it has a way of later rising to the surface in a disguised form which may create mental disturbances.

## The Id

Id is the psychic part which strives for the immediate satisfaction of instinctual needs on the basis of the pleasure principle. It is the child's subjective reality at the unconscious level. It is the *primary process of thinking*, which is the mental process directly involved with the functioning of primitive life forces from the unconscious.

Id is unorganised thinking that does not follow logic. It has no contact with reality. Id only creates needs and cannot do anything more than that. It seeks pleasure and avoids pain. It is impulsive. It has no discipline or control.

## The Ego

The Ego serves to cope with the problems of external reality and the Id's urge for immediate gratification.

It is the child's objective reality at the conscious level. Freud described the Ego as the regulating agent. It meets the demands of the Id by coordinating with the world of reality. It works on the basis of the *reality principle*. Ego is the *secondary process of thinking*, which is the learned and acquired mental process. Ego delays the immediate gratification of the Id, recognising higher or more pressing needs.

Its functioning is characterised by conscious mental activity marked by logical thinking. It is reality-oriented, aware of the self, and willing to put in effort, hard work and intent to act.

## The Superego

A mature adult has a mature Ego. Till the Ego matures, the various demands of the world and the Id are dealt with by the function of the Superego.

The Superego is an internalised model of social reality. It is the authority figure; in that reality it is the voice of a parental figure. It includes a conscious set of ideals and an unconscious set of prohibitions. Superego is the psychic structure which regulates the relationship between the instinctual drives of the Id, Ego and outside world.

A mature adult has a strong and mature Ego. A child has a weak and immature Ego controlled by the Id. A mature adult has an inner-directed person who is able to look at reality objectively and rationally in order to fulfil the needs of life.

The process of education aims to develop the personality of a child into a mature adult.

The process of personality development takes place through the 5 stages of early childhood development.

## Oral Stage (from birth to age one)

The fundamental requirements of this stage are food, warmth and security. The child needs a close link with her mother to experience the same warmth and security she enjoyed during the nine months in the womb. Bonding must happen. If the child does not experience or form a bond with her mother at this stage, her capacity to form emotional bonds as an adult will be severely affected.

Her need for food has to be satisfied. She experiences hunger. She learns that her hunger is not satisfied automatically and that she needs to make an effort, so she cries. Next, she learns to suck milk. This not only satisfies her hunger but causes her to experience pleasure.

In the first stage of personality development, the libido is centred on a baby's mouth, where her first source of pleasure is oral.

When the three needs are adequately fulfilled, she experiences satisfaction. She sleeps peacefully, contentedly. She willingly learns to adapt to her reality.

On the other hand, if the basic requirements of this stage are not satisfied, she gets frustrated, becomes irritable and feels insecure. She expresses this dissatisfaction and her uncomfortable feelings by crying, and is unwilling to leave her mother's hold. She expects her mother to carry her all the time.

Frustration and overindulgence lead to *fixation*. Fixation refers to the situation where a portion of the libido is permanently stuck in a particular stage of development. As a result, later on in life when the individual faces stressful situations she might behave in ways that are characteristic of infancy or early childhood. Dissatisfied oral pleasure leads to oral fixation, which manifests itself in the form of thumb sucking, nail biting, finger or handkerchief chewing, pencil chewing, sucking and biting—actions taken to satisfy the libido and the demands of the child's Id.

It is at this point that the work of education is essential. Preschool plays an important role in helping children get over this emotional block.

The school environment should help the child trust the teacher and the school. The teacher should mean what he says. The child should experience the warmth and security she needs to overcome her mental block. She should experience feeling loved and accepted.

Instead of rebuking a child for sucking their thumb or biting their nails, the teacher should understand the reason for her behaviour. Then he will show compassionate and be kind to her. This itself will have a large impact on the child's personality development.

## Anal Stage (ages two to three)

In the second stage, the infant's source of pleasure and focus of libido changes from the mouth to the anus. The urge to urinate or defecate builds tension in the libido, and when the infant urinates or defecates, this tension is relieved and the experience is pleasurable.

A common sight which we may have observed is of a child sitting very quietly while urinating, completely absorbed in his task. After relieving himself he looks at his urine, something he produced, and splashes it with his hands. He enjoys this action. Similarly, when defecating, he is absorbed and experiencing pleasure. Afterwards he squeezes the faeces in his hands and may even put some in his mouth. He does this because the mouth was the first organ from which he experienced pleasure.

His mother appears. What happens next?

The child looks at the mother with a smile. She is the person with whom he shares a bond. While sucking milk from her breast his eyes were fixed on her happy, loving, calm and giving face. Along with the milk he drank, he took into his psyche the face of his mother. For him, she is the world.

Full of happiness, he generously offers this gift to her. He shares with her what his body was able to make.

Now, how does the mother receive this gift? What is her reaction?

If she is an understanding mother who knows what it all means, then she will share in the infant's happiness. She will smilingly accept the gift offered to her and gradually, with patience, wash and clean the child and give him a warm hug to reciprocate the gesture.

This will help build the child's ego, self-confidence and self-worth. This, in turn, will help develop the child's personality so that he is more loving and pleasant; he becomes a person who confidently and generously shares himself and what he has with others.

Now take the mother who does not know the meaning of her child's interest in faeces.

Her immediate reaction is to be very disturbed by what her child is doing. She exhibits repulsion, admonishes the child, makes him realise what he did was something she does not approve of and something she considers 'bad'. She even hits his hand and, with obvious dislike and disgust, washes him. She sincerely feels that she is teaching the child cleanliness and good behaviour.

What happens to the image of the mother the child has in his mind? What does he feel? Does he learn what his mother wanted to teach him?

It is likely the child experiences rejection and fear. This can impact his confidence and lower the image he has of himself. He may be hesitant to share with others his love and gifts.

Nursery school provides an environment for the child where fixation in this stage is relieved.

Children are provided with soft potter's clay. They pour plenty of water into the clay mix and use their hands to squeeze and smash the clay. They enjoy the feeling of squeezing clay between their fingers, hysterically laughing as they shout 'kaka, kaka'. They repeat this process again and again. They also enjoy the sound made while squeezing the clay. They get a chance to experience pleasure which used to be forbidden. A lot of energy is used during this activity. When they are finished, they heave a sigh of satisfaction. What a relief!

Next comes toilet training. The ego of the child is developing. It is his first experience with the external regulation of an instinctual impulse, where pleasure experienced from relieving anal tension is postponed. The child is aware that he is a person in his own right. He distinguishes 'me' from 'not me', and his wishes bring him into conflict with the demands of the outside world.

His conflict is with adult-imposed restrictions regarding toilet training. If the parents impose their authority and force the child to relieve himself according to a time and place they have fixed, then there is going to be conflict. The child's wish is ignored. He suppresses his urge and becomes stubborn. If he is forced to relieve himself against his wishes, then later in life he may develop a weak sense of self, grow self-indulgent and possess a compulsive personality.

Bed-wetting, withholding, stubbornness are examples of behavioural disorders from toilet training.

If the parents are understanding, they will be supportive and help the child patiently adjust to external regulation, rewarding him for his actions. Then, later on in life, the child develops a good sense of self-control.

At the age of about one-and-a-half to two years, one also notices that the child experiences pleasure by playing with his genitals. The action absorbs him, and he is completely unaware of anything around him.

Many young parents, especially mothers, are very disturbed when they see their children exhibit such behaviour. They consider it bad behaviour and worry or even feel guilty.

If they admonish the child—thinking that the child is doing something bad—and discourage him from doing such a thing, then the child gets the message that he is bad and his parents dislike him. He experiences rejection and feels guilty. At the same time, the pleasure he experienced from this act is suppressed, only to come up later on in the form of masturbation and other self-directed sexual behaviour.

If the parents do not get anxious and leave the child alone, then after a short period he grows out of this behaviour. Parents need to understand this is part of the child's growth process.

Two young mothers, who were very disturbed by the behaviour of their children, tearfully shared with me their anxiety and pain. Once they realised it was a normal growth process and were willing to leave the children alone without showing any negative feelings, the children grew out of this behaviour very normally and naturally. Later, with surprise and joy, they shared their experiences with me, telling me that their children were now well behaved; their children were not 'bad' as they had previously believed them to be.

## Phallic Stage (ages four to five)

This is the third stage of infantile development. Sensitivity now becomes concentrated in the genitals in both sexes and it also becomes the source of pleasure.

This is a difficult stage for children, and also for the teacher and young parents who handle them. Three-year-olds who were working silently by themselves turn four and suddenly become restless, noisy, aggressive, and chaotic.

At this stage the children become aware of their bodies and the bodies of others. They learn the physical sexual differences between a boy and a girl. To satisfy their curiosity, they undress and examine each other and their genitals.

It is in the phallic stage that the sexuality of early childhood reaches its greatest intensity. The instinctive urge is objective and aggressive. Masturbation is a subjective experience at this stage.

If this stage is handled carefully by parents and teachers, the child works through her problems successfully without suffering any ill effects.

If the child is not threatened by adults, understands she is experiencing a stage of growth, and satisfies her curiosity through honest, unperturbed answers from the adults, then the child resolves her problems and uses her energy to further develop the self.

In our nursery school, the four-year-olds used to ask all sorts of questions. In the dolls corner they lifted the dresses of dolls to see whether they had genitals—to determine whether it was a boy or a girl. They had discussions amongst themselves about how a boy, unlike a girl, has a penis.

One grandmother shared with me a conversation she overheard while her grandchildren were playing outside. She was a bit disturbed by the conversation and did not know what to make of it. There were two little girls and a boy, all roughly four-and-a-half years old. The girls were discussing how the boy had something which they didn't have. They asked him to show them what he had. The boy showed them and told the girls that they had been naughty and that their father had cut theirs off. He also told them that he was scared his father might cut his off if he was naughty. The girls inspected themselves and said it was true; theirs were cut off and they had holes instead of what the boy had. The boy stood up, lifted his penis and urinated. He told the girls that they could not do that because they did not have one. The girls stood up and urinated and said that they too could stand and urinate.

Fortunately the grandmother, though perturbed, did not punish the little children. By discussing the matter with me, she was able to understand the situation better. The children grew up with no ill effect.

On another occasion I observed, during snack-time, the four-year-olds in our nursery having a discussion. One little girl in the group had swallowed a plum from a bun.

Vinod told the girl, Rani, 'Now you will have a baby in your stomach and it will grow and become big.' The girl began to cry.

They had noticed the pregnant ayah. They discussed amongst themselves how her stomach was growing bigger and bigger every day.

The group asked the teacher whether the plum seed would grow in Rani's stomach and become a baby. The teacher said 'No'.

Their next question was 'how will the baby come out of the ayah's stomach?'

One of the girls immediately said, 'I know how it will come out.' The group asked her how. She said, 'There is a hole where you make "ucha" and the baby comes out through it.'

A boy said, 'In that case, only girls will have babies growing in their stomach.'

Another boy asked, 'Alright, we know how babies come out of the stomach. But how did they get in?' At this point the teacher told him that he should ask his mother and she would tell him.

The children would observe the genitals of dogs, cats and other animals, and then discuss this topic in their groups in class.

In their drawings, they would draw humans or animals with a penis. In their clay work, they rolled clay and made snakes and talked about the penis. They broke the long snake into smaller pieces and stood those pieces on cement slabs. They called the pieces by each other's names and teased each other.

It appeared that at the age of four their curiosity was centred mainly on genitals. Most of the time their questions and discussions were about sexual curiosity.

One day, during snack time, one of the boys announced that he teased his mother. He then softly whispered in the teacher's ear 'then I kissed her, daddy didn't see.' He sat leaning on the wall, stretched his legs as much as he could, then announced, 'Look,

I am daddy. I am so big. Now I am sleeping. Okay. I snore and sleep like daddy.' He mimed the action of sleeping.

On another day, a girl announced that she sat on her father's lap, asked her mummy to go away and then kissed her father.

This sort of talk was very common among children of this age group.

The girls usually act the role of a mother, feeding the baby and putting it to sleep, washing clothes and cooking food.

In the beginning I was very sceptical of Freud's theory of psychosexual development—that during the phallic stage the genitals become the source of pleasure for children, or his theory of the Oedipus complex—the object of desire for a little boy is his mother, with him jealous of and fearing his father. The boy develops a fear of being castrated by his father. Gradually, the child realises and accepts his father is more powerful, so he represses his desire for his mother and begins to identify with his father.

As a result of this realisation and identification with his father, the boy's conflict is resolved. Similarly, the girl resolves her desire for her father and identifies with her mother.

All this seemed somewhat unbelievable and perhaps imaginative or unrealistic for me.

But when a secure, free environment was provided, children did express their fears, doubts, anxieties and curiosities. They spoke freely, to their satisfaction, and received answers which helped provide clarity regarding their behaviour and thinking. This greatly helped the children when they turned six or seven years old. Teachers observed that children who went through this process in their nursery years showed better concentration in their studies, were well disciplined and behaved maturely.

## Points to Reflect on

Sexuality is part of a child's normal development. Freud introduced the notion of sexuality being central to and normal in infancy and childhood.

Sexual explorations shape a child's sexual knowledge in an important way and, as Freud believed, are a child's first major step in achieving orientation. Infantile sexuality, sexual impulses and wishes are common elements which make up the human constitution (Freud 170). The desire to learn and understand appears to be inseparable from sexual curiosity (173).

What children talk about and express is not necessarily something bad. It is natural talk, which all human beings have gone through and will go through. If their curiosity is satisfied, then their energy is released to help develop the self and be creative and productive in the world.

But what is the message children receive if they are admonished for expressing themselves, or told not to talk about something or to consider that they have behaved poorly? Their suppressed and dissatisfied curiosities will not die out but will surge up later in life in potentially undesirable forms.

Id must be controlled in order to satisfy social demands. This sets up a conflict between frustrated wishes and social norms.

Ego and superego develop in order to exercise this control and direct the need for gratification into socially accepted channels.

Each psychosexual stage involves a particular conflict that must be resolved before the individual can successfully advance to the next stage.

# 6

# Classification of Activities

As children progress through different developmental stages, they face hurdles which may block their emotional growth process. Children are, to a certain extent, instinctually able to overcome these hurdles through self-initiated play.

Play is a very important medium through which children acquire knowledge about the world around them. They also use play as a form of therapy to help deal with emotional issues. Through play, they are able to externalise especially painful feelings, get it out of their system, and look and deal with these issues objectively.

We have seen that imagination plays an important role in children's play. They love make-believe, role play, fantasy and myth, which are all necessary for their ego formation and their ability to identify themselves with others.

Though play is a vital part of a child's developmental process, it can become aimless and chaotic without the careful guidance and observation of a mature adult. By observing children play, the materials they use and the content of their play, teachers can provide an environment in the classroom for healthy emotional development. This allows children to express their feelings in different forms, not just through words but also through creative activities which serve as an outlet for their emotions.

In the beginning, when I chose this methodology for our nursery section, I had to make some drastic changes. Timetables, examinations and prescribed textbooks were abolished. Parents and members of staff raised concerns, but in time those problems were all resolved.

The nursery was set up so that activities were assigned their own distinct place or corner (somewhat like the sample layout given in Chapter 12). We started with one class and gradually introduced this method to all the classes in the nursery.

The first class had twenty-five children who were four years old. The children were told about the change in the layout, then they were taken round the classroom and shown all the activities and the specific place for each activity. They were told they could do any activity they wanted, for as long as they wanted. Once they finished with an activity, they needed to put the materials back in the same place. They could either play alone or with their friends.

The children were surprised. No fixed timetable and no fixed activity for a particular time. The first week was chaos; the children, on their own, didn't know which activity to choose. There was a lot of trial and error. Over time, they got the hang of things.

What I noticed then was that almost all the children chose to play with dolls, or smear clay, or daub paint, or play with sand and wooden building blocks. The children did not choose activities like drawing, threading beads, painting, colouring, cutting paper, completing puzzles or reading picture books and storybooks, Not only that, they spent most of their time on the same activity, every day, without changing activities. Some liked roaming about doing nothing. For more than a month this pattern of working continued.

Though I believed in the theoretical concepts I had learnt, I was a bit tense when I saw the children were not learning as they used to before introducing this methodology. When parents asked the children what they did at school, they said, 'We did nothing today, but we played all the time. We are very happy.'

Parents grew worried. They asked the principal, 'What's happening to the nursery section of the school? Is it going to the dogs?'

I asked the children, 'Don't you like to read, don't you like to thread beads?'

The spontaneous answer was, 'No, we don't want to do that now. We want to play with dolls.'

'What if your parents ask?'

'We tell them, "you don't worry". We will learn after we finish playing.'

This was indeed the case. Once the children got what they wanted from an activity, they moved on to other activities. This was their own choice, and they wholeheartedly took part in all of the activities. There was interest, life and enjoyment in the work.

From this experience, and subsequent experiences with different groups of children from different backgrounds, I came to understand that there are a few important and necessary activities which all the children opt for. Through these activities they perform role play, imaginative play, identification play and fantasy to help solve their emotional problems.

The activities are doll play, kitchen play, smearing clay, daubing paint and scribbling.

So, for the sake of convenience, we teachers classified these activities as *therapeutic activities*. Having classified these activities, we proceeded to classify the remaining activities based on how children used the medium. This system of classification was for the teachers and not for the children.

Giving importance to play content, the activities are classified as follows.

1. Therapeutic activities
2. Creative activities
3. Constructive activities
4. Cultural activities
5. Outdoor activities
6. Learning activities

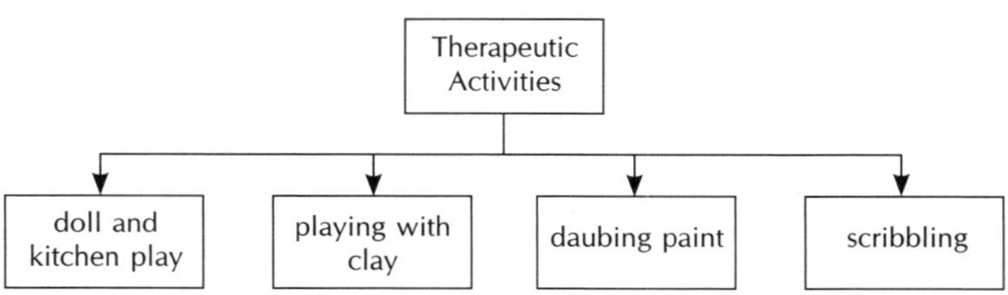

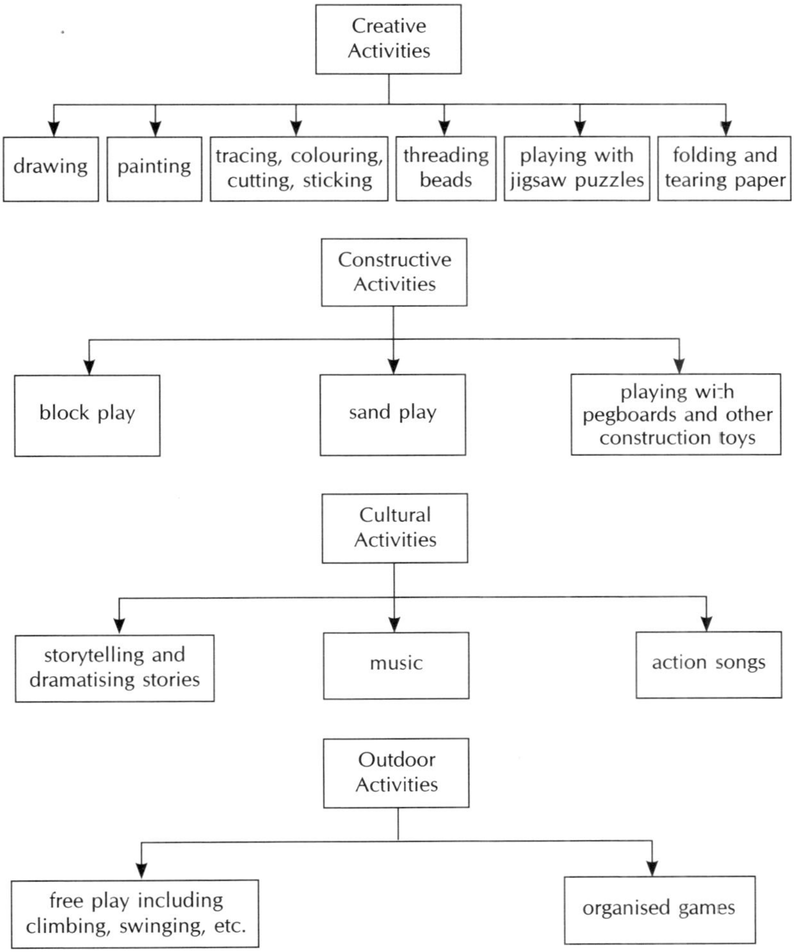


There is no hard-and-fast rule that one has to follow regarding the order of these activities. It is simply a guide for teachers. Some of these activities overlap, as every activity involves learning.

# 7

# Therapeutic Activities

I mentioned in *The Open Classroom* that, 'In an educational system, children who are given a chance to express their emotions and feelings, without being judged and disapproved of, gain inner strength and stability in life' (70). Providing this space and opportunity is the primary objective of all therapeutic activities.

From my experience of working with young children and observing them during their play, I have found there are specific activities which help them work through their emotional issues. Such activities provide an opportunity and space for children to express their feelings, thereby helping them to relax.

Since these activities are used as a medium for healing emotional wounds, we have called them *therapeutic* activities. Once children have expressed themselves and released their negative emotions and energy, they are able to examine these issues objectively.

The following are therapeutic activities: doll and kitchen play, playing with clay, daubing paint and scribbling.

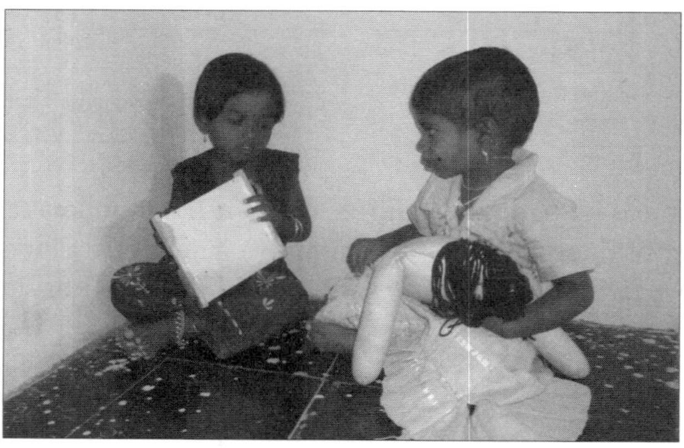

Three-year-olds playing with a doll

A four-year-old playing with clay

A five-year-old daubing paint

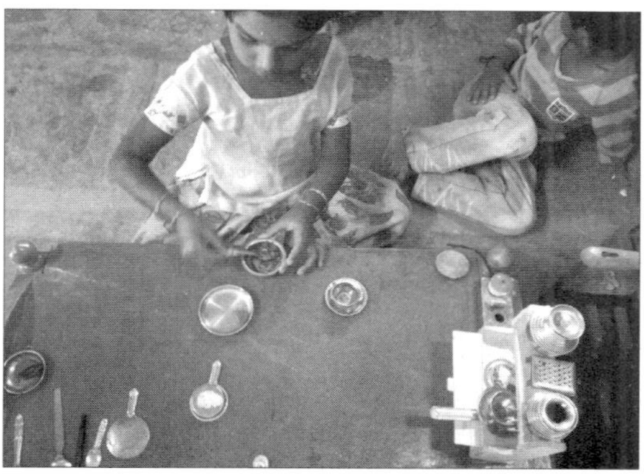

A five-year-old playing with a kitchen set

One may wonder why so much importance is given to therapeutic activities for this age group of children. In an adult's eyes, children are simple, spontaneous, trusting and innocent human beings—what problems can they have? But in reality all of us face problems from birth till death. Successfully coping with these problems makes life more meaningful and shapes a person into being his truest self.

Young children's behaviour is uncomplicated. In an atmosphere free from the pressures of adult control, they reveal who they really are by unreservedly following their instincts, natural impulses and interests. Their fantasies are self-centred and they express these fantasies through dramatic or imaginative play, using any material which they choose.

They *externally* work through *internal* conflicts. This reduces anxiety, tension and guilty feelings. Their imaginative play is a bridge for them to pass from their subjective instinctual reality to an objective outer reality. Later on it also makes it easier for children to control their instinctual behaviour and to accept the limitations of the real world. The ego thus develops.

Children need time and space to express themselves—to get angry, to be sad, to remain silent, to reflect, to rectify and to come to terms with themselves and others. It is a tremendous boon to not check or reprimand children but to allow them to freely express their feelings towards others because it allows the children to gain an awareness of their own behaviour. This helps them to externally process and rectify any issues with their behaviour.

A lot of energy is used in therapeutic activities. Since there is no fixed time for these activities, children play for as long as they need to till they are satisfied. After this release of energy they usually lie down, relax, stretch their hands and legs and heave a sigh of relief.

Usually three-year-olds play for forty-five minutes to an hour. Four-year-olds play for a longer time, roughly an hour to an hour-and-a-quarter, or an hour-and-a-half. Five-year-olds play for an hour-and-forty-five minutes.

The three-year-olds and four-year-olds play with dolls or kitchen sets every day. As soon as they come to school they say: 'We want to play with dolls.'

The five-year-olds are more interested in observing things and completing tasks, but on and off they say: 'Today we don't want to do this. We want to play with dolls, clay and paint.'

If this practice is granted to these children in their nursery years, then they will grow to solve their problems positively and honestly.

A few guidelines for therapeutic activities:

1. The primary role of the teacher is to provide a secure environment where the children can be themselves and freely express their feelings. Teachers who witnessed and experienced this process during their training were able to better understand children's needs and give them the environment they required.
2. It is important for the teacher to *accept the child as she is*. The child needs to feel accepted in order to trust the teacher. She must be able to feel like she can be herself in front of the teacher.
3. There need not be any additional or excessive input from the teacher. If the child is overly praised, she will feel a compulsive need to please the teacher. If the child is criticised, she will feel demotivated. It is important for the child to understand that the teacher loves the child's *person*, which is separate from the child's *behaviour*. It is the child's behaviour which requires change and modification. Separate the child from her actions.
4. If a child asks a question about whether something is right or wrong, or good or bad, the teacher should take care to avoid giving the child any conclusive answers. This is so that the child can learn for herself. One approach to such a situation could be to acknowledge what the child feels. I remember a child once asking me, 'Is it okay to hit the doll?' Answering the question might have led to

the child unquestioningly accepting what I said. Instead, I asked the child the very same question she had asked me: 'You tell me: Is it okay to hit the doll?' Here, the child was not trying to understand whether her action was right or wrong, but was looking for reassurance from the adult that she could go ahead with expressing her feelings. This way allowed the child to take responsibility for her actions.

## Doll and Kitchen Play

Doll play is widely recognised as a medium for children's social development, aiding in clear thinking and in language development. However, its role in emotional development has largely been ignored.

In this type of play, children re-enact everyday situations they've witnessed at home. Doll play allows the children to objectively view and confront topics like their relationship with their family, drunken fathers, marriage, fighting, festivals and death. It is a medium which enables children to express the life they experience and, in so doing, gain a sense of satisfaction, relief and contentment.

Usually three-year-olds carry dolls with them wherever they go. They bathe the doll, comb its hair, change its dress, feed it and put it to sleep in a cradle. Then the child goes to play with the kitchen set, making chapattis or tea, or washing vessels and sweeping the floor. Periodically, the child will check on the doll and rock its cradle.

The child will at times take the doll from the cradle, talk to it, console it (pretend as though it is crying) and balance it on her lap as she plays with the kitchen set.

Their play is quiet and calm. They play alone but talk to the doll. Sometimes they scold the doll, then kiss it, put it on their shoulder and carry it up and down the room. When they sleep with the doll, they put the doll on their chest and pretend to feed it.

Three-year-olds play with their dolls in a caring, tender and loving manner.

In comparison, four-year-olds are aggressive, noisy, restless and chaotic. They play alone as well as with others. Most of their play is with other children in their group (only four children play at a time in the dolls' corner).

As soon as the four-year-olds enter the dolls' corner, there is a sort of funny, uneasy laughter in their group. They mockingly look at all the dolls and say, 'Look, this is the father doll, this is the mother doll, this is the baby, this is the girl.' They comment and joke about the dolls.

Next, they lift the dresses of the dolls to check and see if they are boys or girls. They discuss this topic within their group: 'The doll does not have a penis, so it isn't a boy, but it isn't real, so it cannot have a penis.' Curiosity to look at each other's genitals and the genitals of animals and other people are expressed in this play activity.

As a teacher, when you hear this sort of conversation among children, it is possible you worry about whether you are encouraging something undesirable. The children may get into the habit of talking and behaving like this. In the beginning, I too had such fears. Later I realised it is a natural curiosity of growing children. When they are given a chance to satisfy this curiosity without being held in contempt or made to feel guilty, they come out of this behaviour quite successfully. They show signs of maturity and confidence.

Parents, family and other adults often induce feelings of fear, anxiety, insecurity, mixed love and hatred in the children, who are able to express their emotions through role play. The dolls take on different roles.

It is safe to use dolls to play the roles of parents or adults because dolls are not a threat to the children. The children can hit the dolls, kick them and even kill them. Then they bury them and afterwards brings them back to life. The children announce, 'Now the dying is over. All the dead people are okay.'

Here is an incident I once observed: While playing with dolls, Shiva told his group, 'I do not like Raja.' Raja is Shiva's friend and they recently quarrelled. Shiva took a doll and said, 'This is not a doll. It is Raja. Now I am going to kick him.'

He kicked the doll. He kicked the doll many times till he was exhausted. He threw the doll. Then he rested. After a while he relaxed, got up and put the doll back in its place. 'Now I am satisfied,' he said.

He told the doll, 'Sorry, I won't hit you. I put you back in your house. Okay? Stay there.'

Then he went and sat next to Raja, who was grumpy, and hugged him and said, 'You are my friend. I won't hit you. I hit the doll, okay?'

Friends again, they resumed playing together.

A visitor who observed children's aggressive play in the dolls' corner asked whether violence was permitted. Justifying violence and encouraging an eye for an eye or a tooth for a tooth is not allowed. Without being aware of it, we have negative emotions like anger, hatred, jealousy and vengeance in us, either caused or inflamed by the outer world. These emotions manifest through negative behaviour. Since we are not always aware of the cause of our behaviour, we justify our actions and believe what we are doing is right. This is dangerous.

In the nursery, children are given a chance to bring out and discard such negatives emotions. This cleanses their spirit. So doll play is not about allowing or encouraging violence but escaping the bondages of violence. It is a process of healing, hence a therapeutic activity.

According to Gregory Mitchell, in his article "Sigmund Freud and Freudian Psychoanalysis", catharsis is when repressed ideas and the emotions associated with them are allowed an opportunity to discharge their energy. Once released, they are no longer a source of disturbance.

In my experience as a teacher, I observed that playing with dolls was a powerful means by which children could release repressed feelings.

Doll play corner

Dolls children can play with

Kitchen playset

## Playing with Clay

Potter's clay is a medium which almost all young children are attracted to and choose spontaneously for their play. They enjoy the feeling of squeezing soft clay with their hands and in-between their fingers, and they play by smearing it across the floor.

In my experience, three-year-olds pour plenty of water in the clay and spread it across the floor. They enjoy squeezing this liquid clay between their fingers. They usually play alone and silently, and appear completely absorbed in their play.

Four-year-olds also pour plenty of water in the clay, though they make their clay semisolid. They enjoy squeezing clay and listening to its squelching sound. They repeat this action, again and again, screeching 'kaka, kaka' and laughing. Additionally, they happily smear clay on their hands and legs. They experience satisfaction and pleasure in this play, and a lot of energy—both physical and emotional—is used up. They play to their heart's content, unmindful of the presence of others watching them.

Five-year-olds usually use enough water to make the clay into a soft dough, which they use to mould a few simple objects. Common objects which most five-year-olds make include rectangles, snakes, ovens, ladders, aeroplanes, devil-like figures with horns, human beings with long noses or attached clay penises.

Once in a while these children also pour plenty of water in the clay and squeeze it with their hands.

In our nursery, Navin, who was four-and-a-half years old, used to make aeroplanes by crossing two pieces of clay he had rolled. His clay board was covered with aeroplanes, and if he had playmates who were nice to him, he would play with them and their clay models. Usually his aeroplanes flew overhead and crashed in mid-air. He made aeroplanes every day. I felt the urge to ask him to make something else, but I did not and instead continued to observe his behaviour. Later, I realised that he related aeroplanes with his father, who passed away from a heart attack while travelling in a plane. Once he shared this information with the teacher, he moved on to making other objects.

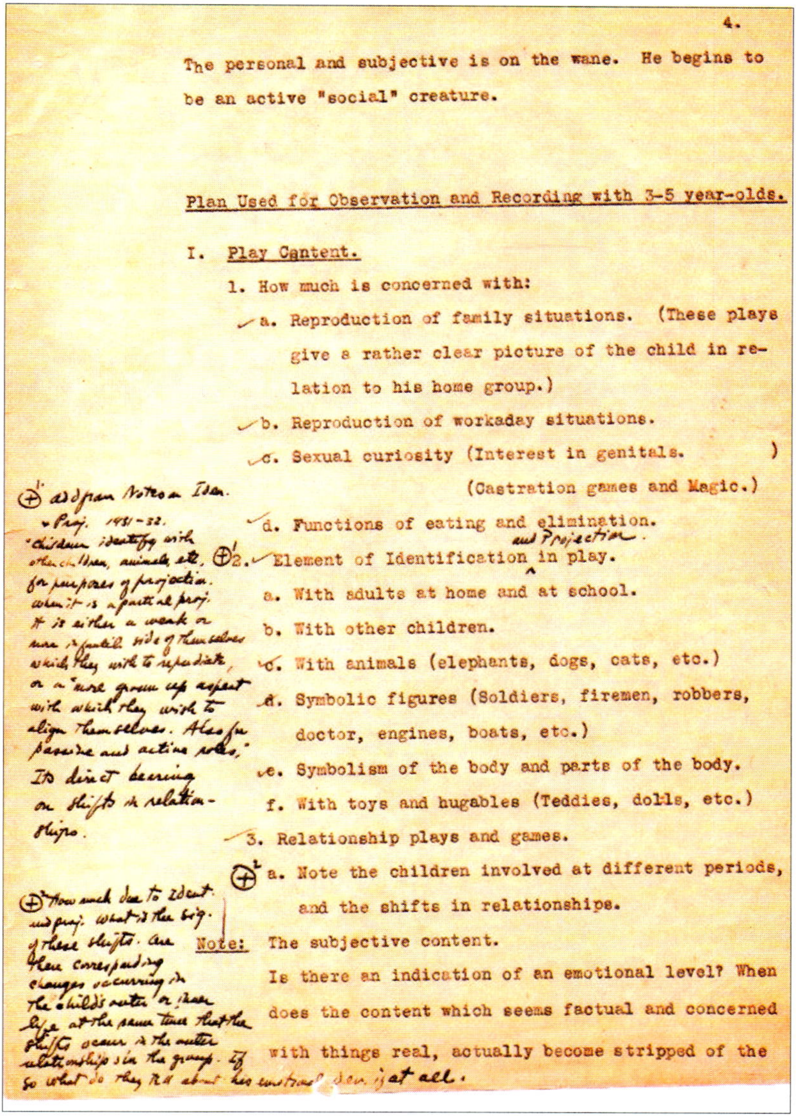

4.

The personal and subjective is on the wane. He begins to be an active "social" creature.

Plan Used for Observation and Recording with 3-5 year-olds.

I. Play Content.

1. How much is concerned with:

a. Reproduction of family situations. (These plays give a rather clear picture of the child in relation to his home group.)

b. Reproduction of workaday situations.

c. Sexual curiosity (Interest in genitals. )
(Castration games and Magic.)

d. Functions of eating and elimination.

2. Element of Identification and Projection in play.

a. With adults at home and at school.

b. With other children.

c. With animals (elephants, dogs, cats, etc.)

d. Symbolic figures (Soldiers, firemen, robbers, doctor, engines, boats, etc.)

e. Symbolism of the body and parts of the body.

f. With toys and hugables (Teddies, dolls, etc.)

3. Relationship plays and games.

a. Note the children involved at different periods, and the shifts in relationships.

Note: The subjective content.
Is there an indication of an emotional level? When does the content which seems factual and concerned with things real, actually become stripped of the

(+)1 add from Notes on Iden. & Proj. 1931-32. "Children identify with other children, animals, etc. for purposes of projection. When it is a partial proj. it is either a weak or more infantile side of themselves which they wish to repudiate, or a "more grown up" aspect with which they wish to align themselves. Also for passive and active roles." Its direct bearing on shifts in relationships.

(+)2 How much due to Ident. and proj: what is the sig. of these shifts. Are there corresponding changes occurring in the child's outer or home life at the same time that the shifts occur in the outer relationships in the group. If so what do they tell about his emotional dev. if at all.

Figure 1: Sample page from Nadya's unpublished *Outline*.

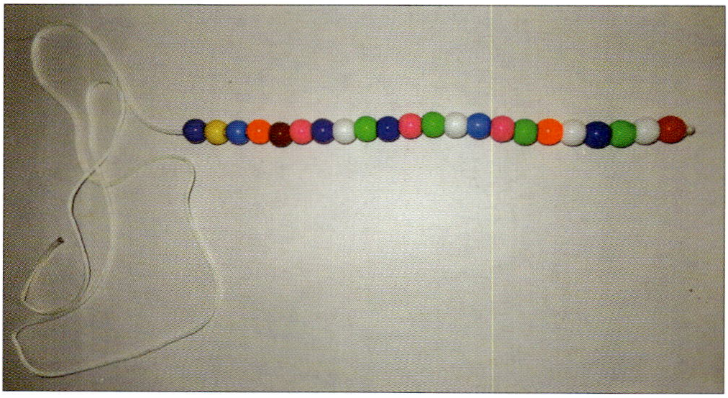

Figure 18: Threading by two-year-olds.

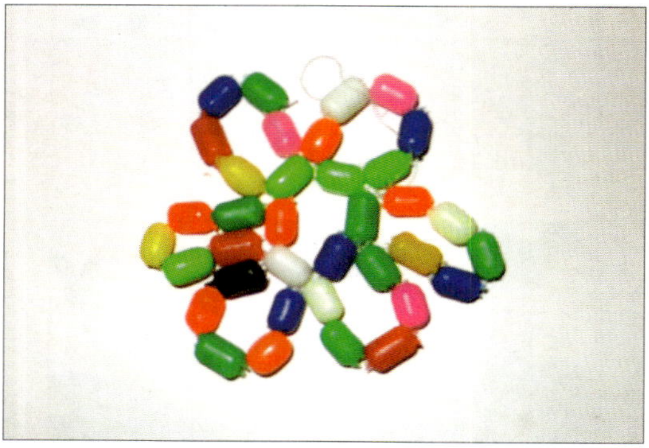

Figure 19: Threading by three-year-olds.

Figure 20: Threading by four-year-olds.

Potter's clay, raw

Potter's clay, fine powder

Potter's clay, smooth dough

## Daubing Paint

This activity is similar to playing with clay and gives children a sense of relief and satisfaction. It has the additional advantage of colours. Observing and blending different shades of colours adds to the children's excitement (though some children also enjoy mixing paints to get a blackish-brown colour).

After playing, children appear to have exhausted all their energy and sit quietly for a while, looking relaxed and calm.

Adult teachers who have played with clay and paint along with their children agreed that they too felt a release of energy. They felt lighter, as though a burden had been lifted from their shoulders, and they experienced a sense of peace and satisfaction.

Three-years-olds usually smear paint across the floor and enjoy the feel of it. They tend to use one colour.

Four-year-olds play like they do with clay. They mix paint colours. Usually they mix all the paints and get a dark brown colour, which they call 'kaka'. They pour more water, splash the paint and smear it across their face and hands.

Five-year-olds do not add any water but take the paint, smear it across the floor and make patterns with their fingers. They usually mix two colours and by chance discover a new colour. Mixing yellow and blue makes green, mixing red and blue makes purple, mixing red and yellow makes orange. They very much enjoy discovering these new colours. When they feel an urge to daub paint like four-year-olds, they do so.

Materials for daubing paint

## Scribbling

This is another medium which helps a child bring out any unpleasant experiences or issues they have stored in their mind, and allows the child to honestly observe and release themselves from such emotional bonds.

Florence Cane writes in *The Artist in Each of Us* about how the scribble is a line drawn on paper without any plan or design. Because of this, it may be straight and simple or it may be tangled and intertwined (56). It removes any stiffness and helps the child relax.

At such a young age, a child derives much pleasure from scribbling and use of colour, regardless of form. A few children do develop further and begin to express their ideas more clearly.

A scribble reflects the state of mind and subconscious thoughts and emotions of the person who is drawing. Children use it to solve problems on their own. Usually five-year-olds and above enjoy scribbling.

Children make random continuous lines and strokes when scribbling in their book. Some children start noticing certain objects in their scribble. The objects can be highlighted by darkening them with a contrasting colour. See page 48, Figures 2, 3 and 4 for examples of scribbles by children I taught.

## Conclusion

In the beginning the children's play was spontaneous and uninhibited. Gradually I began to notice a change in their behaviour. They were no longer spontaneous, nor were they that comfortable playing freely. I could sense that their behaviour was restricted by some adult expectation.

One day little Maria went round watching children playing with clay. Her hands were behind her back and she announced: 'Today I will not play with clay. My hands will get dirty. Mummy told me not to get my hands dirty.' A child who used to spontaneously play and express her feelings through clay no longer wanted to play with clay.

Another example was of Vinod, whose mother usually dropped him off at school. Vinod told the teacher, 'Teacher, tell my mummy to go home. I want to play with paint. I don't want her here.'

A few parents met with me and told me, 'Miss M, don't allow the children to mess with clay and paint. Instead of potter's clay, you can get Plasticine and they can play with that. Let them use brushes to paint. These are young children, you must teach them to be clean.'

We arranged meetings with the parents and tried to explain the methodology we were using and how it would help their children emotionally, socially and intellectually. Parents reacted by saying, 'Don't encourage children to talk about all these things, admonish them and show that you do not like this behaviour. Tell them good children will not talk like this, they should instead study well and score high marks.' I realised parents were not yet ready for this type of education. Two years later, when these children did well in their primary class, their parents appreciated their academic progress but didn't touch upon their emotional growth.

One mother was very disturbed by her four-and-a-half-year-old son's behaviour. She told me, 'Miss M, I am very upset. My son, Arun, is such a bad boy. We took him with us to a relative's wedding reception. In the hall, in front of so many people, he loudly shouted that the uncle and aunt were married, and now they will have a baby. I was so ashamed, I did not know what to do.'

The methodology unfortunately couldn't be implemented fully because there were limitations we faced from adult expectations and the outside environment. I faced my own limitations as well. As a result, I didn't have the courage and confidence to go ahead and fully apply the methodology. But we did have more freedom than other schools, and so were able to implement part of the methodology, which proved to have a positive impact on the children.

# 8

# Creative Activities

Once the children have addressed their emotional issues through therapeutic activities, they begin to pay attention to other creative activities found in the classroom.

It is important to remember that even if, at the very beginning, the teacher gives the children the freedom to choose any activity they want, and even if different activities are arranged in the classroom so that they are easily accessible to the children, all of the children will first choose therapeutic activities. None of them will want to do any of the other activities. Instead, they will spend most of their time on therapeutic activities and, once satisfied, relax. Having expended most of their energy, they will not choose any other activity which requires their concentration.

This pattern of working will continue for many days, perhaps even weeks or months. If the teacher worries that during this stage the children are not learning and are not performing any creative activities, she might forcefully instruct the children to try other activities. Some children will refuse to do so. Others will oblige the teacher's requests, but their work will be slipshod and they will not show any real interest in what they are doing. They will hand over their work and say, 'Here. Take it. Enough?' It may appear as if they are doing the teacher a favour and satisfying her needs rather than their own.

If however, the teacher does not get perturbed during this stage and understands the needs of the children and gives them the chance to pursue the activities they choose, then the children will, in time, move on from therapeutic activities. They will show a genuine interest and desire to learn from creative activities.

Creative activities help develop children's hand-eye coordination. They also test children's small-muscle skills, which improves concentration and precision. As time goes by, the children gradually discover and attempt new ways of doing the activities. Their creativity is aroused. The following are classified as *creative* activities:

- Drawing
- Painting
- Tracing, colouring, cutting and gluing
- Threading beads
- Jigsaw puzzles
- Folding and tearing paper

## Guidelines for Creative Activities

Creative activities require teacher supervision and intervention. The teacher provides guidance when needed. If the teacher notices a new initiative by the child, input and guidance should be provided to enrich the activity. This helps develop the child's self-confidence. Here are a few guidelines to follow for creative activities:

1. At the age of 5, it is important children cultivate habits such as orderliness and cleanliness. Once they have finished playing, they must put things back in the right place. They must also clean up any mess they have made. This helps inculcate good habits.
2. **Drawing:** Through this medium a child expresses his conception of the world and his relationships. Drawing provides a picture of his intellectual development and observational power. It is an effective and healing medium through which he may express emotions from the unconscious.
3. **Painting:** This medium is similar to drawing in its form and benefits.

4. **Tracing, colouring, cutting and gluing:** Only a few children begin to trace at the age of five. At the age of four, children draw outlines of their hands. At the age of four, children also begin to colour and fill in their drawings. This develops their fine motor skills, hand-eye coordination, concentration and accuracy. Cutting paper develops their ability to hold scissors, and gluing paper teaches them to carefully and neatly apply glue.
5. **Threading beads:** This activity develops children's fine motor skills and hand-eye coordination. It also develops tastes and aesthetics, as the children try different colour arrangements and patterns.
6. **Jigsaw puzzles:** Solving these puzzles helps children develop their powers of thinking, perseverance and discipline. It also builds their self-confidence.
7. **Folding and tearing paper:** This is a useful activity for young children who have never used scissors before. It helps improve hand-eye coordination.

## Drawing

There is an artist in each of us. A child's inner urges are expressed through free drawing, which is a powerful medium for self-expression. Several aspects of a child and their development are revealed through their drawings. In my experience, children use a lot of black when they are disturbed, orange when happy, red when aggressive, yellow or blue when calm and brown when confused.

Three-year-olds often draw lines and dots, which develop into circles and squares. Gradually, at around ages four and five, these further develop into objects such as flowers or the sun and the moon. Most children draw snakes, balloons, people, the sun and the moon, flowers and vehicles. After turning five, these scattered and isolated pictures start gaining coherence to form a whole. Sometimes children describe their drawings to the teacher and ask her to write what they say. Usually children go on drawing the same thing every day for several days before they draw something different.

Suggestions and corrections should be avoided during this time as they inhibit the child's spontaneity and self-expression. After they turn six and show their drawings to the teacher, they may be directed on how to observe and draw better. For instance, six-year-olds sometimes draw flowerpots with an upside-down triangular base. The teacher could ask the child to carefully look at the base of a real pot and ask what would happen if the base was balanced on a point, as drawn by them. At this age, drawings should be accompanied by encouragement to observe the things around them. Outings and nature walks help.

Some children prefer to sit and draw alone, while others enjoy drawing with a group. Groups tend to have a lot of conversation, comments and jokes. Some children prefer to lie down and draw.

Three-year-olds usually scribble. Their drawings usually do not have any shapes. By the time they turn four, their drawings start to show some patterns and later they begin to draw random objects. By the time they turn five, their drawings have objects that make a 'complete' or 'whole' picture. See pages 49–52, Figures 5–15 for examples of drawings by children I taught. These examples highlight the children's progression.

To get a complete sense of a child's development, one needs to go through the sequence of drawings done by the child and, along with this, look for patterns made by the child when they used other materials like clay, paints, building blocks, etc.

## Painting

This is another art form children enjoy and use for self-expression. It is similar to drawing, though it involves mixing colours, which is something the children very much enjoy seeing and doing. In the beginning children tend to paint with their fingers. Later, they move on to using bamboo brushes, which is ideal for rough work.

The children may sometimes approach and ask the teacher to write down a description of what they have painted. The teacher writes down what the child describes. The children are not forced to describe or explain what they have painted.

Four-year-olds painting with bamboo brushes.

Similar to drawing, children at first smudge different colours together and enjoy the effect and act of mixing colours. Gradually patterns begin to emerge in their paintings. By the time they turn five, individual objects or parts no longer remain separate and pictures start becoming 'complete' or 'whole'. See page 53, Figures 16 and 17 for examples of paintings by children I taught.

## Tracing, Colouring, Cutting, and Gluing

This activity is provided primarily to develop children's intellect and hand-eye coordination. Children are given outlines of simple objects. They colour the object, cut along the outline of the object and glue the cutout in a book. A great deal of concentration is required to colour the object evenly and to stay within the outline while colouring. Children are taught how to use a pair of scissors. They learn to carefully pour glue into a dish. Teachers help them use a brush to neatly apply the glue to the back of the cutout, stick the cutout in a book, and wipe excess glue away with a piece of cloth.

This activity is for four-year-olds and five-year-olds, not for three-year-olds.

Four-year-olds usually place one hand on a sheet of paper and trace its outline. Then they colour the drawing. They enjoy filling in the outlines of objects, though their colouring can be very clumsy. Most of them do not have the skill to hold a pair of scissors and cut along the outline of their drawings. They usually tear the paper with their hands. They are capable of sticking their cutouts in a book but sometimes require help from the teacher.

The five-year-olds have somewhat steady hands and are able to colour their drawings more neatly. At this stage the teacher gives them guidance on how to slowly and evenly colour the drawings. In the beginning they are not able to hold a pair of scissors or neatly cut out an outline, but as they continue to learn, with guidance from the teacher, they quickly develop this skill. Five-year-olds know how to use glue. They stick pictures in their books. The teacher shows them how to neatly glue cutouts in their books.

A teacher shows a child how to cut along the outline of a drawing.

## Threading Beads

Threading beads involves the use of fine motor skills, in particular, the use of smaller and more precise movements of the wrists and fingers. It also improves concentration.

Children are excited to thread beads. Three-year-olds thread long lengths of beads and do not worry about arranging the colours in any order. They wear these threaded beads around their necks and compare each other's work in a group. The teacher displays some of these threaded beads on a wall. Children are happy to see their work put up.

Four-year-olds thread using specific colours. They make simple patterns.

Five-year-olds thread medium-sized plastic beads and make different patterns. There is creativity in their work.

Threading beads in a group.

The teacher must first observe the patterns made by the children. For four-year-olds, these are likely to be clumsy. Using their work as examples, the teacher should show the children how to thread beads into more distinct patterns. Great care must be taken not to hurt their feelings. The teacher should never criticise their work. At the same time, the children should learn to cheerfully accept suggestions and improve their patterns. At the age of five, the children should have developed the skill of threading small beads through fine plastic wires. See page 54, Figures 18, 19 and 20 for examples of threading by children I taught.

## Jigsaw puzzles

In this activity, children observe the pieces in front of them, compare their different shapes and think about how they fit together. This is an important step in their learning process. Puzzles help improve a child's concentration, reasoning and problem-solving skills. They also develop a child's powers of observation.

Two-piece puzzles for three-year-olds.

Three-piece puzzles for four-year-olds.

Nine-piece puzzle for a five-year-old.

## Folding and Tearing Paper

While this activity is for four-year-olds and five-year-olds, three-year-olds too experience the urge to tear paper. They enjoy the sound and feel of tearing paper, but they do not have the skill to fold paper. Folding paper, especially along lines, requires concentration and good hand-eye coordination.

Children possess an innate creativity, and they may tear paper into shirts or blouses. Some fold paper and pretend to make it fly, calling it a rocket. They make a number of creative things on their own, such as snakes, windmills and bats.

When the children start to show an inclination for such creativity, the teacher should give them newspaper to play with. Gradually, the teacher can show them how to make small objects like aeroplanes or windmills. The children might already know how to make some of these.

The teacher can help them by showing them how to fold the paper in a systematic way. This encourages the children to try and fold and create objects on their own. The teacher can guide them and offer suggestions when necessary.

# 9

# Constructive Activities

All the activities provided in a nursery have one aim: to give the children a chance to explore their true selves.

Children do not classify activities as therapeutic, creative, constructive and so on. They do not think, plan and say, 'Now that I have finished the creative activities, I shall move on to the constructive activities.' They choose the activity which appeals to their spirit.

This classification of activities is meant mainly for the teacher who thinks logically and needs some sense of order to observe and help the children.

For an adult, young children's learning processes may not appear to follow any orderly pattern. This is because young children do not learn from words. Their learning depends on their sensory experiences. They need a chance to live or re-enact their experiences, play with them and express them in various ways using different mediums.

Children express their ideas, feelings and creativity through mediums like drawing, painting, playing with clay, block play, sand play, outdoor play, or music and storytelling. Their learning process is incomplete if they do not get a chance to express themselves through any of these mediums.

Children need time to become familiar with the materials and objects of an activity in order to freely express their ideas during play. This may take several months. The children do not need too much information from the adults. What they really need is time and space—a chance to become familiar with the activity's objects, to gain experience and play with them. This is why we find so much repetition in children's play activities. They are trying to understand the materials.

They should be free to explore at their own pace. This helps them to order and eventually master the world around them. They will be serious, interested and involved, using their time and energy to attempt to make a connection between themselves and the world. In such an environment, the children feel a sense of satisfaction, achievement and well-being.

The teacher should not interrupt them during this time of discovery but should patiently observe and trust them. This attitude supports the children. When they share their achievements with the teacher, he must acknowledge them.

While creative activities involve children playing with colours and expressing their ideas of objects through paper, *constructive* activities give children the chance to hold and feel materials. They can create or construct objects and see the results of their work develop a structure. During constructive activities, children still abundantly use their imagination to indulge in fantasy and drama.

If they play with building blocks, they first pick up the blocks and push them around. If they play with wet sand, they first dig a hole in the sand, cover their legs with sand, or make a mud pie. Their actions are instinctive. They use their muscles.

When their instinctive urges are satisfied, they search for something new and a desire to arrange objects in an orderly way arises. An impulse to create or construct takes shape, and it gives them a sense of fulfilment during their play, which develops their perseverance and hard work. They feel energetic and enjoy work.

Constructive play helps muscular development and physical growth. This play also develops their powers of observation, cooperation, organisation, accuracy and ability to arrange materials.

We classify the following activities as constructive activities:

- Block play
- Sand play

- Playing with construction toys, like pegboards, Legos and Montessori equipment

## Block Play

Wooden building blocks are essential educational materials. They are standard nursery equipment. Most of us fail to appreciate the educational value of these blocks, perhaps because they are neither colourful nor attractive like other nursery equipment. They are solid and heavy. For effective use, blocks should be plain, unpainted and made of good wood which will not splinter.

Usually a set of blocks has blocks of different sizes and shapes. A 'unit' is shaped like a brick. There are units, half units (which are square in shape) and double units. There are also pillars, triangles, arches, spheres, cubes, ramps and curves. A set of these blocks offer children endless possibilities for constructive, creative, imaginative, dramatic and cooperative activity. They bring a child's muscles into play and help with their physical development.

This activity should have its own separate area, away from the other activities of the class. Blocks must be stored on shelves. They must be arranged according to their size and shape so that the children find it easy to select the pieces they need for their play. After play, the teacher should help the children put the blocks back in their correct place.

### THREE-YEAR-OLD BLOCK PLAY

Three-year-olds usually pile the blocks into a heap with no order, form or shape. They fill a cardboard box or a toy wheelbarrow with blocks and pull it round the classroom, or carry it from one place to another, dump it, then refill it and bring it back.

They pile the blocks on top of one another, in no order, and so the structures are shaky and fall. But they keep doing it again and again. They do not have the skill to balance or lay a stable foundation.

They take one block, usually the unit, call it a car or a train and pretend to drive it round the class. They take the accessories provided for block play, usually a wooden animal or vehicle set, tie a string to the hook of the toy and walk or pull it round the classroom. They play alone and silently.

A three-year-old with a toy wheelbarrow filled with wooden blocks.

## FOUR-YEAR-OLD BLOCK PLAY

The four-year-olds arrange blocks in a line. They enjoy making long lines. Usually they arrange them near a wall. Gradually the lines change into squares. They sit quietly in the square and call it a house. They bring dolls and play with them and the kitchen sets within the square structure. As their play progresses, the square develops into a small house with rooms. In one room they lay the dolls to sleep, in another they arrange chairs and tables using wooden blocks, and in another room they play with kitchen sets. They bring accessories from the dolls' corner, like pillows and sheets, and cuddle up with the dolls and pretend to sleep in the 'bedroom'. This play goes on and on. One day the house might change into an airport filled with planes. These planes fly, hit one another and fall down.

They begin to construct vertical shapes. They balance large blocks on a small base. At this age they are not interested in making perfect structures. They do not plan or think about what to create, but instead experience block play. They rely on their muscles and senses. The artist in them acts—the child speaks through her blocks. After making vertical structures which are shaky or unstable, they kick or topple them over and enjoy the sight, sound and feeling of the blocks crashing to the floor.

They make two columns, put a block on top and call the block a roof. This enclosure becomes either a jail or a cage. If it is a jail, they put cardboard cutouts of people in it. If it is a zoo, they put animal cutouts in the cages. The enclosure may also change into a theatre where films are shown (their films usually involve shooting games, as they tend to play in a group and their play can be aggressive).

Most of their play is instinctual and subjective. It is self-centred.

## FIVE-YEAR-OLD BLOCK PLAY

At the age of five, children change their style of play. They seem to be more serious and thoughtful. They have a purpose and plan to their play. They make elaborate constructions using different blocks. They build houses, garages, factories and bridges. Most of the time it is cooperative play. They plan what they want to do in a group and each member takes on their own responsibility. Together, with concentration and perseverance, they build a structure. They put in a lot of hard work and spend more time on block play. Depending on the size and plan of the structure, they may play for an hour to two hours. If they do not complete their work that day, they leave the structure as it is and resume work on it the next day.

Examples of block houses built by five-year-olds.

Block building is an effective medium of expression which develops a child's sense of construction, observation, imagination and cooperation.

Group after group, we notice the same patterns repeated. In the beginning, the structures are very simple and crudely designed. Over time, there is a gradual improvement in the use of blocks, with the children creatively and imaginatively building elaborate structures.

## Sand Play

There are common sights one sees when observing children play with sand: the children stare at their hands and enjoy watching the sand pour through their fingers; they cover their legs with wet sand and pack and press the sand down to make it firm and decorate it with leaves and flowers; they enjoy freeing their legs from the packed sand; they roll in the sand and enjoy the feeling of rolling about; they fill coconut shells with wet sand and call them 'idlis'. Sometimes, I have found two children sitting across from one another and burrowing tunnels in the wet sand. They slide their arms down their tunnels and catch each other's hands. They enjoy this play.

The sandpit is a space where the younger children often explore the texture and properties of sand. As they grow older, they try to explore the possibilities of building structures with sand. The children jump around, build structures and dig, pour, feel and sift through the sand.

Sand play helps improve finer muscle development. It also develops imagination and initiative. The feeling of sand has a calming effect on children. It reduces tension and helps them relax.

Children playing in a sandpit.

## Playing with Construction Toys

Various construction toys and peg boards are available in the market. Children play with these toys by fitting the pieces together on the board and creating objects like trains, schools and houses. These toys add to the colour of children's spaces. Playing with the various pieces, understanding their properties and, through the process of trial and error, trying to fit the different pieces together is something the children very much enjoy.

Children playing with construction toys.

# 10

# Cultural Activities

Songs, music, dance, dramatisation and stories are vital parts of a child's everyday life. These activities are just as important as other activities in aiding the development of a child's personality. When we plan a timetable for the children however, the learning activities take precedence over all other activities, with cultural activities considered secondary and assigned once or twice a week.

In a school environment, where they are happy and satisfied, children joyously skip, dance, chant and move about in the hall. They enjoy rhythmic action songs, nursery rhymes and stories told in rhymes. They make their own songs, stories and verses, and express themselves through sound and rhythm. They sing and chant, even when they are engaged in other activities.

These activities give life and colour to the educational environment of the nursery. The following are classified as *cultural* activities:

- Action songs
- Music and dance
- Stories

## Action Songs

An action song is a song or rhyme with actions and gestures that the children can perform while singing. Children enjoy listening to these songs, singing along and performing the accompanying actions. Some of these songs are also used for reading.

The teacher should prepare charts with illustrations of popular rhymes and put them up on the wall. The children can sing and have conversations amongst themselves about the objects or people or actions illustrated on the charts.

## Music and Dance

A classroom must give children the space to enjoy and appreciate music as it is a significant facet of their personality development. When they hear slow or fast music, their movements change and they naturally and joyfully respond to the rhythm of the music. Simple musical instruments like the tambourine, triangle and bells add to their enjoyment while they sing or dance. These instruments also help children recognise different sounds.

Singing and dancing together help to develop among the children a feeling of belonging to a group or community. Those who are withdrawn, shy and quiet, who may have an innate urge to sing and dance, let go of their inhibitions and totally involve themselves in the rhythmic movements of dancing and the vocal release of singing. This helps them build their self-confidence.

## Stories

Stories are a powerful medium which young children find absorbing and involving. Stories also help in the development of a child's multi-faceted personality.

The content of the stories the young children read should be simple and vividly narrated. They should have a pattern, a series of experiences, and should not focus on plot. For example, the story *Home for a Bunny*, written by Margaret Wise Brown, has a delightful pattern and depicts a series of experiences a bunny goes through while searching for a home for himself. The character of the story appeals to the children. They enjoy the sounds they have to make. They are delighted by the rhyming sentences and chant along. In short, the child is completely involved in the story.

Stories for young children should be closely tied to their lives. Their lives revolve around sensory and motor experiences, and stories should reflect this. This does not mean the stories should lack imagination. A specific word or phrase is enough to stir a child's imagination and create a vivid picture in her mind.

Children love animal stories, and stories about vehicles such as cars, trains, cycles and aeroplanes also interest them. They also enjoy stories about other children. Stories which create anxiety should be avoided.

Five-year-olds are capable of reading or listening to stories which have more text and less pictures, while children below the age of five need their stories to have more pictures and less text. Though the five-year-olds enjoy simple and realistic stories—stories similar to their own experiences—they also enjoy a certain amount of fantasy.

Keeping all these points in mind, the teachers in our nursery section had developed simple stories based on the children's conversations and experiences. These stories were very popular and children enjoyed listening to and dramatising them. This activity also encouraged them to make up their own stories, which were simple and direct. Some of the stories they developed are listed below.

- 'Chetan and the Monkeys': This was a story about monkeys, big and small, which came to Chetan's garden to eat his bananas.
- 'Nithin's Cycle': This tells the story of how little Nithin was happy to get a small cycle, which he enjoyed riding. When one of the wheels was punctured, Nithin and his father repaired it.
- 'Chetan and Moksha Go to School': This story was about two young children going to school.
- 'I Am a Blue Baby': This was a simple story written by a five-year-old girl, Nithya, about how she had a hole in her heart.

The children also narrated simple stories. Some drew pictures for their stories. These stories usually had an element of fantasy in it. Below is a story narrated by a four-and-a-half-year-old.

> There was a forest. There were many wild animals there. They were all friends and lived happily together. They played ring-a-ring-a-rose.
>
> Then there was a man in the forest. He was their manager. Then the animals brought dosai for him one day and jalebi for him another day. Then he took them to a class. Handwriting class. All the animals wrote very nicely, but the monkeys wrote very untidily. Then the manager said 'good' to all the wild animals and to the monkeys he said 'very bad work'.

The teacher and children together prepared simple booklets for these stories.

Stories also help develop children's memory. A teacher narrates a story to a class. When she narrates the story the next time, she may not be able to remember the exact words and phrases she used before. She may use a new word or phrase which may have the same meaning. But children who are listening to the story will not stay quiet. They will immediately correct the teacher. They remember the words, the phrases and the sequence of the story.

# 11

# Outdoor Activities

Children are active by nature. They need plenty of strenuous physical activity, which is their earliest method of self-expression, and enjoy stretching their muscles. Watch a child in a nursery joyously climb the steps of a slide and then swiftly slide down. She will repeat these actions over and over without ever getting bored or tired. An adult however may feel a few times is enough. Children enjoy repeating such actions. They find them mentally stimulating. These activities also help children in their physical development.

Children who climb a jungle gym and jump down are simultaneously trying and learning to calculate distance to see whether they have the physical ability to complete such actions. They are learning to solve problems.

Running, jumping, climbing and other vigorous activities are relaxing and gratifying. The joy of motion that comes from strenuous activity gives them a feeling of accomplishment and releases inbuilt tension. The children use their entire body for physical activity. They therefore need space. If the school has limited space, then periodic visits to nearby parks are required. These parks should be child-friendly, with equipment for climbing and jumping and plenty of space to run, skip and play.

Physical activity for young children should not be during 'breaks'. It is an essential part of the nursery programme. The following may be classified as *outdoor* activities:

- Free play
- Organised games

## Free Play

Climbing, running, pushing, jumping, skipping, rolling and going on the slides or swings are part of free play. Children need a lot of space, interesting objects and equipment to explore and test their physical limits.

We find young children trying to climb sofas and other furniture in the house. When they join school they try to do the same things along with the other children. They run around and try to explore their physical strength when they climb a ladder, get a sense of weight and balance on seesaws and experience a sense of freedom when they use the swings. They play until they are tired. These activities help release a lot of energy.

Another enjoyable game for young children is to imitate the actions and sounds of animals or birds: to fly like a crow, walk like an elephant, hop like a frog, quack like a duck.

## Organised Games

From playing freely, their own way, on their own terms, children are slowly introduced to organised games. These are games with rules which children willingly accept at this age. The more time they have for learning and understanding rules at this age, the easier they will find it to follow and obey rules when older. Following instructions during play is one of the ways in which children realise that they are part of a society and have to sometimes conform to certain laws and rules.

Children enjoy organised games. They make an effort to follow the rules, to cooperate with and listen to others in order to be part of the fun and games. We see a huge difference between children running about freely versus how they behave when a race is organised for them. Both are necessary forms of play.

Organised games are for five-year-olds and above. Here are a few outdoor games which children enjoy playing. The rules are simple, as they must be for the children to understand and follow.

1. In the Pond, on the Bank
    - Participants stand in a circle drawn in the sand.
    - The group selects who will be leader.
    - The leader stands in the middle and calls out, 'In the pond'. The participants must jump inside the circle.
    - The leader calls out, 'On the bank', and the participants must jump outside the circle.
    - The leader may choose to call out the phrases as quickly or as slowly as they want, and may change the order of the phrases.
    - Those who fail to follow the leader's instructions are out.
    - The game continues till all are out.
2. Colour, Colour, What Colour?
    - The group selects who will be leader.
    - The leader stands next to and faces a wall.
    - The rest of the children stand far away from the leader and together choose a colour.
    - Then they ask, 'Colour, colour, what colour?'
    - The leader guesses a colour.
        i. If it is not the colour the group has chosen, then the group says 'No', takes a step towards the leader, and asks the question again.
        ii. If it is the colour the group has chosen, then the group says 'Yes' and runs. The leader tries to catch one of them. The first child to be caught becomes the new leader.
    - The game continues till the children start to lose interest.
3. What's the Time, Mr/Mrs Wolf?
    - The group selects who will be leader. The leader is Mr/Mrs Wolf.
    - The leader stands next to and faces a wall.
    - The group stands in a line far away from the leader.
    - The group asks the leader, 'What's the time Mr/Mrs Wolf?'

- The leader says, 'It is one o'clock.'
- The group takes one step forward and asks the same question again. The leader says, 'It is two o'clock.' This continues till the leader says 'It is five o'clock.'
- When the leader says 'five o'clock,' the group runs away and the leader tries to catch them. The first child to be caught becomes the new wolf.
- The game continues till the children start to lose interest.

In our nursery we had a collection of simple outdoor games for young children. These were prepared by different groups of teacher trainees and teachers. It may be useful for an aspiring teacher to collect games and devise outdoor activities for young children.

# 12
# The Setup

## Choice of Place

Children need a quiet, secure place which is free of interruptions from others—a place where they can be themselves. It must be a place which the children feel is their own, and is meant solely for them and their learning materials. This could be an entire room or part of a room. It should not be a make-shift arrangement.

## Arrangement of Materials for Activities

All the materials required for the children's activities should be arranged and kept in order. Each activity should have its own place and space. Each corner should be allocated a specific activity. The children should be able to see and recognise the materials in the classroom. They should have access to what they need without depending on the adult all the time. This will help the children develop a sense of ownership and responsibility. A simple sketch provided here may help you understand how to arrange a classroom for young children.

This is only a rough arrangement meant to give you an idea about how a classroom could be set up. You could use your imagination to make your own arrangement more attractive. The most important factor is that the space is not organised for adults and should instead be organised to help young children learn. Children should be able to freely move about from one activity to another.

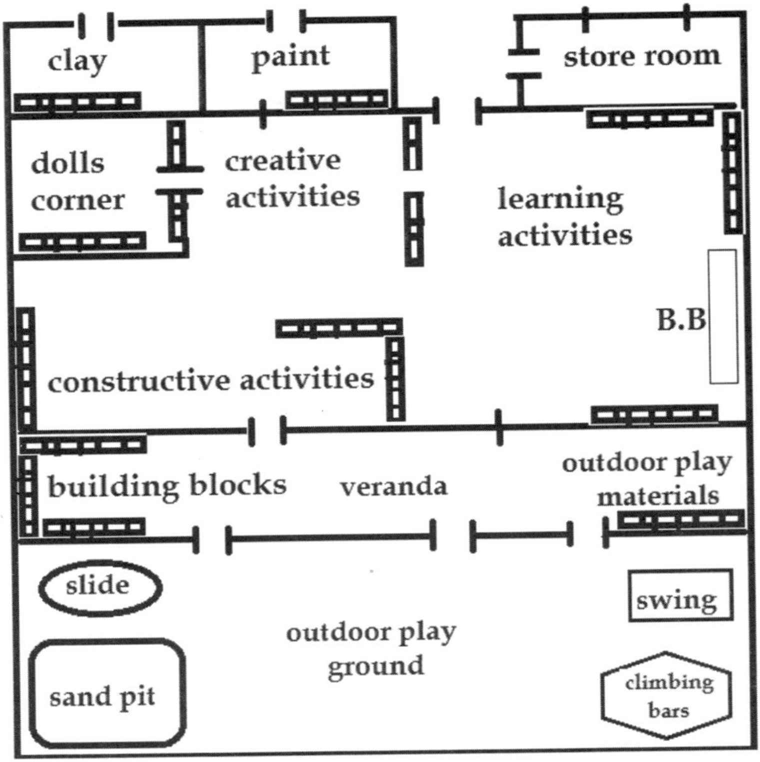


## Display of Teaching Materials

Activity charts should not be randomly located but instead displayed on the walls of their respective areas in the room. Children's drawings, paintings, bead work, and craft work should also be displayed on the walls. There should be an order to the display.

## Atmosphere

The classroom should be bright, lively, attractive and have an environment conducive to learning. The atmosphere should be

Dolls Corner

Wooden block play

peaceful, calm and happy. Children need to feel safe and content in the classroom.

## The Teacher

The teacher is the most important person in the setup. It is his personality which will bring cheerfulness, life and joy to the whole setup. The teacher should also be observant and attentive to what the children say and do, and must respond to their needs.

Ideally, the teacher reaches school before the children and arranges the classroom for the day's learning. He happily welcomes them as they arrive and shares a pleasant exchange with each child.

If this happens, then the children, from the moment they enter the premises, experience acceptance and warmth from their teacher and the adults in the school. They need this in order to go through various activities, to courageously face hurdles and to build their personalities.

## Time to Begin

Now everything is ready. How to start? Where to start? How does the day begin? When does one introduce the lesson plans, timetable and syllabus?

Introducing the lesson plan in the beginning itself will have no impact on the child. It will not mean anything to them. It satisfies adult logic. Children need time and space to adapt to a new environment, that is, the school. A slogan worth remembering is: 'Begin where the child is.'

Children come to school with their own unresolved emotional problems, fears and questions. Time has to be given to them to solve these problems before they plunge into intellectual learning activities. A proper environment can help children overcome these hurdles and ready them for the next stage of activities. As a result, they will soon exhibit a hunger and eagerness to learn.

# 13

# Suggested Materials and Directions

Split into five categories—therapeutic activities, creative activities, constructive activities, outdoor activities and cultural activities—this chapter lists the various materials that I believe and recommend every nursery should carry.

## Therapeutic Activities

These are activities designed to help relieve a child's tension and stress. Some of the activities also help the children confront and understand domestic situations which they daily face.

### DOLL AND KITCHEN PLAY

Doll play requires a quiet corner with two shelves. The corner must be like a small room within the classroom, secure and protected from the noise of other activities. The materials for this play, listed below, should be arranged on the shelves in such a way that they are easily accessible.

- Four rag dolls to represent a family of two parents and two children. Rag dolls are suitable for this play as they are soft, bendable and are not damaged if children hit or throw them. In short, they obey the children's wishes and bend to their needs.
- Dresses for these dolls including frocks, skirts, blouses, shorts, shirts, dhotis, saris and blouses.

- Accessories for these dolls including bangles, chains, ribbons, caps, a toy iron, etc.
- A doll house and doll-sized furniture including a cot, mattress (with pillows and bed sheets), cupboard, shelf, table, chair, dressing table, stools, cradle, etc., as well as doll-sized items from a toilet like a bathtub, mug, mirror, comb, soap and soap dish, towels, etc.
- Two small plastic dolls
- Kitchen playset including an oven, a kadai, a tava, spoons, pots, plates, vessels, tumblers, buckets, a chapatti roller and other 'cooking' items such as mud, aluminium, steel or plasticine

## PLAYING WITH CLAY

Materials:

- Potter's clay
- A plastic sheet
- A plastic bag to store the clay (this helps keep the clay soft)
- Bucket of water and a mug
- Floor brush or broom to clean up after play
- Hand towel

How to prepare the clay:

- Powder the clay.
- Sieve and separate the fine powder.
- Mix the fine powder with water and knead it well to make a smooth dough.
- Place the clay on a cement slab meant only for playing with clay.

Directions:

- Show the children the materials. Tell them they can play with the clay however they want, even if that means using more water.

- After play, have the children clean the cement slab, put away the materials, and wash and wipe their hands.

## DAUBING PAINT

Materials:

- Starch powder (available in grocery stores and used to starch clothes made of cotton)
- Packets of red, yellow and blue rangoli powder
- Castor oil
- Six large dishes, three spoons and three small containers
- A towel, soap and a soap dish
- A plastic sheet

How to prepare the paint:

- Mix the starch with water and stir it into a thick batter. Make sure there are no lumps.
- Boil water.
- Pour the prepared batter into the boiling water. Stir well. The consistency should be semisolid. Let it cool.
- Mix the powder with the prepared starch and a few drops of castor oil. Make sure there are no lumps. The castor oil gives the paint a smooth, slippery feeling which the children enjoy.
- Add a little water to dilute the solution.

Directions:

- Pour paints of different colours into dishes large enough for children to place their entire hands in them.
- Leave the dishes on a cement slab used only for paint-related activities. The children can smear paint across the cement slab. They may use both hands, squeeze the paint and pass it through their fingers.
- Allow the children to play till they are satisfied. Do not interrupt them if they smear paint all over their bodies. Some of the more hyperactive children may pour lots of water into the paint and enjoy rolling in the mixture.

- Make sure the children thoroughly clean themselves.
- Help the children clean up.

### SCRIBBLING

Materials:

- Newspaper
- Crayons (used because of their smoothness)
- Scribbling book
- Adhesive tape
- Scissors

Directions:

- Provide the children with sheets of paper. Stick these sheets of paper to the floor using adhesive tape. (This is so that the paper does not move when the child scribbles.)
- Let the children select their crayons. They may use any colour(s) to scribble on the paper.
- Encourage the children to stretch their arms and scribble freely. They release a lot of energy doing so and experience a sense of contentment.
- Instruct the children to scribble continuously without stopping. They may use both hands.

## Creative Activities

Creative activities serve as an outlet for the children's emotions and, as mentioned before, help develop their hand-eye coordination and test their small-muscle skills, which overall improves their concentration and precision.

### DRAWING

Materials:

- Drawing books (each child has their own one with their name written on the cover)

- Crayons (each child has their own set of oil pastels)
- Dishes or jars to store the crayons
- Sheets of paper

Directions:

- Materials for drawing should be easy to access so that the children need not depend on the teacher when they want to draw. Children should be allowed the freedom to draw while seated, lying down or leaning against something. Drawings should be displayed on the wall reserved for children's artwork.

## PAINTING

Materials:

- Sketchbook for the children. This should contain blank white sheets of paper. The cover should list the child's name, age and year.
- Set of poster-colour powders (primary colours)
- Water, gum or paste to mix with the paints
- Four medium-sized dishes for mixing
- Spoons for mixing or pouring paint
- Three small dishes for each child
- Jars for storage
- Rags
- Bamboo brushes (These are made by cutting bamboo sticks into the size of a pencil and then flattening one end with a stone. The flat end is used for painting.)
- Large paintbrushes

Directions:

- Make sure the materials required for painting are arranged so that children have access to them when they want to paint. They should also have time and space to paint.
- Mix paints (red, yellow and blue) with water and pour into separate dishes.

- Place a spoon in each of these dishes.
- Let the children pour the paints from these dishes into their own smaller dishes.
- Children should spread newspapers across the floor before they paint to make sure they do not make too much of a mess.
- Children should be allowed to use any or all of the colours to paint. They should learn to paint first with their fingers, then the bamboo brushes and finally with the large paintbrushes.
- After painting, children should wash and dry their brushes and dishes. They must also clean the place where they painted.

## TRACING, COLOURING, CUTTING AND GLUING

Materials:

- Paper shapes which may be used by the children to trace and draw. (Children must be familiar with the objects and the objects must be easy to draw, like a pot or a leaf, kite, flower, etc.)
- Crayons
- Glue
- Dish for the glue
- Rag to wipe away excess glue
- A book for the children to glue in and collect their drawings
- Scissors
- A dustbin which the children should use to throw away waste paper. (After the activity, children should put away their materials and clean up.)

## THREADING BEADS

Materials:

- Wooden beads of varying sizes, from large to small (large ones are meant for the three-year-olds, medium-sized ones are meant for the four-year-olds)

- Plastic beads of varying sizes, from large to small (the small plastic beads are meant for the five-year-olds)
- Plastic wires of varying thickness
- Scissors
- Four jars to store the beads
- Dishes for when the children play with the beads

Directions:

- Have the children thread wires through the holes in the beads. Let them experiment with colour combinations.
- Younger children should use large wooden beads and thick plastic wire. As their finger coordination improves, they should be gradually introduced to smaller wooden or plastic beads and thinner plastic wires.

## JIGSAW PUZZLES

Materials:

- Two-piece puzzles of animals and birds
- Three-piece and four-piece puzzles of fruits, vegetables and birds
- Five-piece and six-piece puzzles of vehicles and flowers
- Ten-piece and fifteen-piece puzzles of scenes from stories

Directions:

- In the beginning, children are allowed to try and fix the pieces together by themselves. The teacher can then show them how to solve the puzzle.
- Three-year-olds should be given two-piece and then three-piece puzzles. The pictures should be of fruits, vegetables, animals, birds, or common objects.
- Four-year-olds should be given four-piece to six-piece puzzles.
- Five-year-olds should be given ten-piece to fifteen-piece puzzles as long as the pictures are clear and simple and the pieces easily fit together.

### TEARING AND FOLDING PAPER

Materials:

- Old newspapers
- White paper
- Glazed paper
- Glue
- Small scissors for cutting paper
- The bristles of a broom (which the children can use to make windmills)
- Wastepaper basket

## Constructive Activities

### BLOCK PLAY

Materials:

- Plastic building blocks
- Medium-sized wooden building blocks
- Toy wheelbarrow
- Empty boxes (for the children to carry blocks)
- String

### SAND PLAY

Materials:

- Sandpit (The sandpit should be at ground level and should be a protected place which can accommodate five to six children at a time.)
- Accessories including coconut shells, bottle lids, thin bamboo sticks

Directions:

- Remove any large stones from the sandpit. If necessary, sieve the sand.

- Pour water in one section of the sandpit. The children will be able to use the wet sand to build castles and other structures or dig caves and tunnels.

### PLAYING WITH CONSTRUCTION TOYS

Materials:

- Pegboard
- Accessories including cutouts of animals, people, trees, houses and vehicles (car, bus, truck, etc.)

## Outdoor Activities

### OUTDOOR PLAY

Materials:

- Pulling toys
- Pushing toys
- Balls
- Rubber ring which the children can use to throw and catch
- Swings, climbing bar, rocking horses, jungle gym

## Cultural Activities

### MUSIC

Materials:

- Charts for the following: action songs, rhymes, stories, etc.
- Rhyme books
- Storybooks
- Musical instruments including the xylophone, bells, tambourine

# 14

# How to Begin?

## The Importance of Instructions

It is very important that children, from a young age, are trained to follow instructions. Listening is a skill that many find difficult to develop. It is easy to talk, but one needs discipline to listen.

Nursery years are when children could be helped to develop this skill, to make it a part of them, to learn to remember and follow what they are told. They should be encouraged to ask questions, clear doubts, clarify what they hear and then follow instructions.

Instructions should be clear and simple. The children must understand what the teacher says. The teacher must make sure they are not confused.

The teacher can ensure they are not confused by asking them to repeat what he has said and encouraging them to follow the rules he has provided. The teacher should mean what he says. He cannot say something and then later contradict or change what he said. This will confuse the child.

## Getting Familiar with the Setup

There should be a fixed time in the morning when the teacher and all the children gather together to begin the day's work.

Fixing a definite time to be followed every day involves discipline and makes both the teacher and the children give up some of their comforts. The same time should be followed every day. The children should be taught to respect this time. It is something they have to practice every day till it becomes a part of their daily schedule.

Once all have gathered, the teacher should greet the children and they in turn should greet the teacher. Next, everyone should close their eyes and stay silent for two minutes. This is done to avoid sensory distractions and to recollect what activities have been planned for the day. Some may prefer to begin the day with prayer. Either way, the purpose of this time is to help with recollection.

After this, the teacher should take attendance and compliment the children for coming to school on time. In our centre, after taking attendance we would begin with a cleanliness check. This was done with care and tact so that the children did not feel any shame. They are helped to grasp the importance of cleanliness. This motivated them to develop good cleaning habits. The children in our centre also used to have a short and spontaneous conversation after the cleanliness check. They would share news with those children who were absent the previous day and discuss any new developments. This is a sort of anxiety sharing. The teacher should give the children time for this, but not so much time that they end up distracted.

The teacher then should tell them about the classroom, the materials in it and all the activities available to them. They will be interested to know what is in their class, so the teacher should take them around and show them all the different activities available as well as all the materials arranged on the shelves in the room. The teacher should also show the charts on the wall.

The children are allowed to go through all this carefully. They may not understand or be able to take in all that the teacher shows and tells, but each child will register what they need. It is at this point that they should sit quietly and try to decide what they want to do.

## Choosing an Activity

From my experience of working with children, no one usually goes for creative or constructive or learning activities in the beginning. They either opt for doll play or outdoor play. Most of them choose the dolls' corner and spend the whole day there. This is allowed.

In the beginning there will be chaos, indiscipline and noise. This atmosphere is very different from that of a normal classroom. It's like a starving animal finally getting food. The children may not be able to decide what to do and so might run from one activity to another.

Despite this freedom, there are limits. They must not hurt others, should not damage or break any play materials and should put the play materials back in their rightful place after completing an activity.

The teacher's attitude is very important. The teacher should not feel helpless or unable to control the children and should be aware that this disorder is to be expected. Things will settle down after a few days. The teacher should deal with the situation confidently, without fear, tension or anxiety, and this in turn will help the children.

Once the children become aware of the materials in the classroom, they begin to choose activities which appeal to them. The teacher should not suggest activities. The children should decide for themselves. If a particular child is unable to recognise or understand certain play materials, then the teacher may help or guide the child.

Children usually choose doll play or playing with clay or sand or building blocks, and spend most of their time on the activity they chose. They may spend many days on the same activity. As soon as they arrive in the morning, they head straight to the activity they chose. It may look like they even have a plan or purpose in mind for their play.

Usually, boys choose building blocks and girls choose doll play. This however, is not always the case. Sometimes boys choose doll play and girls choose building blocks.

The children need this play. They need time and space and also freedom. They should believe the classroom is a place where they can be themselves without being judged, reprimanded or punished.

The teacher must be like a strong pillar which they can trustingly lean against.

Of course the place will be messy. It will not be the way we expect it to be. Most of us were raised to be tidy and clean—these were considered to be signs of a good upbringing. It will therefore not be easy for an adult who has grown up with that sort of discipline to tolerate this messy situation. The immediate impulse would be to express disgust. This attitude is not helpful. But, however careful we are, we will act as we do. We need to accept this fact and with humility try to acknowledge and modify our approach for the sake of the children. This does not mean the children are allowed to make a mess and leave the classroom like that. After play, they must clean up after themselves. They do this with the teacher. It is a learning process.

What helped me when I first started teaching young children was reminding myself that after play everything would be washed and cleaned. This helped me control my impulses and allowed me to let the children freely play.

The teacher's job during this period is to observe the children and note the activities they take up, the play materials they use and what they say. The teacher must record this information. No comments are necessary. The teacher does not need to scold the children, or make fun of them, or discuss what they do with other adults. The teacher has to *respect* the child. The child trusts the teacher and reveals herself to him. He should not betray the child's trust.

This does not mean the teacher should remain quiet and passive. Children may ask questions and he has to give them honest answers which they can understand. Instead of expressing his opinion, the teacher should encourage the child to reflect on what she asked so that she gains the confidence to answer her own questions.

The teacher must be on the move, observing the children and listening attentively to what they say. If any of the play affects the teacher—touches on his own childhood experiences and creates a disturbance within him—then it is for the best if he shares this information with someone who is aware of children's growth processes. Otherwise the teacher may develop an emotional block. The children are quick to notice and feel this, and this is not helpful for them.

Writing observations every day is very important. Observations should not be subjective. No conclusions, no assumptions, no opinions, no interpretations and no judgments should be made in these observations. The teacher simply writes down what he sees. Further information on writing observations is given in Chapter 16.

Once a child has gained satisfaction from an activity, she feels calm, peaceful, self-confident, and freely moves round the classroom. There is a sense of belonging to the school, a sense of ownership. She is happy and cheerful and so she dances, sings, skips and jumps. She is active, interested in all the events of the school and aware of others in the group. This is a sign for the teacher to know that the child has overcome internal emotional blocks.

Not all children will be at the same stage at the same time. In my experience, those children who were less inhibited, like, for example, children from slums, were spontaneous and responded quicker than others. Some needed time to make sure the school was a safe place for them to use the materials provided to express their feelings.

Those who feel their urge to express their feelings has already been satisfied will not bother to spend much time on therapeutic activities and instead will begin with creative activities. Though they participate with interest and enthusiasm, they may periodically return to doll play or playing with clay or painting. The teacher allows them to do this because she knows the children need this. The children may even like to roam about or just relax and do nothing. This is allowed. The child needs this space. But not for prolonged periods of time.

Lesson plans and a timetable are guidelines for a teacher. They need not be strictly followed. The most important thing is that the teacher offers activities to the children in order to observe them, guide them and help them when they need help. When the children are ready to learn, the teacher discusses with them the importance of selecting two or three activities for a day and completing them as a group.

Children above the age of five are usually able to select activities as a group. In the beginning there are arguments within the group; each child wants their activity to be selected. Gradually they come to an agreement and select two or three activities for the day. These activities are put on the board. The children work together and complete the activities. This exercise is repeated day-by-day for a week, with more activities added and completed.

Next, the teacher asks the group whether they wish to continue in the same pattern or plan for an entire week. There is a discussion in the group about what they did and what they want to do.

If they are ready for it, they talk about their experiences and together, with the teacher, plan for a week. Then a final timetable is drawn up by the teacher and approved by the group. Assuming the children are happy, this timetable is followed for a term.

For children between the ages of three and four, it is better not to have a structured timetable. As they turn five, children could be introduced to a structured timetable. This prepares them for formal learning when they turn six years old.

A structured timetable does not work for very young children. Their activities cannot and should not be confined by an adult's logical planning and timing. Nevertheless, a teacher needs something to use as a guide so that he knows which direction the children are moving in and doesn't lose track of events happening in the classroom.

This guide is one that is *developed*, not planned. After the teacher allows the children to choose their activities and after they play for as long as they want to, he makes a note of the main activities they chose and how long they spent on these activities. The teacher observes the children for a week or two and then gains an approximate idea of the time the children need for each activity.

I have found that during the first three hours of class in the morning, the younger children spend the first hour or hour-and-a-quarter on therapeutic activities. After this they need rest. It takes about 30 minutes. During this time they relax, eat snacks and use the toilet. Then they ask for action songs or stories. They concentrate on this activity for thirty to forty minutes. After that they settle for quiet activities like threading beads, drawing, solving puzzles, colouring the outlines of objects, cutting and gluing these outlines or drawings in their books, or going through storybooks. For this as well they concentrate for about thirty to forty minutes.

Some days they spend a lot of physical and mental energy on therapeutic play. Afterwards, they prefer to be quiet. They silently move about, lie down in the resting room or sit and thoughtfully observe the garden or fish tank.

Below is a model plan that could be loosely followed by children under the age of five.

**Plan**

| | |
|---|---|
| 1. 60 minutes | therapeutic activities |
| 2. 30 minutes | relax, rest, snacks, toilet |
| 3. 30 to 40 minutes | stories or action songs |
| 4. 30 to 40 minutes | creative activities |
| 5. 20 minutes | putting things away, cleaning, reflection, ending the session |

# 15

# Sharing a Few Classroom Experiences

A teacher cannot be satisfied with only a well-prepared, well-arranged classroom. Teaching a group of young children is a real challenge. Each child will possess a unique personality with different interests, skills and behavioural problems which the teacher will need to face and address every day.

In a classroom there are children who respond to teachers and there are those who do not. As a human being, the teacher's immediate reaction might be to pay more attention to those who respond to them and to view those who do not respond to them as a burden they will have to carry.

This is where this methodology helps a teacher. First, do not view those children who do not respond to you as a burden, but instead learn to look at them with compassion and ask yourself why they are different.

If the teacher is alert, attentive and compassionate while handling the children, then there will be innumerable opportunities for her to discover herself and help the children grow and develop their unique personalities. Many incidents which happened in my classroom come to mind at this point. Here, I share a few.

## Nithin

Four-year-old Nithin was a daydreamer and a clumsy and lazy child in my class. My immediate reaction was to be irritated by his behaviour.

One day he asked me to get his drawing book and crayons. I believed he was too lazy to get up and get them by himself—this was my judgment of his character—but still I patiently did what he asked.

He drew a father crow and a baby crow flying in the air, and showed his drawing to me. He told me: 'Teacher, the father crow and the baby crow are flying. Suddenly father crow dies and falls. The baby crow is sad. It is crying.'

A teacher who is serious about the personality growth of a child in her care will not consider this something insignificant. She will ponder what the child is telling her and what should be her response. If she is patient and compassionate, instead of judgmental, and gives the child the time and space and security he needs to work out what disturbs him, then one day the child will slowly reveal what issue has been bothering him.

This was what happened: Nithin told me, 'Teacher, you know my father went to Delhi in an airplane. My mother told him not to go, but he went. In the plane he had a heart attack and died. My mother cried. We took him to a forest and made a fire. I, too, cried. Teacher, I am sad.'

The child burst into tears, sobbing bitterly. I allowed him to cry. I was shocked and did not know what to say.

I began to notice a gradual change in the child after that. He stopped daydreaming. He seemed to be more cheerful and active, less clumsy or lazy.

Not only that, he became a compassionate child who was sensitive to other children's problems and always stepped forward to help them.

One day, during storytelling, the children and I were seated in a circle. Suresh wanted to sit next to me but Manoj pushed him aside and took his place. Suresh was sad and sulked. Nithin immediately got up, went to Suresh, put his arms around him and told him, 'Don't be silly. It's alright, come and sit next to me.' He held Suresh's hand, took him to his place, made him sit next to him, smiled at him and wiped away his tears. Suresh smiled, grew cheerful and listened to the story. Nithin didn't scold Manoj or make him give up his place to Suresh, but consoled Suresh. After the story, the group went out to play together as friends.

This type of situation does not require the teacher to moralise or admonish the children. In an open environment, the children will amicably solve their own problems. Here was a child considered to be lazy and a daydreamer—his behaviour an irritation. But he was not a burden. In a tension-free environment, he was able to solve his own problems. Later, this child grew into a responsible, thoughtful and loving child. That was the report given by his first- and second-standard teachers.

I witnessed many such incidents in the classroom which, on the surface, may have seemed insignificant but were most definitely not so.

## Vishwas

There were also times when I felt helpless and did not know how to deal with a situation in my classroom, as can be seen by the following experience.

During block play, four-year-old Vishwas hoarded all of the blocks and was unwilling to share them with the other children. Padma and Reshmi wanted to play but saw there were no blocks on the shelves. They saw Vishwas sitting with all of the blocks. They approached him and asked him for some blocks, but he refused to give them any. Ignoring his refusal, they forcefully took a few blocks from him and played without him.

Another child, Nithya, needed blocks and asked Vishwas for some. He grew extremely upset and started to kick and scream. He threw the blocks at her and cried and shouted: 'Take them away, take them away, take them all away!' Nithya was frightened and left to thread beads instead.

I watched what happened, then went to Vishwas and tried to talk to him, but he was unwilling to listen. He appeared to be very stubborn. I began to lose patience. I was getting annoyed and felt he had unfairly treated Nithya. I thought Vishwas was selfish, but I controlled these feelings and tried to talk to him. It was no use. I felt helpless. I did not know what to do.

Fortunately, on that day, Nadya was in my class and had silently watched the drama unfold. She came forward and put her arm around Vishwas's shoulder. He tried to push her away. He was inconsolable. Nadya collected the blocks, one by one, and put them in order. She asked Vishwas to pick a block and hand it over to her. Vishwas looked suspiciously at Nadya. She was smiling and humming a song to herself. Vishwas stopped crying, hesitantly took a block and gave it to Nadya. Nadya started building with the blocks and Vishvas slowly joined her. Together they constructed a beautiful block house. Vishwas was astonished. He couldn't believe he had built a structure like that. He stood up, jumped, clapped and laughed, overwhelmed with joy. The children in the classroom wondered what had happened to him. They admired his block house. He proudly showed it to them. He gave away his remaining blocks to three girls.

Vishwas was always by himself in class. He looked very tense and during block play could only pile blocks, not construct anything. He had a short temper and would sulk over small or trivial matters, so other children didn't include him in their groups.

Nadya saw him as a child who needed comfort and support to come out of his cocoon. She helped him emerge from this cocoon and see his own beautiful self, whereas I was trying to logically analyse the problem. I was judgmental and searching for justice over how he had treated the other children. I was stuck on this and so couldn't help the child. Vishwas was stuck as well, but with his own problems.

After this incident, Vishwas no longer played by himself in class. Others accepted him in their groups, and he contributed with enthusiasm. He also went out of his way to help those children who were stuck in their work. He no longer hoarded blocks or other play materials but shared generously. As Barbara Biber mentions:

> For the first five or six years of his life, he needs to be understood as a creature of conflicting feeling, of uncertain control and strong impulses.

> He needs the comfort of feeling that he will not be expected to control his own impulses alone, that the adults who exert control over him will not hurt him or dislike him, that they will not be shocked or offended by inconsistent, uncomfortable behavior that stems from feelings of conflict, that they will give him ways and things with which to release feelings, that they will stand by through the storm as well as the calm. If this part of the education is successful, he will feel loved and valued and the adults can chalk up a good beginning on the construction of a secure and social human being. ("A Dream for the Nursery Years" 1)

Parents and teachers alike need to accept the fact that preschool children are living through a period of fundamental conflict. During this period the children are being asked to renounce a great deal that is dear to them and to accept a great deal that is unfamiliar and perhaps undesirable to them. This does not mean teachers must direct their efforts towards eliminating conflict. These are the experiences that will strengthen the children and help them understand their personalities and capabilities. What we need to do, as teachers and parents, is give the children the time and space to overcome their inner conflicts so they may develop into their true selves.

The teachers in our nursery understood this reality and also recognised that we need to support each other in order to help the children in our care.

## Lakshman

Nadya was there to help me recognise a child's needs in a difficult situation. Other teachers faced similar situations in their classrooms. They needed support and guidance. We worked together, supported each other, and so were able to confidently face and solve problems in our classrooms.

In certain cases, when a teacher mentioned a difficult problem she had faced with a child in her class, we as a group would agree to study the child's behaviour for a year. This included monitoring their behaviour during different activities. We would meet periodically to share our observations, which were recorded every day. The group would discuss any problems and supported the teacher in taking the next step.

I used to take notes when the teachers shared their observations.

These studies helped us gain a holistic picture of the child—their relationships with other children, how they changed, etc. It also allowed us to understand the factors, both within and outside of the classroom, that affected the child's behaviour.

Here I present an abstract of one such study of a child named Lakshman. The class teacher observed Lakshman and read her observations to us. I gave her regular feedback, though I also sought help from Nadya. The abstract is only an outline of how a study was done by our group of teachers.

## ABSTRACT

Lakshman was a four-year-old boy. He was tall for his age, very thin, and looked undernourished. His elbows and knees stuck out from his body. He stomped around the class in shoes that were too big and too heavy for him.

Lakshman had a very sweet smile, though the expression on his face was usually not a happy one. He seemed to be a very frightened child and his large eyes reflected his anxiety.

Lakshman did not play with any children in the classroom except Raghu, his cousin. When Raghu finished an activity, Lakshman would rush to finish the same activity. In his hurry to do what Raghu did, he would leave his materials all over the place

The teacher felt Lakshman should not depend on Raghu but work independently, so she would ask him to arrange and put away the materials he used before leaving. With great effort, and struggling to control his impatience, Lakshman would put the materials in order and back on the shelves.

Note: It is not advisable to arbitrarily break a child's relationships. There is value in closely observing how these relationships develop.

Lakshman would not go to the toilet by himself. He would take Raghu with him. He didn't allow Raghu to play with the other children, and when Raghu tried to play with the other children, Lakshman would call him back. If Raghu didn't come back, then Lakshman would kick him and beat him. Raghu didn't react, he kept silent. After this, Lakshman would once again be friendly with Raghu and the two would play together.

In the middle of the term, a new boy called Shiva joined the group. He tried to become Lakshman and Raghu's friend. When he and Raghu played together, Lakshman angrily hit him. Shiva left to play with the other boys.

Before school closed for the year, Raghu and Lakshman's mothers met with the teacher and asked about their child's performance.

The teacher felt Lakshman's mother was very stern, withdrawn and tight-lipped. The teacher told her that Lakshman was a frightened child. Lakshman's mother immediately reacted by saying, 'He was not like that last year.'

The teacher told her that even the teacher who taught him last year said he was a frightened child. Lakshman's mother appeared sad and upset and asked the teacher for suggestions to help the child. The teacher told her to read stories to Lakshman and to give him the time, space and materials to draw and paint.

The next day, Lakshman arrived at school and told the teacher that he was not frightened.

Note: On answering parents' questions—talk about the child's progress in a tactful way that does not make the parents feel uncomfortable.

Below are observations the teacher made of Lakshman's work during play activities.

- **Doll and kitchen play:** In the dolls' corner, he sometimes played by himself and sometimes played with Raghu and other children. He usually played with the kitchen set and not with the dolls. He brought water in a big pot and poured it into the tumblers, cups and small pots. Then he poured the water again from these small vessels into the big pot. When he played, the floor and the shelves would get wet. The teacher showed him how to dry the place. He dried the floors and shelves and did it well. He made chapattis with plasticine.

- **Playing with clay:** He poured plenty of water in the clay to make it soggy and mushy. He was immersed in this activity. He would sometimes wet the clay with spit.
- **Scribbling and drawing:** He usually drew with black, brown, and purple pens. He scribbled, and the finished drawings were a mixture of these colours. During the process he completely obliterated his drawings as he scribbled so hard that the paper often tore.
- **Tracing, colouring, cutting and gluing:** He used to take a sheet of paper and first cut it into strips before cutting the strips into small squares. He stuffed the squares of paper into his pocket. He preferred straight lines to curved lines, and when given the drawing of a circle, struggled to cut along its outline.
- **Block play:** He played with building blocks near the passage where the large blocks were placed. He liked to act like a traffic police officer directing traffic. If any child passed that way he would hit the child. Once, he threw a block at Raghu. The block hit Raghu in the face, causing the skin around his eye to swell up and turn blue. Raghu did not react. The teacher showed Lakshman Raghu's eye and told him that she would not let him hurt other children. He kept quiet and did not look at Raghu's eye.
- **Outdoor play:** Every day, for all of his time spent during outdoor play, he played on the rocking horse. He would not let any of the children use the rocking horse. If they went near him, he would hit them.
- **Drama:** The children had to stage a play and Lakshman would either run or walk around the group that was singing or acting. He would quickly walk around the group

and then sit in his place before the song had finished. He did not listen to the teachers who tried to make him join the group. He repeated the same behaviour on the stage.

- **School medical examination:** When it was his turn to go to the doctor for a medical checkup, he stomped around the room. The doctor called him but he wouldn't go for the medical examination. His mother was with him. She did not say anything. The teacher spoke with the child, pacified him and helped the doctor examine him.
- **Parent-teacher meeting:** Lakshman's parents were called to the school to discuss his progress. His father said they used to read a lot of stories to him, but he would always interrupt and ask a lot of questions about the story. Finally, they stopped reading to him. He also said Lakshman was quick to grasp things.

The teacher told the parents that they should continue narrating stories to Lakshman, and if they did not know the answers to his questions then they could tell him they would find out and let him know later. This would make him curious and encourage him to look for answers too. It would also help the boy if he was not always prevented from doing the things he liked. Instead of immediately saying 'no', they could explain the consequences of his actions.

The parents were aware that their son was frightened and sometimes hurt other children. They tried telling him not to do that, but later expressed their disapproval by angrily staring at him and eventually hitting him.

His father said they did not allow Lakshman to play outside with other children or to even go up to the terrace. This was because they had sent Lakshman's sister, who was a year or so older than him, to play in the neighbourhood, and while playing she had fallen headfirst into a small construction tank filled with water and drowned. They said that since then they had been very protective and

> frightened about Lakshman's safety, as he was their only son.

After this meeting, Lakshman began to show a slight improvement in his behaviour. He would draw on his own, even when Raghu was playing outside. He would draw three or four pages with interest. His drawings began to show patterns and themes. For the rest of that term, he painted only twice, but his paintings now had form and were not mashed up like before.

He traced the outlines of animals and learned to do so correctly. He was more relaxed and freer in his movements. The teacher also noticed Lakshman and Raghu at times playing separately.

On the last day of term, just before the children dispersed, the teacher prepared them for the next year of school. When the bell rang, she asked the children to form a line to go home and handed each one their progress card. Then she felt someone come from behind, take her hand, kiss it and run away. It was Lakshman.

A good rapport between the teacher and the child's parents is necessary for the healthy development of the child. Just like the children, the parents also need time and space to trust the teacher and share their fears, anxieties and feelings of guilt.

It is very, very difficult for a parent to accept any negative criticism about their child, especially from a teacher. This doesn't mean the teacher should tell the parents only positive things about the child. The teacher and the parents cooperate and work together to help the child develop, so they have to be honest with each other.

Since parents are placed in a vulnerable position and worry about their children, it is better if the teacher initiates the conversation and paves the way for a trusting, honest and comfortable relationship. The teacher could begin by informing the parents of their child's progress and praising the positive developments she has observed in their child. This puts the parents at ease and makes them feel comfortable. They become more open to listening to and talking about their child's negative behaviour, and are more likely to consider suggestions put forward by the teacher.

In spite of all this, the teacher cannot expect miracles to happen. For the first two or three meetings, the parents are likely to try and convince the teacher that their child is good and there is nothing wrong with him, and that they are good parents who do their best for the child.

When parents talk like this, the teacher should not try to confront or contradict them. Instead, she should patiently listen to them and trust that they will be able to honestly speak about what bothers them when the time is right. This attitude will create an atmosphere of trust and honesty.

All parents, whether rich or poor, illiterate or well educated, drunkards or teetotallers, are all basically good human beings with good intentions who want the best for their children. They all need time and space to express this basic good in them. If the teacher truly wishes to develop the children in her care, she must make it her responsibility to provide, with compassion and understanding, this space for the parents.

Lakshman's parents were fearful and their fear was transferred to their child. They experienced tragic and painful trauma, and it badly affected their lives. They retained their fear and protected their son through fear. As a result, Lakshman couldn't be himself and be free and this created anger in him, which was reflected in his behaviour.

Once Lakshman's parents were able to share with the teacher their pain and fear, which they had kept to themselves for so long, there were able to begin the process of healing. The teacher was empathetic, not judgmental. His parents feared they would be blamed for this unfortunate incident and felt guilty that perhaps they could have done more to prevent the death of their daughter. Because of this, they couldn't share their feelings with anyone, tried to evade talking about it and spoke only about the good things they had done.

After a few meetings with Lakshman's teacher, they were able to tell the teacher what bothered them. As a result, they were freed from the fear that had gripped them, and this led to a change in their behaviour with their son, which brought about a change in the child as well.

Lakshman's friendship with Raghu was also a good source of support in helping him conquer his fears. Despite the possessiveness and anger that Lakshman expressed, Raghu remained a calm and affectionate companion who patiently dealt with any difficult situations. This helped Lakshman calm down many times.

It is easier to work with and help a young child than an adult. The first five or six years of his life are years of fundamental growth and adaptability. During this stage the child is gaining a feeling or understanding of himself. As Biber mentions in "Nursery School as the Beginning of Education": 'In these early years the fundamental groundwork of a child's personality is laid down. He meets decisive problems. His ways of meeting his nursery age problems, the residue of feelings, attitudes, inclinations, laid down in the course of his childhood victories and defeats will contribute a basic pattern to his later growth' (4).

## Bharat

Here is another story about a child, one who was slightly older than Lakshman.

Bharat was a very responsible and reliable child who was capable of patiently doing very good work. All the adults relied on him for help with any work in the school. When he was angry however, he was very destructive. Whenever he was confronted about something or criticised in order to make him aware of his behaviour, he chose to leave the school and go home, thereby sweeping the issue under the carpet. (This took place in a learning centre for children from a poor community. Children were allowed to go home during class hours to have food with their family or to help their parents. This was allowed because most of the children were dropouts.) He avoided facing negative comments and instead chose to run away. He would return after a few days, once the issue was forgotten, and would behave as though nothing had happened.

This was a situation where the intensity of the issue would periodically and temporarily reduce, but the child remained incapable of overcoming his weakness.

In his case, the process of learning was like an unconnected chain. If he faced his behavioural issues, then the links in the chain would connect and be continuous, and his personality and maturity would develop.

If Bharat continued to handle issues the way he had been doing so, then his behaviour would have handicapped his personality growth and prevented him from truly developing his potential and skills. Since he was quite young, we were able to help him get out of this behaviour. He gradually learnt and became aware of his own actions.

Confrontation may be an unpleasant experience for a child, but if he has the courage and willingness to face it and in the process become aware of his own issues, then it is possible to help him work on his issues and eventually change. This is one of the most important functions of a school. For adults, it is far more difficult to undergo such a process.

I witnessed this when teaching a child from the slums. The child was active and interested in learning, and over time grew to become an honest individual, though she did behave negatively in one way—she refused to share her work with others. It disturbed her. She would not let me help her work through this problem. It appeared to be very painful for her to change. As an adult, this behaviour has affected her in many ways, both in her career and in her family life. She is aware of it now and realises that she couldn't face it as a child. She had a great fear that if she shared her work with others, she would lose something precious. Even now, she does not want to deal with this issue. She says what she got from the centre was enough for her and she is happy. So she chooses to be happy and stand on one foot rather than on two feet.

As mentioned before, in these early years the child's behaviour is primarily naïve and instinctual. It does not matter what form they take, what matters is that we, as adults, do not feel outrage when one child physically attacks another or slaps or kicks an adult. As long as we do not take these as signs of our own failure, we will be free to help the child.

It is this environment which must be provided in a classroom. The methodologies I have outlined in this book help facilitate this process and provide the space for children like Bharat to deal with the problems that could prevent them from reaching their full potential.

## Guidance for a Young Teacher

The following are some basic guidelines which I found helpful during my time as a teacher:

1. 'Begin where the child is.' Instead of bringing to the class ideas of teaching and imposing them upon the children, the teacher should begin where the child is. The needs of the children, what stage of development they are at and what disturbs them have to be understood by the teacher. All children have an innate urge to grow and develop and they look for opportunities around them which help fulfil this urge. The teacher has to recognise this and provide an environment in which the children can choose what they need for their development.
2. The primary role of a teacher is that of a keen observer who is attentive to the child's needs and listens to what the child is verbally or physically communicating. The teacher must provide assurance and support for the child.
3. Lessons planned for the children should not be based on adult logic but should connect with the children's emotional needs.
4. This does not mean the teacher should come to class without any preparation. The teacher must know the materials young children use in their play. These materials need to be prepared and arranged in the class. The teacher must, however, give the children the freedom to choose

what they want to do. For example, while drawing materials are available in class, the teacher should accept that the children might not want to draw on that day but instead play with clay.

5. The teacher need not worry if children do not choose the activities he has planned and hoped the children would choose. He need not feel that, by not doing the activity, which he believes is important, the children are missing something vital to their learning. Not allowing a child to choose what they feel comfortable working with might curb the child's growth process, so the teacher must believe and accept the child has an innate urge to choose materials they need for their learning.
6. The teacher must be sensitive to emotions, including his own, that arise in the classroom. He must accept children as people who, like himself, are creatures of feeling. He must also be aware of and accept his own emotions in a situation.

# 16

# Observation Records

An observation record is a very important document for those teachers concerned about the personality development of the children under their care.

Usually teachers find recording to be a tedious job. It involves discipline and the willingness to sacrifice a bit of personal time. Teachers prefer to talk about the children, their behaviour, their problems and their achievements without recording their behaviour on the spot. The problem with this is that a verbal report changes according to the mood and mental state of the teacher.

When I went through my old records (only fragments remain—many students borrowed my records and then forgot to return them or lost them), I didn't know whether to believe they were written by me or by someone else. This is because the way I remember and think about the incidents recorded is very different from what I had actually recorded. This holds true for children's drawings, paintings, photographs of clay work, block play and sand play as well.

It is true that writing down observations can be a tedious job, especially when a teacher's energy is spent taking care of the children and then, after work, attending to household and personal responsibilities. That doesn't mean one shouldn't do it. Doesn't a research worker or discoverer work hard and take risks to overcome difficulties and satisfy their curiosity? A teacher is in many ways a discoverer of human behaviour. The raw data the teacher collects helps in the search to discover and develop a child's personality.

In this modern age, with equipment like cameras, microphones, mobile phones and video recorders available, recording is not as cumbersome as it used to be twenty or thirty years ago.

That being said, a teacher should know what to record, how to record and when to record. Without a proper understanding and knowledge of observation records, teachers and trainees will record material of no substance—monotonous notes on what the children did every day. So, what are the things a teacher has to know about observation records?

1. The record should be in relation to the background of the actual educational methodology used. Here is what is needed:
    - A summary of the main activities based on the methodology given to the group for a specific time (six months, one year, etc.).
    - A full record of two or three sample weeks.
2. The teacher should record behaviour the children exhibit at any particular stage, rather than changes in their behaviour. It should show what the children *are* by nature and not what the children ought to be (or what the teacher wants them to be).
3. The teacher must observe the children without influencing their behaviour. For the children, even the slightest of actions by a teacher is full of meaning. The teacher listens without comment, withholding suggestions or questions as these might affect the children's spontaneous behaviour. This passivity on the part of the teacher will help her objectively record and will also allow her to focus on the children's responses to parental influences and adult pressures. Observations must be dispassionately recorded, free of assumptions and not according to the likes or dislikes of the teacher.
4. Only observed behaviour should be recorded. There should be no interpretation of the children's behaviour in the observation records. Impulsive, casual remarks will not help a teacher understand the child's problems (and so will not help the teacher help the child). For example, when I observed Vishwas hoarding all the wooden blocks (Chapter 15), I thought he was being selfish. My judgment

didn't help Vishwas, and I, as a teacher, was stuck not knowing how to help the child. Instead of drawing vague conclusions like the child is selfish, lazy, quarrelsome, clever, smart, etc., the teacher should observe the child's behaviour as it happens and record only that. Situations which give rise to a particular behaviour should be recorded. Records immediately written are more effective and useful in helping understand children than those written at leisure.

5. Other teachers interested in working with young children, when reading these records, should be able to refer to them. For this reason, judgments and interpretations should not be present in observation records.

Usually most young teachers are very reluctant to write observation records. They appear diffident. Perhaps the instructions given to them on how to write observation records make them feel as though it is something they cannot do. One has to get out of this fear and just start writing in a very simple and concise manner. It will not be perfect. There will be mistakes, but mistakes help us learn.

Records are of two types: *psychological observations* and *pedagogic achievements*. This chapter deals with how to record psychological observations.

For psychological observations, children are given the freedom to express their feelings and views through words, and to satisfy or release their urges and impulses through dramatisation, imagination, fantasy and myth. Once given this freedom, the teacher's observation should not be swayed by pedagogic influences and moral judgments. Approvals or disapproval should not control the children's behaviour. Morals and manners should not be imposed upon the children. There are certain conditions that affect the observation and recording of children's psychological behaviour. These are listed below:

- The children: The number of children in a class, their age group, the time, whether children are in day school or (and) residential, and the number of teachers involved in handling the class.

- The school: a building with large, well-lit and spacious rooms for children to perform different activities.
- The materials: Are the materials for different activities arranged in different places and are they easily accessible for the children?

When a teacher is fully engaged—mentally, emotionally and physically—with a bunch of children in the classroom, she cannot always be objective in her understanding and dealings with the children. When she is out of the classroom, relaxed and by herself, she will be able to clearly think. Then, if she goes through her observation records, she will be able to see the drama which unfolded in her classroom in an unbiased and detached way. This objectivity will help her learn to better deal with the class next time. This develops her self-confidence and motivation to teach.

Here I share with you a few extracts from the observation records which I wrote in the early years of my teaching career. In the beginning, I too was very reluctant and didn't have the confidence to write down my observations. But, when I made up my mind to write in a simple and concise way, and persevered, I realised the value of these observations in understanding children's behaviour.

I am not presenting a template or an ideal record, but one which I hope will encourage young teachers to start writing down their observations.

## Sample Observation Record

### CLASSROOM SETUP

In this class there were 25 boys and girls who were around the age of four. Lessons were for three hours in the morning. The teacher had two helpers to keep the rooms tidy, prepare snacks and materials for the class and wash and clean the children after their play.

The school building had a large central hall connected to two rooms, with a veranda at the front and at the back. The rooms were spacious to accommodate the children's various activities. The veranda at the back led to a large quadrangle which led to an outdoor playground. This outdoor playground went round the entire building and so connected with the front veranda.

Dolls' corner and creative activities were located in the central hall. One of the rooms was used as a library while the other room was where the children could rest. Toilets were attached to the latter.

Materials for painting and playing with clay were arranged in the veranda at the back. There were taps and water facilities there. In the quadrangle, wooden building blocks with accessories were arranged on shelves.

The playground at the back was used for playing with solid blocks, and there was a tree ladder tied to the branch of a big tree. The sandpit, jungle gym and slide were in the playground by the front of the building.

## TIMETABLE

The children typically followed this schedule:

They would assemble in the hall, sing a prayer, then sit quietly for a few seconds to reflect on what they wanted to do that day (they could choose any activity for as long as they wanted).

In the first hour, nobody would choose creative activities or reading. Usually, the boys would play outdoors or play with building blocks, and the girls would go to the dolls' corner. Sometimes the boys would also choose to play with the dolls, while the girls would play with blocks.

After an hour-and-a-half, the children would relax. They would eat their snacks and enjoy a short break.

After their break, they preferred quiet and more peaceful activities like reading stories or singing action songs. They would have no desire to play anymore. Some would go through storybooks, either by themselves or with friends. Some would choose to solve puzzles, thread beads or play with cards.

Twenty minutes before the end of the session, they would tidy up and put away everything. Then they would sit in a group and share how they felt about themselves and the day.

After hearing instructions for the next day, they would go home.

## OBSERVATION RECORD

| | |
|---|---|
| 13 June<br><br>Outdoor play<br>Wild animals<br>• Initiator<br>• Participants<br>• Description of play | Arun, Ashwin, Rohit, Kiran, Roshan and Rahul chose outdoor play.<br><br>Rani, Meena, Mini and Nithya chose dolls' corner.<br><br>Vinod, Vishwas, Nithin, Ravi, Murali, Shanker and Ramesh chose to play with building blocks.<br><br>Arun was in the jungle gym pretending to be a wild animal. Pointing at the jungle gym, he announced 'This is my cage.' He frightened the girls who were playing in the sandpit. The girls ran helter-skelter. The other boys, who were watching Arun, joined the game. They too became wild animals—walking on four legs and trying to frighten the girls.<br><br>Ravi climbed a small tree near the jungle gym. He sat on a branch. The others saw this and stopped their game to climb the tree and the jungle gym. They jumped from one branch to another, making monkey sounds and saying 'We are monkeys!' Arun sat on a branch and sang:<br><br>We are monkeys<br>We jumped into trees<br>Our tails are cut. |
| 16 June | The same boys chose outdoor play. Ashwin, Rahul and Rohit took bats and rings to play outside. Using the bats, they played a shooting game. They ran with the 'guns' in their hands, shouting 'tosu, tosu' and pretending to fire at each other.<br><br>Roshan and Kiran joined the game. They carried long sticks. They always carry long sticks with them during outdoor play. |

| | |
|---|---|
| | The boys stopped 'shooting' and started hitting and kicking each other. The teacher intervened and stopped their fight, saying, 'I will not let you hurt others, nor will I let others hurt you.' Rahul said, 'Miss, it is not a real fight,' and the teacher said, 'Nevertheless, you hurt each other and I cannot let you do that.'<br><br>Rahul said, 'Okay, let us play the train game,' and Rohit and Roshan agreed. Vinod stopped playing with blocks to join them. The others climbed the jungle gym, sat there and made animal sounds. They looked at the girls playing in the sandpit and tried to frighten them.<br><br>Rahul and his group sat on a parapet and pretended it was a train. They used bats to connect compartments and tennis-court rings as a steering wheel. Rahul was the engine driver and the others were passengers. Rahul was always the engine driver. He said, 'All of you should be passengers, okay?' The others didn't mind being passengers.<br><br>Rani and Mini left the dolls' corner and joined Rahul's group. Rahul announced, 'If girls want to come on the train, they should sit in a different compartment, not in our compartment.' The girls agreed to this condition. |
| 18 June<br><br>Film show | Roshan left his group and joined Vinod to play with blocks. These two children constructed a film show with the small building blocks. They invited the girls in the dolls' corner to their show, issued tickets and allowed them to see the film. It was a film where they were 'shooting' each other. |
| 25 June<br><br>Animal game<br><br>Shooting game | Arun and Arshad played the animal game. They went round frightening the other children. Later on they put their bats and rings under the slide and played house.<br><br>Ramesh made a jail with big building blocks. He put all the cutouts of people in the jail and announced, 'Look, now I have jailed them all. Let them stay there.' Roshan from the animal group joined them.<br><br>Ramesh. Rohit, Vinod and Rahul also joined them. After imprisoning the people, Ramesh played the shooting game. The others in the group joined him and they all 'shot' at each other. |

| | |
|---|---|
| | Ravi, Ashwin and Kiran, during outdoor play, made poison water using coloured chalk powder. Ravi gave this 'poison' to Ashwin to drink and said that he would die if he drank it. Ashwin mimed drinking the water and said that he didn't die.<br><br>Arun joined Ravi, Ashwin and Kiran and made poison water with pink chalk powder. He said, 'This is poison. I'll give it to the snakes.' After some time he said, 'This is not poison water, it is tea.' Rani left the dolls' corner and joined Arun's group. She asked Arun, 'Is it poison?' Arun said, 'Who said it is poison? It is tea.' Then they both used plasticine to make pancakes and pretended to have tea and pancakes. |
| 1 July | Nithin, Vinod, Rahul, Roshan, Arun and Ramesh chose to play with building blocks and planned to make a zoo. They needed animals for the zoo. Nithin told the group, 'Come, let us make cutouts of animals.' The others joined him.<br><br>Nithin made an elephant cutout. Vinod made a lion, Roshan and Rahul made tiger cutouts. Arun and Ramesh watched the others. When the children finished cutting and colouring their pictures, they built a zoo with big wooden blocks and scattered their animal cutouts within the zoo.<br><br>Nithin kept his elephant in a special, separate cage away from all the other animals. He directed the play and helped the group build the zoo, but once he built a cage for his animal, his attention was focused only on it. He stood near his cage, watching it and protecting it from others.<br><br>The group said, 'Let us call the girls to come and see our zoo.' Nithin showed no interest. He remained silent but was protecting his elephant in the cage. |

This observation record does not include my observations of children's behaviour in the dolls' corner, or while playing with clay or paint—activities which were happening while I was taking notes. I didn't include these observations because during such play, deep and personal feelings and emotions were expressed.

Once you start writing down observations that are objective and not influenced by your personal emotions, you begin to write in detail all that takes place in your classroom.

From such records we can gather play content which will help us understand the behaviour and developmental changes in young children.

Not only is their behaviour important but also what they say. This observation record would be a very useful document if the teacher was to continue writing the record for a year. At the end of the year she could go through the record and, if she wants to make a case study of a particular child—Arun, for example—she could underline all of his activities for the year. She could copy these underlined notes in another book, and these observations would offer a clear and complete record of what Arun did, what he said, how he interacted within a group or with his parents. This book may also include his parents remarks from meetings. All of this can be used by the teacher to try and get a clear and honest picture of who Arun is as a person.

If records are so complete that a teacher has three years' worth of observation records of a child, from age three to age five, as well as records of their drawings, paintings, clay and block constructions, then studying these records will offer the teacher a rewarding and in-depth understanding of the behavioural patterns of young children.

# 17

# Learning Activities

## The Process of Learning

Though the heading of this chapter is 'Learning Activities', it first deals with the most important aspect of learning, that is, the *process* of learning. Once the process is understood, it will be easier to know what activities will help children learn.

Note: The various activities outlined in the previous chapters prepare the children for the life-long process of learning *with understanding*.

The most common form of learning which takes place in schools today is rote learning, where children memorise the content they are studying without truly understanding what it means. It is a mechanical process, involving repetition, and so can become laborious, time-consuming and unappealing. There is no practical application of what is learnt, and so no true intellectual development. Worse, over time what is learnt may be easily forgotten.

But there is another form of learning called intelligent learning, or learning with understanding. This form of learning is more creative and engaging, which means the children do not find it burdensome or boring, and this in turn means the children are less likely to forget what they have learnt.

Intelligent learning involves the formation of conceptual structures which are communicated and operated by means of symbols.

What does this mean and how does it happen? To understand these two points it is useful if we have an idea about what is intelligence. Richard R. Skemp, in his book *The Psychology of*

*Learning Mathematics*, explains this in a clear, meaningful way which helped me understand the functioning of intelligence and the process of learning. Skemp uses findings by the Canadian psychologist D. O. Hebb to define intelligence as having two meanings: the first (A), is possessing a brain and body capable of development; the second (B), is the use of a brain which has already shown signs of development (16).

The function of intelligence B is to understand, interpret, predict and control one's environment. The process of this mental function is through *concepts*.

But what are these concepts? How are concepts formed? How do concepts help the learning process?

A concept is an idea. It is therefore invisible and inaudible. To form a concept one needs to interact with the outer world and undergo a number of sensory and motor experiences.

These experiences should have something in common. For example:

> *A child sees something which walks on four legs, has a tail and two ears and barks. The child saves a mental picture of this moving object. Then he sees another one which is similar yet larger. Later he sees another one which is furrier than the first two. The idea formed in the child's mind from his sensory experiences is the <u>concept</u> of a dog.*

## How are Concepts Formed?

Many sensory and motor experiences are put together in groups on the basis of similarity. In other words, we say the experiences are *classified*. New experiences which have similar or overlapping qualities are added to these various forms of classification.

Once these experiences are classified based on similarity, the *invariant property* (the property which does not change and thus is used to identify something) is abstracted.

Abstraction is an activity by which one becomes *aware* of the similarity. The end product of abstraction is a concept. Abstraction is a lasting mental change. It enables one to recognise new experiences as sharing similarities with earlier experiences which have already been classified.

The illustrations below explain abstraction. $C^1$, $C^2$, $C^3$ and $C^4$ are sensory experiences.

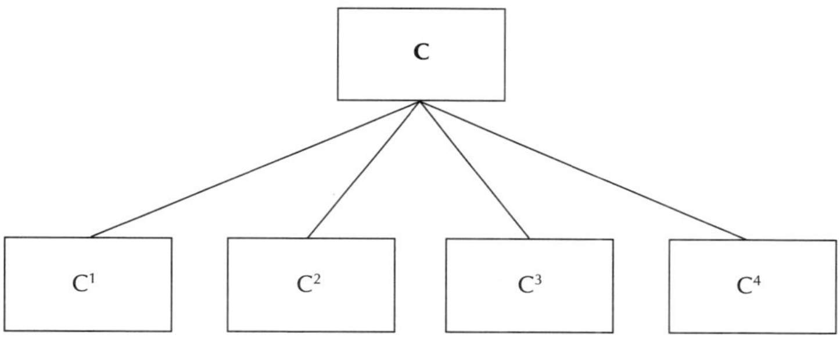

Figure 21

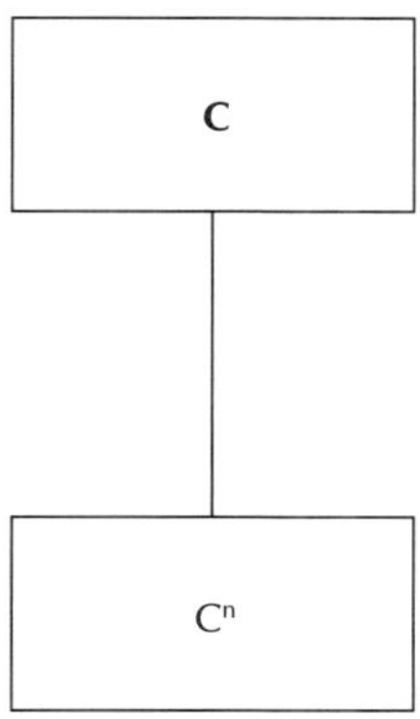

Figure 22

1. In Figure 21, C is the abstracted concept from $C^1$, $C^2$, $C^3$, $C^4$ based on certain similarities.
2. Once the abstraction is formed, new experiences—$C^n$—bring to mind the concept C.

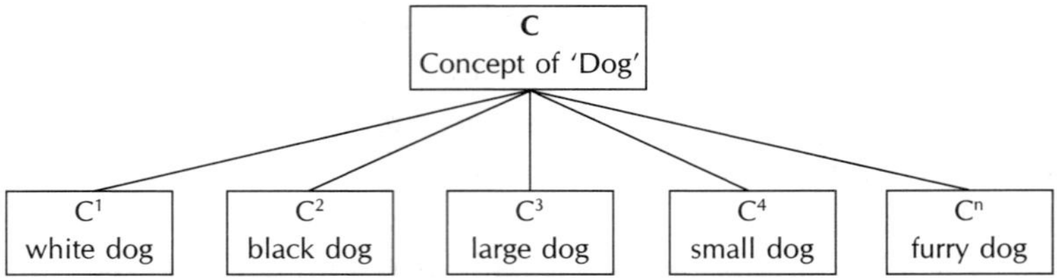


Figure 23

3. $C^n$ and C are similar in experience. Children find it easier to see similarities not differences.
4. The new experience, $C^n$, is sorted under the classification C along with $C^1$, $C^2$, $C^3$ and $C^4$.

Carrying forward the example that we used earlier in the chapter:

> *The child abstracts in his mind the idea of a dog from the invariant qualities of something which walks on four legs, has a tail and two ears and barks.*

Since a concept is an idea, we have no way of knowing or observing the idea existing in another person's mind. I am unable to know or observe the idea formed in your mind, nor are you able to know or observe the idea in my mind.

A concept therefore needs a visible or audible symbol for everyone to recognise it. Naming a concept is making it audible, writing down a concept is making it visible. The word we speak or the symbols we write become associated with the concept, and this in turn gives them meaning.

> *The child who abstracted the concept of dog now begins to hear people around him referring to this object as 'dog'.*

He hears the word (the spoken sound) 'dog' in different situations. It is used to refer to types of dogs which may be different in terms of fur colour, size or shape, but which all share a common quality or *invariant factor*—they all walk on four legs, have a tail and two ears and bark. Variant factors may change from dog to dog, but an invariant factor is the similarity which identifies the object, in a person's mind, as a dog. He associates this spoken sound 'dog', which he hears many times, with the concept he has formed in his mind. He begins to use the spoken sound and learns to say 'dog' whenever he sees one.

Naming thus classifies a concept and also enables him to talk about the concept.

Naming is an essential factor in the process of abstraction. Without a concept attached to a symbol or name, the symbol or name is meaningless.

*The word 'dog' now means something to the child, and he is able to use the word whenever he sees or wishes to identify one.*

Let us look at the process of forming the concept 'dog' in a child's mind, and how that leads to the child using the word 'dog' to represent the concept.

Through sensory and motor experiences the child is exposed to a number of situations which involve an animal. On the basis of similarity (has four legs, a tail, two ears and barks) these experiences are abstracted and classified. Thus, whenever the child sees a dog he recognises it by associating it with the idea or concept he has formed in his mind.

When he hears others refer to this animal as a 'dog', he associates the word with the concept in his mind. Without the concept, the word would have no meaning. He would have nothing to refer to. But now, because he does have a concept of dog, when he sees one he is able to identify it by saying 'dog'. This is a significant moment because the child has used a word to consciously name a concept. This is intelligent learning. It involves learning through understanding.

Let us look at the opposite of this. Let us look at an example where a symbol or name is attached to something the child has not experienced and thus is not, in their minds, a concept.

*In class, a teacher is trying to teach the letters of the alphabet to the children. She says 'A is for Apple, B is for Bat, C is for Cat, D is for Dog' and so on. As she speaks she shows picture cards of the letters and objects. One of the students, a five-year-old named Karthik, is asked to read aloud the words on the cards. He does so, but when he comes to the letter 'd', he does not read aloud the word 'dog' but instead says 'Rocky'.*

The reason this happened was because when Kartik saw the picture of a dog, he did not connect it with the word 'dog' but with the mental picture he had of Rocky, a dog in his school. He played with Rocky, fed him, petted him, talked to him. He liked Rocky's company. And Rocky was fond of Karthik. Whenever Rocky saw Karthik he would wag his tail and run up to him. Rocky was Karthik's friend.

The word 'dog' held no meaning for Karthik. It didn't exist for him. But the picture reminded him of Rocky because he had an emotional bond with the dog.

The teacher was trying to teach using adult logic. My understanding is that children do not learn by logic. They learn from sensory experiences which involve touching, tasting, seeing, smelling and hearing. Emotions play an important part in their learning.

When you teach young children, you must make sure the process involves sensory experiences and that the children can form an emotional bond with the content they are learning.

If a symbol or name is seen or heard each time an example of a concept is encountered, then by the time a concept is formed the name has become so closely associated with it that it is mistaken for the concept itself. This is what happened with Karthik. He mistook the name 'Rocky' to mean the concept 'dog'. It is difficult to separate a concept from its name.

Once the child has learnt to say the word 'dog' with understanding and with meaning, he has to be led to read and write the word 'dog', and to complete activities which will help him learn the complete meaning of the word. Listed below are the different steps involved in the process of intellectual learning:

1. Sensory and motor experiences
   - Forming an emotional bond
2. Classification of sensory and motor experiences (based on similarities)
3. Abstraction of the invariant property
4. Naming the abstracted concept
   - Associating name (sound) with concept
5. Reading
6. Associating symbol (word) and picture with concept
   - Matching the word with the picture and reading aloud
   - Reading the word without the picture
7. Writing the word
8. Recognising the letters in the word
   - Recognising these letters in the names of other objects
9. Completing class activities connected with the word
10. Group learning and individual learning
11. Group testing and individual testing

## Sample Method of Intellectual Learning

### STEP 1: SENSORY AND MOTOR EXPERIENCES

The goal is to introduce the concept of 'red' to young children. The teacher arranges and introduces a collection of experiences to the children in the hope that they will abstract the common property—'red'.

What is in the collection of experiences?

The teacher brings to class a number of different objects which share the similarity of the colour red (some of these objects are familiar to the children and contribute to the children's classification of known experiences). They may include, for example, a red pencil, a red bag, a red ball, a red box or a red ribbon. The teacher shows the objects to the children and repeatedly asks them, 'What is this?'

## STEPS 2 AND 3: CLASSIFICATION AND ABSTRACTION

The teacher once again takes the objects and shows them to the class, one by one, only this time she does not ask them to identify each object but instead tells them to listen carefully. She introduces each object and emphasises the colour of each object: 'This is a bag. It is red. This is a box. It is red. This is a pencil. It is red.'

By doing so, the teacher introduces the children to a similarity. Now, from their exposure to these different objects, the children are able to abstract one invariant property—the concept 'red'.

This stays in their memory far longer than the meanings of the objects.

Now the teacher asks the children to look for this quality in objects inside and outside of the classroom. The children look around and recognise this invariant quality in new objects. They collect these new objects and add them to the classified concept 'red'.

Thus the invariant property (the colour red) is abstracted from the classification of all these variant objects to form a concept. The teacher identifies the invariant property and gives the concept a name: 'red'.

## STEP 4: NAMING

The children associate this name (the sound of the word 'red') with the visible colour of red. They learn the name of the concept while they are forming it. To strengthen this learning the teacher gives them plenty of exercises which extend their understand of the world of 'red'. These exercises may be in the form of activities, games, songs, stories, conversations, making things, group learning or individual learning. Examples of such activities and further discussion on how to introduce the class to colours may be found in Chapter 22.

## STEP 5: READING

The next step is to read. The teacher hands out a picture card which shows the colour red along with the word 'red' written underneath.

The children touch the colour on the card and then touch the word and say 'red'.

This connects the act of identifying the colour with the acts of reading and saying the name of the colour. The teacher helps the children to do this in a way that is not mechanical. The children should understand the connection between identifying the colour and reading and speaking the word.

After enough practice the children are able to dissociate the written word from the picture. The teacher does this by giving the children cards which only carry the name of the colour, and not the colour itself. The children are asked to match the word on their card with the concept it names. Therefore children are able to take a card with only the word 'red' written on it, and match it with a picture card which shows only the colour red. The children are now at a stage where, when they see the word 'red', they immediately think of the concept 'red' and are able to identify the colour and speak its name. As Skemp discusses in his book, human's superiority over other species lies in being able to detach concepts from sensory experiences and attach them instead to language. This act hints at the vast potential of greater intelligence (28).

When the children are taken on an outing—either walking on the footpath or travelling by bus or train—they get very excited when they see the word 'red' on a poster or sign. They will read the word aloud, talk to each other and count the number of times they see it during the trip. This is the case not just for the word 'red' but for all the other words and numbers they have learnt. Spotting these words in the outside world leads to plenty of noise, talking and excitement.

They also recognise this word in their storybooks and on the charts in the classroom. They realise that what they have learnt has meaning and is connected with their lives outside of school. They begin to recall and connect the words they have learnt with past experiences.

### STEP 6: WRITING

The next step is for the teacher to encourage the children to try to copy the word 'red' from the picture card into their exercise books. The individual letters which spell the word are shown to the children, and the teacher helps them correctly write these letters. This is done during handwriting-practice time. The children learn to correctly write and spell the word, conscious of what the word they are writing means.

### STEP 7: RECOGNISING LETTERS

Gradually the children learn to recognise the letters in the word 'red' ('r', 'e' and 'd') and pronounce them as well. This is how teachers should teach children the letters of the alphabet.

The children begin to see these letters in other items like the names of actions, animals, flowers, moving objects, vehicles and so on. They begin to read these words with ease because of the connection they have made with the words they have learnt.

Initially, the children are slow in learning to read and write. The process takes time. But once learnt, the children are capable of reading quickly and with understanding. After a point, they will no longer need the teacher all the time during a reading lesson.

Teaching the children to read and write by showing them the letters in their names has proven effective. The children were keen to learn to spell their own names, and thus learnt how to do so quickly and with interest. Examples of such activities and further discussion on how to introduce the class to names may be found in Chapter 21.

## Kinds of Concepts

Red is not the only concept a child learns from her sensory and motor experiences. There are other similar concepts belonging to this category, such as the concepts of blue, yellow, green, etc.

These concepts are learnt the same way the child learns of 'red'.

Now she has learnt to read and write the words 'red', 'yellow', 'blue' and 'green' and understands, from her rich experiences with these colours, what they mean.

What next?

She cannot hide them in her pocket and stay quiet. She has to express her thoughts about these concept-words to others. They have to become functional in her life. Human's use of language is what makes us different from other species.

Alone, these basic concepts will not help her to communicate. She needs another set of concepts which will help her talk about the concepts she has learnt. So, for example, the concepts 'red', 'yellow', 'blue' and 'green' all fall under the broader concept of 'colours'.

The concept of 'colours' is not abstracted from sensory and motor experiences but from *other concepts*.

The teacher must explain this to the children, perhaps by following the model below.

Teacher: 'Children, you have learnt about red, yellow, blue and green. Now you should know that they are all members of a family. They are like you and your families. And just as you have a surname, they have a family name. The name of the family they belong to is called "colours". So red belongs to the family of colours. We call red a "colour". Likewise, we call blue a colour, yellow a colour, green a colour.'

Such an introduction to this new concept of 'colour' helps the children hold a conversation on colours:

Karthik: I like yellow. Lemons are yellow. I like lemon juice. Which colour do you like, Kiran?
Kiran: I like red because I like apples. Apples are red.

The conversation progresses. The children ask questions like, 'What colour is your bag? What are the colours you see in our classroom?' They may even begin to draw while conversing: 'Now I will draw a flower and colour it red and yellow. Your colour and my colour for this flower.'

The children now have the freedom to fluently express their thoughts and feelings about colours.

It is important to remember that abstracting basic concepts from sensory and motor experiences is only a step in the process of intellectual learning. These concepts need a structure.

Any developmental process needs a structure. Intelligent learning also requires and possesses a structure. It is called a *conceptual* structure. This structure is arranged in a hierarchy with many branching subcategories, as can be seen in Figure 24. This structure helps enrich the learning process.

Let us continue to use our example of 'red', 'yellow', 'blue' and 'green' as concepts abstracted from sensory and motor experiences, with the broader concept of 'colour' abstracted from the abstracted concepts of 'red', 'yellow', 'blue' and 'green'.

The concepts red, yellow, blue and green are called *primary concepts*. The concept of colour is called a *secondary concept*.

Primary concepts are lower-level concepts, while secondary concepts are higher-order concepts.

As already mentioned, higher-order concepts are not abstracted from sensory or motor experiences but from other concepts. They are thus 'more abstract' (which means, more removed from sensory or motor experiences).

Now, imagine if another concept is abstracted from higher-order concepts (this can be seen in Figure 24)—the meaning grows more abstract as the concept is more removed from sensory or motor experiences.

Primary and secondary concepts of the same class form a hierarchy of concepts. In this case, the primary concepts of red, yellow, blue and green fall under the secondary concept of colour, though they all belong to the same hierarchy.

There are different hierarchies and these hierarchies are interrelated to form a conceptual structure, as can be seen in Figure 24.

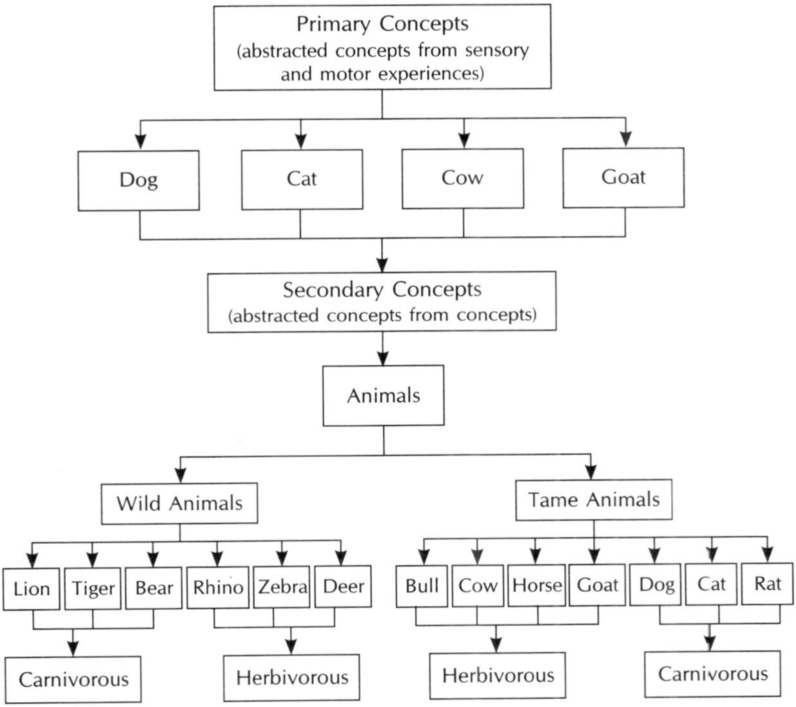


Figure 24: Conceptual structure

Two things happen in this process of learning. First, there is a recognition of a concept through the classification of various experiences and by abstraction of the invariant property. Second, being made conscious of the name for the concept. This second step is something only human beings have proven capable of doing. This is because of our ability to isolate concepts from sensory or motor experiences or examples which give rise to them.

Only once concepts have been detached from their sensory experiences can they be collected as examples (dog, cat, cow, goat) from which one can form new concepts of greater abstraction (animals) (Skemp 28). Children are able to abstract the concept 'red' from their experiences, and name the concept 'red' when they hear the word being used. They read and write down this word and soon are capable of recognising the word and its meaning immediately. They learn other concepts and words simultaneously. This is intelligent learning as their minds are active and functional. Once they detach concepts from sensory or motor experiences (which led to these concepts being formed in the first place), they are capable of putting these concepts together to form a new level of classification. They abstract from these concepts a new concept, in this case: 'colour'. This is a higher-order concept formed from greater abstraction.

At this point conceptual learning takes place and the developmental process of intelligence, once started, continues to form higher-order concepts of increasing abstractions. Unlike rote learning, the mind is active. It will not remain dormant or work mechanically but will begin to actively form multiple interconnected hierarchies of concepts, thus building a strong learning structure.

## Importance of Language

Speech is essential for the formation and use of higher-order concepts.

Let us look at a simple example: When learning a language, humans have a store of accumulated concepts like the alphabet or names, words, grammar, etc., which help them learn and which have all been inherited from previous generations. This is true not just for language but for other fields like mathematics where there already exist concepts like numbers, decimals, addition, subtraction, multiplication, division, etc.

Children should therefore be given plenty of sensory and motor experiences. They can then classify these experiences and abstract concepts. The work of previous generations will help them identify and understand these concepts. This is the foundation or base of the conceptual structure. A solid foundation means the children understand lower concepts and, over time, will be able to build on that foundation and grasp higher-order concepts. In conceptual learning, if the base or foundation of the structure is not

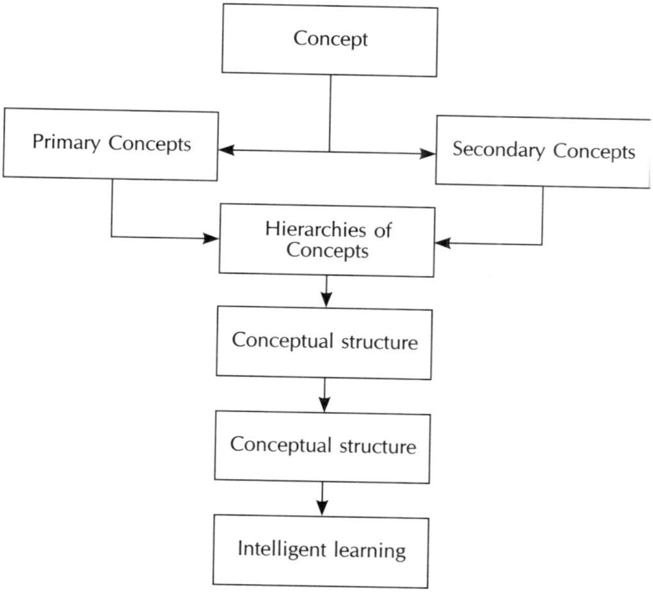


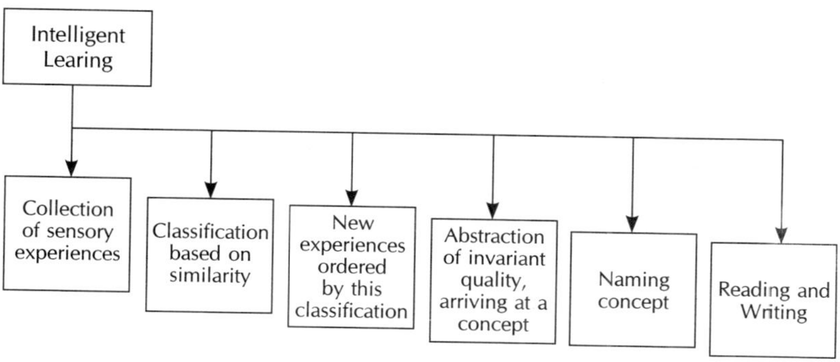


solid and reliable, then the whole structure will be shaky. Higher-order concepts therefore *cannot* be taught without the children first learning about lower-level concepts.

Higher learning depends on the basics of reading, writing and speaking.

We adults are so used to symbols, definitions and rules that we take them for granted. The result is that we fail to understand what they mean to children. We try to teach them these symbols, definitions and rules and in so doing forget to begin where the child is.

## Basic Learning Activities

1. Collecting and classifying objects based on similarities.
2. Labelling groups, naming objects.
3. Matching objects using domino cards or matching cards. Children enjoy playing with these cards. These cards could include colours, letters, the names of children, fruits, vegetables, animals, etc.

A five-year-old learns to read by matching words with pictures.

4. Reading the letters and names of objects from cards.
5. Song charts, matching strips.
6. First letters of names, picture cards—match and read.
7. Writing.
    a. Hand exercises.
    b. Writing or drawing shapes in sand.

c. Writing these shapes on paper using crayons.
d. Writing on paper using a pencil.

# 18

# Pre-lesson Plans

What are pre-lesson plans?

I am not sure whether it is appropriate to use the prefix 'pre' for this chapter. I suppose I use it to help readers differentiate between structured, formal lessons used to teach six-year-olds and above, and the more unstructured and activity-based lessons used for younger children. Since these plans come before formal lessons, I decided to call them 'pre-lesson' plans.

The pre-lesson plans in this chapter are designed for five-year-olds. Who are these five-year-olds and how do they learn?

They are children who have gone through the emotional upheavals of being a four-year-old; they've endured getting into all sorts of problems and overcoming confusing personal trials, and now appear to be happier and more settled. They've moved from subjective infantile behaviour (exhibited when they were three or four years old) into an objective factual reality. They are active, curious and want to understand 'how' and 'why' things are the way they are. What is striking about the nature of their learning at this age is that they learn through direct experiences and active experimentation, which is to say, they learn through the use of their senses. In particular, they are keen observers. They notice (by seeing, smelling, tasting, touching and hearing) differences in the size, shape and quality of various physical objects, and share these observations with their classmates. Through this they improve their vocabulary.

This is the right time to introduce the basics of reading, writing and mathematics to the children.

Taking into consideration the fact that they are still only five years old, their learning environment should be one which makes it possible for them to learn with interest and enjoyment, allowing them the opportunity to freely participate and converse with one another. They learn quickly, enthusiastically and independently in such an environment. They also learn to work in groups.

Children between the ages of six to eleven begin to experience intellectual and social developments and during this time may settle down and concentrate more on their learning—working longer hours and trying to absorb more information. Five-year-olds require adequate preparation for this; they need to learn how to concentrate and follow instructions. They are thus at an important age when the foundation for intelligent conceptual learning is laid.

Since five-year-olds struggle to focus on one thing for a long time, they must learn in an informal way. This could be done by reading a story, visiting a park or zoo, preparing an activity for the class or having the children bring objects to class for show-and-tell.

Any of these usually incites a lively conversation between the children and the teacher. From these conversations they move on to active learning using their senses, and from there they gradually move on to learning the basics of reading, writing and mathematics. This learning is not static and is done with interest. It is not restricted to abstract ideas but is made to encompass everything around them.

As adults, we can understand the concept of activity-centred learning, but only when we actually *experience* this sort of learning are we capable of grasping what it really involves and gain the confidence required to provide such an environment for the children to learn.

Since most of us are used to a formal, structured plan for teaching, we dare not deviate from a familiar routine to try something so informal.

Change is a very difficult thing for human beings, it can take us out of our comfort zone, and we teachers are not exempt from this reality. In my experience, I found teachers usually felt insecure using such an informal activity method in their class. It was a terrible experience for them to dismantle or abandon known and safe methods of teaching. While pursuing such endeavours, teachers require the support and understanding of the school authorities.

The section that follows is an example of what I am trying to say about the nature of a five-year-old's process of learning. This was an actual learning experience which took place in the nursery school I worked at, where both children and teachers underwent a rich learning experience which I will never forget. The events are still fresh in my mind, as if it they are taking place as I write.

## Teaching Five-year-old Children: A Sample Class

Once Nadya, who was a consultant to our Nursery school, held a class for the five-year-olds. I did not know what exactly was the topic, but when I entered the class I saw they were in the midst of an exciting conversation. They were having a discussion on Vinod, a boy in their class, who was not sure where he belonged.

Vinod explained that the reason for his confusion was because he was not always living with his parents in one house. He would spend one day at his grandparents' house, another day at his uncle's, another day at his aunt's, and so he was moving from house to house and did not know where he really belonged.

He asked the group: 'Which is my real home? Where do I belong?'

The group was surprised but also curious. It was a lively and serious conversation involving all the children actively participating. Nadya was the catalyst. That day the class ended with everyone wondering how to answer Vinod's questions.

The next week, Nadya held the same class. This time she brought with her the storybook *Home For a Bunny* by Margaret Wise Brown. She told the class that she had brought a story and hoped they would enjoy it.

The story was very interesting; even we teachers were so engrossed by what Nadya narrated.

The story went like this: a bunny was in search of a home. During his search he came across a robin, a frog and a groundhog. He asked each one if he could live with them. They refused. How could they live with a bunny? Finally, he met another bunny who agreed to let him live in her burrow. They both happily lived together. At last the bunny had found a home.

Vinod was attentively listening to the story. He looked anxious and tense. When the story ended, he jumped up and exclaimed, 'Now the bunny has found a home of his own!' He was happy. This led to him talking to his parents and discovering the answers to his questions. He thanked Nadya and his classmates and told them, 'Now I too have a home of my own like the bunny.'

The story spread like wildfire in the nursery school, and the children soon had memorised all the catchy sentences and words that rhymed in the story. They began to chant parts of the story while they were playing outside or climbing up and down the stairs.

Though the story had been told to only the five-year-olds, the whole nursery school seemed to know it and enjoyed chanting lines about spring.

Nadya's narration of the story marked the beginning of a festive mood in the nursery school.

When Nadya noticed the children chanting parts of the story, she selected a few passages which rhymed and wrote them down on sheets of paper. She stuck these sheets of paper on the walls of the veranda, staircase, corridor and classroom.

These sheets of paper attracted the children's attention and they asked their teachers to help them read the verses. They ran their fingers along the lines of verse and tried to match the lines with what they were chanting. It was very exciting for them. They enjoyed this activity and soon were able to read words and entire sentences from the verses.

During conversations they would each explain which verse was their favourite and why. There was even a healthy competition amongst the children to find out who could read and identify words chanted by a group, or to even identify those words which rhymed with words chanted by the group.

What did the children do next? Did their interest end with reading and chanting the verses on the sheets of paper? Not at all! They created a list of words which rhymed and added their own words to that list. They pestered their parents and teachers to help them do this. Below are a few lists made by the children:

| | | | |
|---|---|---|---|
| hog | dog | bun | fun |
| log | bog | gun | run |
| wog | frog | sun | bunny |

The children's interest in reading verses had changed to rhyming words, and they enjoyed reading aloud words which rhymed to their classmates. Nadya noticed this and asked the teachers to make a list of words which rhymed for the children. These lists were glued to the walls of the classroom.

| | | |
|---|---|---|
| pot | top | dog |
| hot | hop | bog |
| lot | shop | jog |
| shot | crop | frog |
| | | |
| pat | bag | tap |
| hat | wag | cap |
| bat | rag | lap |
| fat | tag | map |
| mat | flag | |
| | | |
| pit | tip | dig |
| hit | hip | big |
| lit | ship | pig |
| drip | wig | |

Children liked reading these words. They would ask for help from the teachers whenever they wanted to learn the meanings of certain unfamiliar words. They read these words aloud by chanting them, or expressed them by miming actions.

They recognised changes in pronunciation when different vowels were used, and therefore knew the difference, for example, between 'pot', 'pit' and 'pat', or 'top', 'tip' and 'tap'.

Here, the teachers helped them by showing how combinations of vowels and consonants could be used to form words. The children were taught combinations like 'ot', 'op', 'og', 'it', 'ip', 'ig', 'at', 'ap' and 'ag', which could all be added to letters to form a complete word. This encouraged the children to make their own words using these combinations. They found some of the words they created were funny because of how they sounded, even though they were meaningless. Examples of such funny words included 'yot', 'zot', 'dop', 'zat'. The children enjoyed creating funny words and even gave them their own funny meanings. They discussed all the words they created with their teacher and understood why some words held no meaning.

Following this, the teacher would introduce individual letters to the children and teach them how to correctly pronounce these letters. Children began to read, pronounce and spell words. They enjoyed chanting words as well, and cracked plenty of jokes in their group while doing this exercise.

The idea of this class was to create a relaxed atmosphere where the children could connect their learning with as many things they knew and understood. Children brought to class new words which they shared with their groups, and this led to plenty of lively conversations. Their enjoyment and enthusiasm meant the children soon began to read and understand words and sentences without effort.

In class, readings took place and both the children and the teachers actively participated and held meaningful conversation. They discussed what they read and together made their own games, action songs and activities. For the first time, the teachers were given the chance to behave like the children.

While the children were busy bringing new words and ideas to the classroom, Nadya, when she next visited, brought with her a few flowers that were just beginning to bloom. She also brought a peapod which had opened and was bursting with peas. When she showed the flowers and pods to the class, there was much excitement. It generated an animated discussion on how peapods split when ripe, and how other plants have pods which, when dry, crack open to release seeds.

From there the children began to talk about how robins and chickens hatch from eggs. The conversation moved to other living creatures hatching from eggs, like lizards, snakes, frogs, etc. They also spoke about living things which did not come from eggs like dogs, cats, cows, rabbits, etc. These conversations were short; their span of interest is short, and so they did not have an in-depth discussion on the topics. All the while Nadya remained a silent listener, a keen observer, only asking a question when she found it was necessary to ignite the conversation. She was the catalyst.

What surprised the teachers was that after Nadya's lesson the children began to collect and bring to class all sorts of different things like leaves or stones of various sizes and shapes, flowers, flower buds, the eggs of a butterfly in a shoe box, two lizard eggs on cotton in a coconut shell, frog spawn in a small water tank, snakeskin, and shells. Day by day their collection in the nursery school increased.

The most interesting part of this activity was that even the parents took an active interest in the collection project. They helped their children. Even helpers at school joined in, so that it become an activity we all shared and participated in.

Nadya visited the school once in a week, and whenever she did she would take the children and teachers with her to classify everything which had been collected. Each teacher helped organise the collection by taking charge of a particular type of item. For example, one teacher would be in charge of leaves and would take all the leaves to her classroom. Along with the children, she would sort through the leaves and classify and label them.

Similarly, other teachers would take the items they were in charge of to their classrooms to classify and label them.

Thus the collection was split into smaller categories. Each classroom would contain a different category of items (which were classified and labelled according to size, shape, variety, etc.), and a sign by the entrance indicated which category was stored in the classroom. Some of the categories included 'Leaves', 'Flowers', 'Eggs', 'Seeds', 'Stones', etc.

Children were thus able to easily classify items by matching. All this helped the children learn to read without much effort and with great enjoyment.

They also watched with excitement and with surprise when the lizard eggs hatched and tiny lizards crawled out. Tadpoles swam out of the frogspawn. Caterpillars crawled from the eggs in the shoebox. Oh, there was such excitement in the nursery school!

Things didn't stop there. Arts and crafts classes flourished—the children were busy drawing, painting, tracing, and cutting and pasting the outlines of flowers, leaves, trees, birds, animals and the nests of birds and the homes of animals. They put their artwork on the walls of the classroom.

The teachers and children also prepared charts. These charts had pictures of beautiful scenery, or forests with trees and birds' nests, or snakes, animals, etc. They were hung up in the classrooms according to the category they matched.

The children went through all the items exhibited in the various classrooms and enjoyed plenty of interesting conversations in their groups.

The conversations did not focus on one specific thing but on broader topics. The aim was to motivate the children and to arouse an interest in developing their powers of observation. We wanted them to be curious about the world around them, and to sustain this curiosity to try and answer the 'how' and 'why' of things.

During Nadya's classes the children continued to have lively conversations about the story. These conversations—about spring, the homes of different animals, wild and tame animals, nature—were reflected in their outdoor play, where they identified themselves with different animals and acted out parts of the story.

When teachers observed their interest in acting out parts of the story, they spoke with the children and suggested maybe they should organise an event where the children perform the entire story. The children liked the idea.

The children chose animals they identified with and memorised their parts. One child volunteered to be the narrator and she had to memorise her lines. The teachers and children made simple costumes. Even some of the parents offered to help. They also made cutouts of trees, nests and baby robins which they painted and stuck to cardboard. Together, these formed a tree prop which could stand by itself. Rehearsals took place during classes.

The parents were invited to the play. Children made simple invitation cards for their parents. They, along with the teachers, prepared a simple stage. They performed the story for their parents and for the other children in the school. This developed their self-confidence and their motivation to do and learn more. They experienced a great sense of success for their efforts.

Just as Nadya's narration of the story of the bunny led to the children chanting and learning to read and write, so too did the process of creating a collection nurture the children's curiosity. As a result, there were other activities which they picked up in an attempt to learn more.

There was a children's library close to the nursery school. Most of the children visited the library to go through picture books on different topics. Their parents were heartened by this interest and signed up with the library so that the children could borrow books. Together, the children and the parents would go through the books. The children also brought books from the library to school, and would sit quietly in the library corner and read. They learnt to borrow and return books.

Children also prepared a small plot in the corner of their playground. There they grew beans and tomatoes. They also observed the germination of bean seeds in a glass tumbler using water and blotting paper. They keenly watched the process of germination every day as the bean seeds soaked in water begin to swell, then sprout. The children found the process engrossing.

When the beans and tomatoes grew, they harvested the crop (it was a very small harvest). The children, supervised by the teachers, cooked the beans and also made tomato jam. With excitement they discussed the process of making jam. They drew pictures of this process in their drawing books to try and explain the steps involved. The teacher made use of some of these drawings (which were very simple) to make a small book on how to make jam. The instructions were simple and easy to read, and the children read this book with great interest.

After one year the children's interest in reading and writing had flourished. Their vocabulary had improved. They even began to read simple story books and write simple sentences about things which interested them.

A word on writing and numbers: The children found it difficult trying to write down verses from the sheets of paper on the walls. They asked the teachers to do it for them. The teachers helped them. The teachers used this opportunity to motivate the children to improve both their writing skills and their handwriting. The various steps involved in learning how to write were introduced. Children were taught basic hand exercises, then practicing writing on sand, then on sheets of paper, and then in exercise books. The steps on how to improve children's handwriting could fill an entire book, and I won't list those steps here, but suffice to say that by the end of the year the children's handwriting had vastly improved.

Though I have placed a lot of importance on the process of reading in this sample, numbers and mathematics played just as important a role in the process of learning.

Informally, the children were taught the concepts of big/small, tall/short, less/more. They began to measure things they collected using their feet, palms and arms. They made a simple weighing balance and enjoyed weighing their collection of stones. They learnt the concept of same/equal through this activity.

Nadya's discussion with her class and her decision to narrate *Home for a Bunny* brought about a great change in the concept of teaching and learning in the nursery section. It wasn't just that the children came out of their shells, but so too did the teachers, thereby breaking the monotony of structured learning.

It may appear that such a form of teaching could eventually grow out of control and chaotic, but the truth is that in the nursery school there was a *healthy* chaos. There was curiosity, desire, and an intent to learn. We were all working towards accomplishing that one aim of learning. It was not a static situation involving mindless repetition, but one where the children learnt through *doing*, and, by doing, filled their lives with meaning and enjoyment.

Children from all backgrounds benefit from this process of learning; I discovered similar results working with children from slums or children with disabilities. Some of these children did not have the same level of parental support and economic comfort as the children in our nursery school. This did slow down the learning process, but it did not affect the children's enthusiasm or intent to learn.

As teachers, we must remember that children, no matter their background, have the same innate capacity for learning. All they need is an understanding, loving catalyst.

# 19

# Teaching Language

## (first steps towards formal learning)

Children should not permanently follow the informal, unstructured type of learning discussed in the preceding chapter. There will be no progress if they do. Once satisfied with such an experience (which they needed at that particular stage of development), they will want to take the next step. I have noticed that five-year-olds, towards the end of their academic year, show signs of being ready for the initial stage of formal learning.

The teacher needs to be alert to this. She needs to be observant and recognise when the children have arrived at such a point.

In their final term, the five-year-olds are introduced to formal learning through reading, writing and numbers. But care is taken not to leap ahead and try to teach the children about abstractions like the alphabet or numerals. This is important. The children, in the first step, were exposed to enough sensory and motor activities that they could abstract concepts, then transform these concepts into symbols by naming them. Without this first step, the children would have no experiences to draw from when taught abstractions, and without this personal connection would find the process of learning laborious and uninteresting.

Trying to teach the children without first providing them with plenty of sensory and motor experiences can lead to the children growing frustrated or anxious during class.

At this point I would like to share an experience I had during my college years.

Mathematics was a subject I liked very much. In school, we had arithmetic, algebra, and geometry. In college, some new subjects were added to this list. One was trigonometry. I was absent for the first two lessons in trigonometry, and when I attended the third class I saw the lecturer writing on the blackboard: sin$\theta$; cos$\theta$; $\sin^2\theta + \cos^2\theta = 1$.

I couldn't understand what she was writing. What did sin$\theta$ and cos$\theta$ mean and how, when squared, did they equal one? When I asked the lecturer, she repeated the formula like it was a slogan. This did not help, and when I asked her again, she again only repeated the formula. It meant nothing to me. When I asked my friends they said they too did not understand how the formula was arrived at but chose to memorise it nonetheless.

I began to dislike my trigonometry classes. I was like a blind person listening to a teacher describe colours. It went on for some time before I decided I could not carry on like this. I went to the library and borrowed a few books on the basics of trigonometry. I carefully read these books. What dawned on me was that trigonometry is all about right-angled triangles and the Pythagoras theorem. This was a theorem I liked very much and I quickly realised that sine and cosine were terms used to name the relationship shared between the three sides of a right-angled triangle. I made a sketch of this idea:

$$\frac{AB}{AC} = \sin\theta \qquad \frac{BC}{AC} = \text{cosin}\theta$$

$$AB^2 + BC^2 = AC^2$$

$$\left(\frac{AB}{AC}\right)^2 + \left(\frac{BC}{AC}\right)^2 = \left(\frac{AC}{AC}\right)^2$$

$$\left(\frac{9}{25}\right)^2 + \left(\frac{16}{25}\right)^2 = \left(\frac{25}{25}\right)^2$$

$$\therefore \sin^2\theta + \cos^2\theta = 1$$

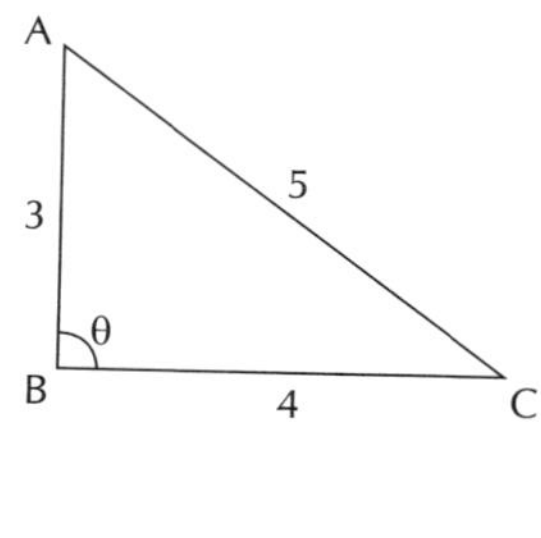


What a joy! I was now able to successfully solve a number of trigonometry problems. From then on I enjoyed my trigonometry classes.

In this example of learning, I was aware of the concept of right-angled triangles, but I had missed the crucial step of abstraction and naming. Thus the words 'sine' and 'cosine' meant nothing to me. Without this step, trigonometry made no sense to me.

We may believe that if we teach children the letters of the alphabet or introduce them to numerals, then they are learning. The problem is that this is teaching which relies on adult logic. The reality is that learning this way is a slow, laborious process. It results in the children merely repeating symbols and names we give them. The children parrot the teacher's words and end up depending on the teacher instead of learning by themselves.

To recap: children, usually at the age of five, are ready for factual learning. This is done through participation and sensory or motor activities, leading to them classifying their experiences and abstracting concepts. The next step is abstracting from concepts (not experiences), and these abstractions are names or symbols which can be used when needed to form higher concepts and greater abstractions. Intellectual growth is achieved by building higher concepts and greater abstractions based on abstractions and concepts made during the early stages of learning.

Keeping in mind the process of intellectual development, we could say the teaching methodology looks a bit like this:

Step 1

- Sensory or motor activities
- Active participation
- Experiences
- Classification of experiences
- Formation of concepts

Step 2

- Making abstractions from formed concepts through conceptual learning

Step 3 (occurs after the children turn six years old)

- Abstractions formed during early stages of conceptual learning are registered in the mind and recalled to form higher concepts and greater abstractions

This book deals with only the first two steps. In the preceding chapters we have seen how to introduce Step 1. Now we must move on to Step 2.

## How to Introduce Step 2?

In my experience, I have noticed that one of the most effective ways to teach the letters of the alphabet to the children is through the use of their names.

Why use their names?

Because it establishes a personal and powerful connection. We use names to identify ourselves or others, and the children are invested in learning about something which is so closely connected to them. For example, a girl called 'Swapna' may show active interest in the letter 'S' if the teacher were to say 'S is for Swapna'. Her interest may lead to her recognising other children whose names begin with the same letter, or she may look up words beginning with the letter 'S'. Either way, she is engaged with the material being taught and is actively trying to learn. It is therefore more effective to first attach significance to individual letters—so that the children remember them—before trying to teach the entire alphabet from A to Z.

In addition to names, I have found children take an active interest in learning about things which attract their eye and mind—colours, shapes and parts of the body.

Moving objects attract children. It is not uncommon to see a child following a butterfly, trying to catch it to better observe it. Or perhaps playing with a puppy or kitten. Even moving vehicles hold their attention.

Regarding numbers: when two children are given sweets, or play materials, or anything for that matter, their immediate impulse is to compare how much they have. It is not uncommon to find children saying things like, 'he has a larger marble than mine,' or, 'I got less milk than she did,' or, 'they've got so many pencils, and we've only got one!' If you ask a child a question related to numbers, quantity, size, etc., they respond through comparison. They do not use numbers but may instead answer by using their hands to indicate amounts. This is their mathematical concept.

From here, children proceed to the second step, which is to move from 'more' or 'less' to naming numerals like '1, 2, and 3'. These numbers are abstractions. They are abstracted from the children's pre-existing mathematical concepts.

In the next part of the book I share a few simple lesson plans which I have developed over the course of my career as a teacher. I have found these lesson plans improved children's interest in learning to read, write and understand numbers, and also developed their creativity.

They are only suggestions. They are not lesson plans to be strictly followed. A creative teacher could use the ideas to make her class lively and interesting.

Though my lesson plans are organised according to 'names', 'colours', 'numbers', etc., this does not mean they should be taught separately. Teachers should not complete one lesson plan before moving on to another. As the image on the next page shows, these topics are all interconnected.

Teaching these lessons simultaneously will mean the children will learn to identify connections between separate concepts and will discover the interrelatedness of all things around them. This is intelligent learning, as it is learning through understanding.

# Lesson Plan on Names

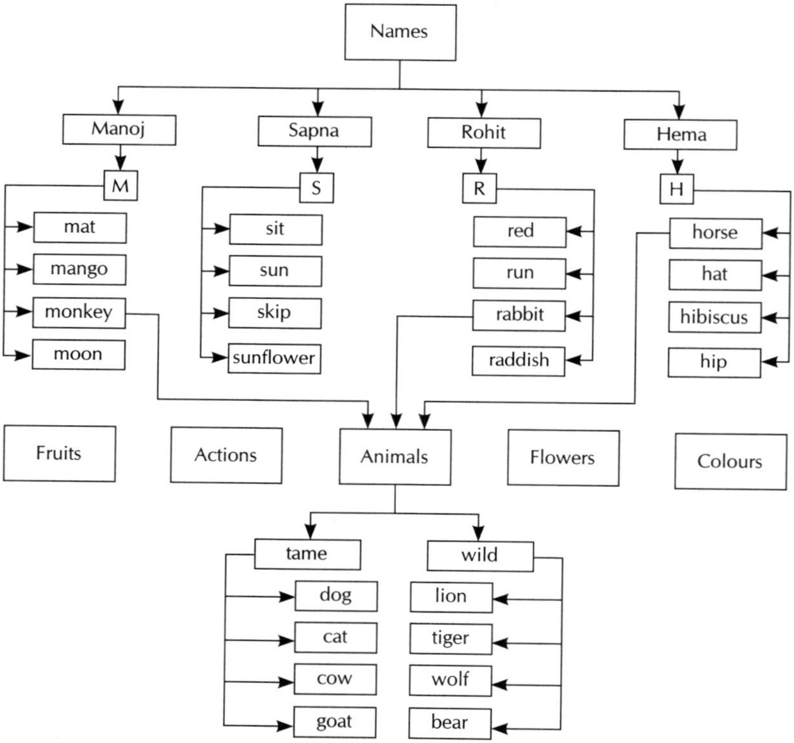

# 20

# Teaching Mathematics

## (Introduction)

Mathematics is an interesting subject to learn, yet many children do not enjoy studying it. The concepts of mathematics are far more abstract and precise than those of language, which means that students who learn without understanding are likely to find it tedious.

What do I mean by more precise?

A child may draw on her experiences involving blue-coloured objects to abstract the concept 'blue'. But this is not precise because there are many shades of blue. A child may draw on her experiences involving chairs to abstract the concept 'chair', but that too is not precise as there are different types and shapes of chairs. Number concepts are not like that. They are precise because numbers do not come in different shades, shapes or sizes.

Teaching and learning a language is different from teaching and learning mathematics. Language is a skill subject (a subject in which children develop certain skills in order to learn; in the case of language, these skills include reading and writing) whereas mathematics involves greater abstractions.

Knowing mathematics is not enough to teach mathematics. Nowadays, most teachers appear to lack the ability to teach mathematics in an engaging way. Because of this, many children dislike or fear the subject.

The main ability required for learning mathematics is the ability to abstract and manipulate abstracted concepts.

In most schools, children are taught the manipulation of symbols in a mechanical way—through rote learning—without attaching concepts to symbols. For children, symbols without concepts attached to them are meaningless. Since the children do not have a connection with the material being studied, they are not mentally engaged. They are memorising definitions and rules about how symbols operate but are learning without understanding. This means the learning process becomes laborious and the children lose interest in the subject.

By the age of two, children are able to count to six or seven, some might even be able to count till ten. But they learn to do so through imitation. They copy words, phrases and even numbers from adults. The adults are very proud to have their young children reciting numbers. Sadly, the children, like parrots, are reciting words or numbers without understanding their meaning. Though there are now smart-classes, television programmes and textbooks containing exercises and explanations, children will only truly learn mathematics if they are mentally engaged and learning with understanding. This requires the abstraction of concepts.

What are the basic concepts in mathematics?

Numbers are concepts whereas numerals are symbols. Therefore a number is an idea, a numeral is how we write that idea. We have seen that a symbol without a concept attached to it is empty and meaningless for a child. Reciting numbers and writing numerals in their exercise books doesn't help children understand numbers. We often make the mistake of believing children understand what numbers and numerals are if they are capable of reciting 1, 2, 3, 4, etc.

We've already seen that in language, for a child to be able to speak, read or write with understanding, he must first be exposed to a number of sensory or motor activities. He classifies these experiences and then abstracts a concept. He hears others identifying the concept and over time he names the concept. Doing so produces a connection between the spoken and written word and his personal experiences with that concept. Thus, he learns to speak, read and write the word with understanding and meaning.

But what about number concepts? How are they abstracted and then attached to symbols (or numerals)? Number concepts are not taught to us. They are something we gradually become aware of, bring to the surface, link with sensory experiences and abstract and name.

As mentioned in the previous chapter, children tend to compare objects. They use words like 'larger' or 'smaller', 'more' or 'less'. This sense of scale is not taught to them but something which children of all backgrounds seem to intuitively grasp. They are number concepts.

Children also match objects or sets of objects. For example, a three-year-old child I knew was presented with a kitchen set on her birthday. Every day, as soon as she got up, she would play with her set. One day she unpacked the set and started screaming. Her mother asked her what happened. The child started taking out all of the items, one by one. As she did, she matched each item with one of her toes and said, 'this one is here, this one is there...' But she did not match an item with her last toe. There were only nine out of her ten items. She wasn't counting but was matching, and according to her grasp of mathematics, there was one item missing. Her mother was surprised because she had taken one of the items to use in her kitchen and had assumed the child would not notice.

The child did not count, as she had no connection with such an experience. She kept track of the number of items in the kitchen set by matching them with invariant or unchanging objects—her toes. This is the number concept in children: matching a set of objects with a standard set.

Here's another example: in the nursery school, a four-year-old girl was arranging bricks around her to create a small, rectangular-shaped garden. She needed one more brick to complete the rectangle. There was a gap. The teacher asked her, 'Why is there a gap?'

The child sat down and first showed the teacher her ten toes, then showed the teacher eight fingers and a thumb and said 'This is how many bricks I used.' She pointed at her remaining thumb and said, 'This one is not there.'

Though the child could recite numbers, she did not associate this form of counting with the number of bricks she needed or used for her plot. She did not say, 'I used nineteen bricks and now I need one more.'

As can be seen from the two examples, for children, matching is an important activity associated with number concepts.

In our nursery school we often found that children playing with wooden building blocks matched the number of accessories they used with the number of constructions they built. For example, the children built three cages, and in each cage placed a toy animal and said 'this one goes here, this one goes in this one.' They matched the number of toy animals with the number of cages. This was not always the case and sometimes they were left with more cages or more animals.

This process of matching also happened during doll play. Children matched cups with saucers. The number of tea cups they filled with imaginary tea would match the number in their group.

Matching is an ongoing activity in nursery school and is very much part of the children's play, no matter if they are alone, in a group or in class with the teacher. Through this they learn numbers.

It is not only young children in nurseries who understand numbers by matching.

A milkman I knew used to milk his cow and leave a litre of milk at a house. On the days when he delivered milk, he would use charcoal to draw a line on a wall, while the woman in the house would mark her calendar. At the end of the month he would match the marks on the wall with the marks on her calendar so that they both knew how much money she owed him. This was his way of calculating.

When I shared this experience with a group of teachers, one of them told me about how his mother, when she prepares tea for visitors, will pour tea into tumblers and say the name of each guest. After she's done she will say 'there are eight tumblers of tea, and there are eight people in the hall.'

In the remote villages of North Karnataka I have seen a shepherd boy (who attended night school) open his shed to let out his sheep. For each sheep that was let out he would place a stone on the ground beside the shed, slowly forming a pile. When they were all out he would close the door and lead the sheep into the fields, where they could graze. When he returned, he would make sure the sheep entered the shed one by one. For each sheep that went inside he would remove a stone from the pile he had made. If all the sheep were there then there would be no stones left.

The shepherd boy was not counting but was using his number concepts to match a standard set (the fixed number of stones) with a set of objects (his sheep). Though he did not know how to count or add, he still possessed an understanding of numbers.

## Number Concepts and Number Names

'A few/many', 'more/less', 'big/small' are number concepts abstracted from sensory experiences. The names of these concepts are not precise and cannot be used as a standard. What is 'big' in one situation may be 'small' in another situation.

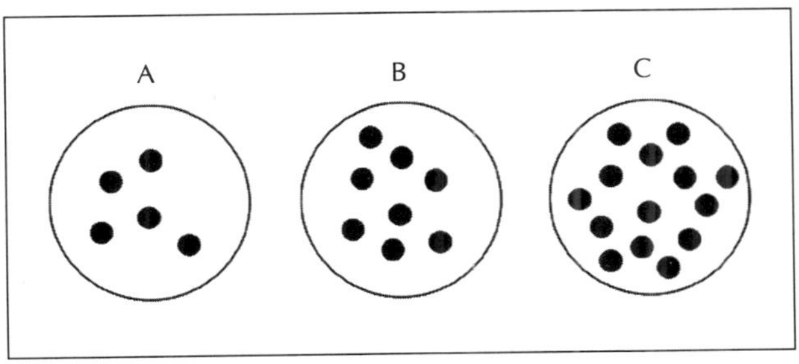


If you were to compare the number of dots in B with the number of dots in A, you'd say there are more in B. However, if you compare the number of dots in B with the number of dots in C, you'd say there are fewer in B. Thus 'more' and 'fewer' are imprecise names dependent on the situation. They cannot be used as a standard.

Not only that, how does one abstract a number concept, name it and use it as a standard? It is not enough to name concepts, the children also have to order them. This is where the problem of teaching number concepts lies.

Usually most teachers teach numerals first. That is the symbols of number concepts. Children learn to recite these symbols. Then the concept is introduced. 'One' for head, 'two' for eyes, 'three' for wheels of an auto rickshaw, etc.

In the beginning there was a lot of hesitation and uncertainty, but the children soon began to grasp number concepts and learnt with ease and understanding.

This is how it was done.

There are two groups: group A and group B. A few objects were placed in group A, while many objects were placed in group B.

The teacher would remove an object from group A. This led to the quantity in the group reducing (as can be seen in Figure 26, row 2). The teacher would continue to remove an object from group A, one at a time, so that the amount in the group reduced until only one object remained (as can be seen in Figure 26, row 5). If the final object was removed, then there would be nothing in the group. Therefore group A in row 5 of Figure 26 represents the 'smallest' possible unit.

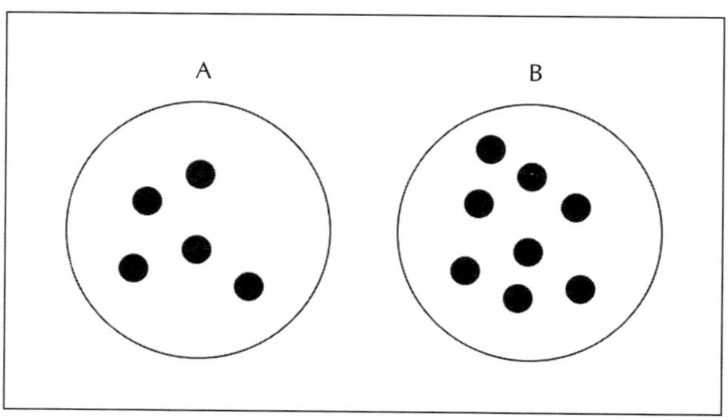


Figure 25

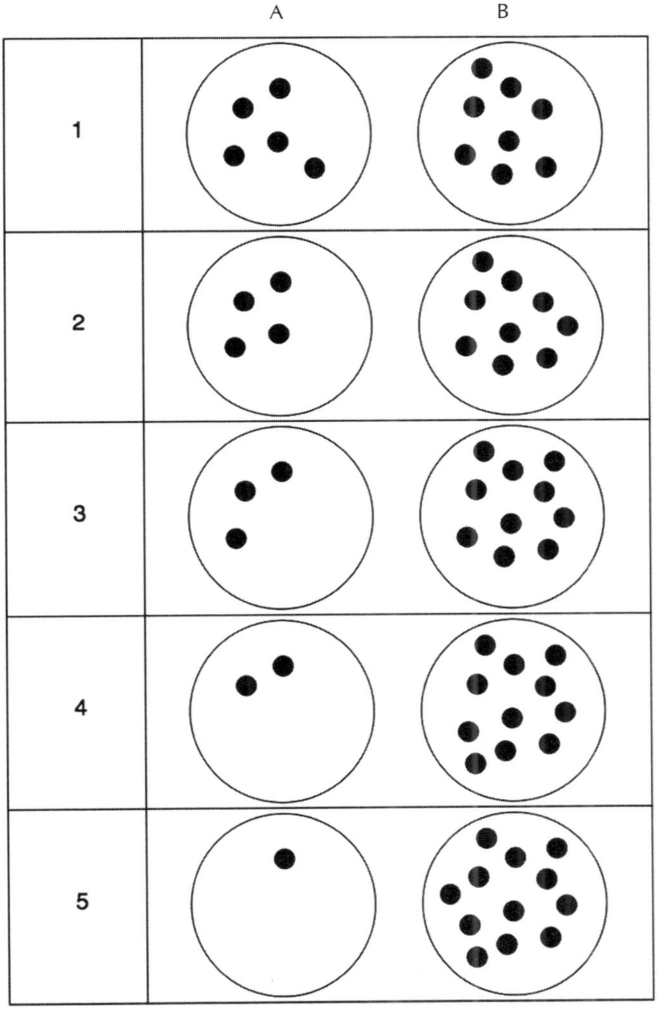


Figure 26

This group is taken as the standard to match other groups of objects.

Plenty of actual objects are collected and matched with this standard. For example:

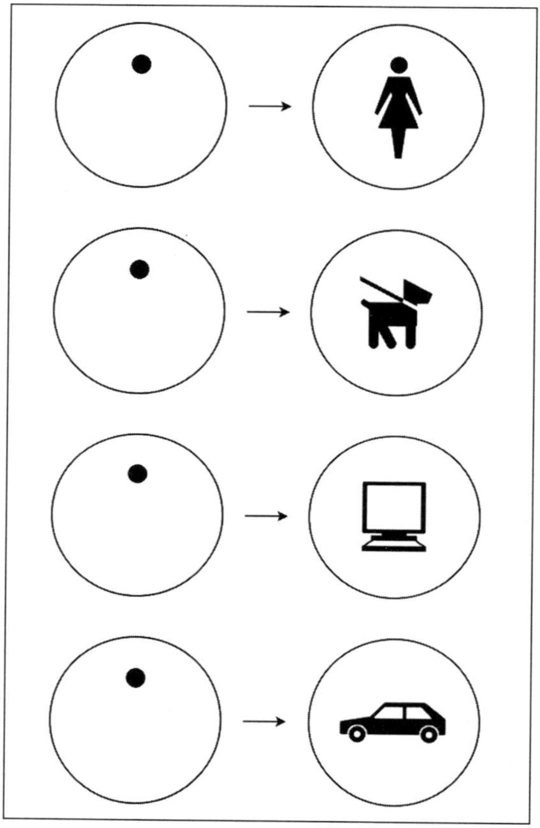

The symbol of this set is taught by associating the concept with the symbol. Once a standard is abstracted, the concept is given a symbol, a name. In this case, the name is 'one'. It is written as '1'.

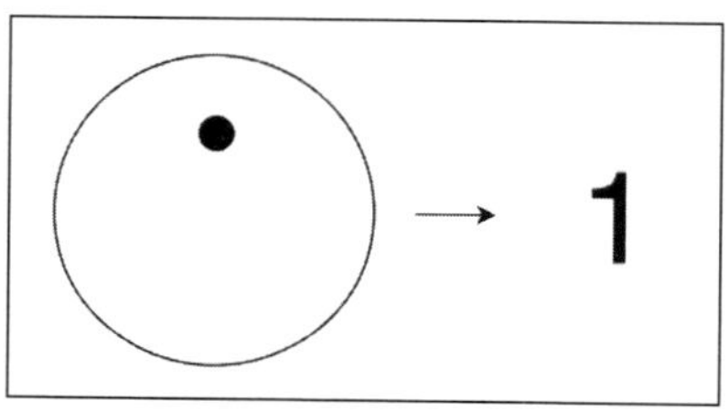

Making use of the symbol as a standard, the next number concept can be taught.

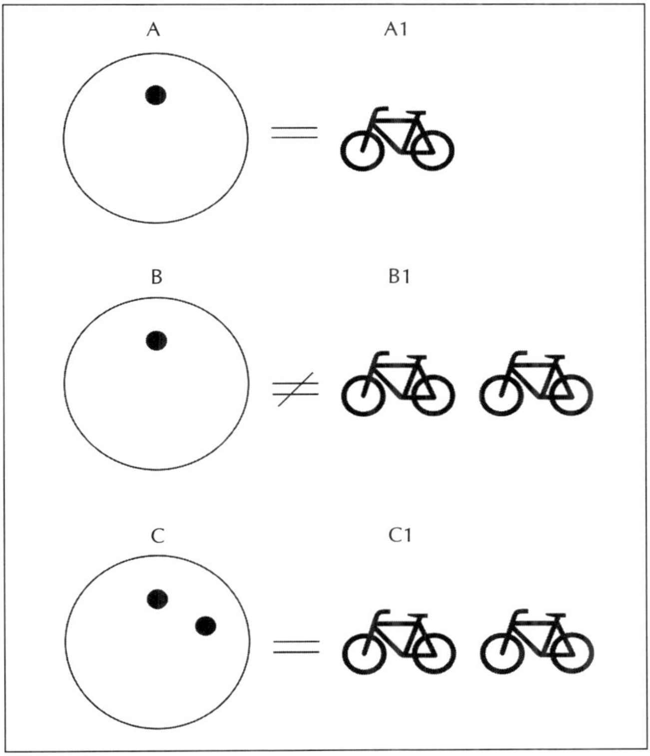


In the above image, A and A1 match. This is because both A and A1 contain the same number of dots/cycles. Now, B and B1 do not match. This is because B has one dot and B1 has two cycles. If a child was asked to make them match, then the child would need to draw a dot in B. Doing so would make the groups look like C and C1, which do match.

Now, the smallest group from the category of 'few' and another smallest group from the category of few make a slightly larger group still in the category 'few'. This can be seen on the next page and in Figure 26 row 4.

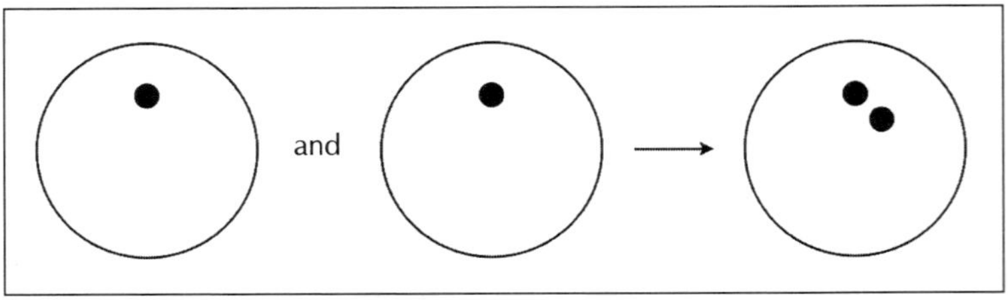


This becomes the next number concept abstracted from the category of 'few'. The name for this concept is 'two', and its written symbol is '2'.

Thus, relying on the categories of 'few' and 'many', the children are introduced to the smallest group (one/1), then the second smallest group (two/2), and so on. In this way, the numerals 1 to 5 are introduced.

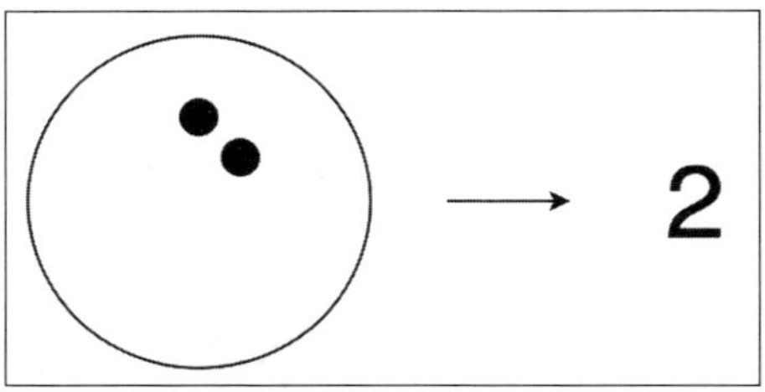


The mathematics lesson plans will explain in detail how numbers and numerals should be introduced to the children.

Once the basic concept of the smallest group is abstracted from their life experiences and associated with the symbol 'one/1', then the process of teaching numerals and other mathematical concepts becomes a lot easier. It may appear as though a lot of time needs to be invested in teaching the children the numerals 1 to 5, but this is essential to their learning and understanding mathematics. With such a strong foundation, the subject becomes an enjoyable and meaningful activity. And, there are long-term rewards as the children, with this foundation, might not struggle as much while dealing with greater abstractions.

The second number concept is addition and subtraction—introducing the idea that a large number is made up of small numbers, or small numbers put together make a large number.

These are the two number concepts introduced to children between the ages of three to five.

## Language Classes

We found that it was best to first teach the written form of the numbers 'one, two, three, four, five' in language classes to help children understand numbers. Doing this meant that when it came to mathematics, the children didn't have to face the difficulty of learning the name of a numeral while also attempting to associate the number concept of the symbol for the smallest group in the category of 'few' with the numeral '1'. Moreover, the written form of the numbers 'one, two, three, etc.' is less useful in mathematics than the numerals '1, 2, 3, etc.' which may be used in the abstraction of higher-order concepts.

In language classes the children were taught the names of numerals by associating the written word for a numeral with their experiences with that number. This is done for the numerals 1 to 5.

We found that teaching the written form of the numbers 'one, two, three, four, five' in language classes helped the overall learning process. Children already knew the numerals '1, 2, 3, 4, 5' which were associated with the number concept.

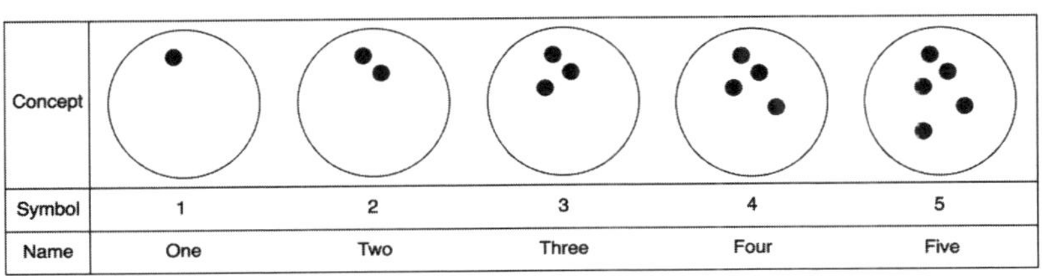

## Recap

To recap using points from Skemp's *The Psychology of Learning*, these are the activities that need to be completed for the children to build a solid foundation in mathematics:

1. Collecting objects into sets on the basis of a common property. (For example, all red items collected in one set, pictures of fruits collected in another, etc.)
   a. Comparing two sets to see whether they match.
   b. Ordering. (Numeration is the systematic naming of numbers.)
2. Completing plenty of the above exercises before learning to count.
3. Concept building through experimental and manipulative activities. (To transition to written work after reciting numbers without essential contributory concepts is to begin learning mathematics on the shakiest of foundations.)
4. Lay a well-structured foundation of basic mathematical ideas. (Keep in mind that mathematics cannot be learnt directly from the everyday environment but only indirectly from other mathematicians.)

# 21

# Names

The lesson plans which follow offer content on how to teach specific themes or topics to children between the ages of three to five. Topics have been selected based on the nature and emotions of children from this age group.

Lesson plans are organised such that each topic, for example 'Names', has its own unit. The teacher may wish to go through the entire unit on 'Names' and then decide how much time should be assigned to teach the topic. It is important to remember that children from this age group have a short attention span. Learning has to alternate with activities. A rigidly structured formal lesson plan does not work well for children from this age group.

The main features of these lesson plans are:

1. Children are led to reading, writing and learning numbers through themes which interest or have an emotional appeal to them.
2. Teaching is done through association and matching. Conversations, practical work, games, storybooks, singing, acting and outings are all part of this form of learning.
3. The teacher is not the sole authority in the classroom.
4. The children have the freedom to learn on their own, with their friends or from one another. Individual and group learning are important to the child understanding concepts.

While conducting these lesson plans, it is a good idea to record your observations and the outcomes of each activity in a notebook. Your notebook will prove invaluable in offering clues to help you understand the children and better tailor your content for future lessons.

| Content | Method | Teaching materials |
|---|---|---|
| Introducing the topic of names | • Have a brief conversation with the children on the topic of names. Things that could be discussed include how the children got their names, the importance of names, and why people have names.<br>• At some point in the discussion, explain how human beings are capable of using their vocal chords to produce different sounds. These different sounds can be used to identify people, places and things. We can thus *hear* our names. | |
| Discussing the idea of being able to both hear and see names | • Encourage the children to imitate sounds made by different animals. Through this activity they recognise that humans can make different sounds, whereas animals tend to only make one type of sound (a cow moos, a crow caws, a toad croaks).<br>• It is important to explain that we can both *hear* and *see* our names. To see a name requires drawing the shapes of the sounds we use to say the name. These shapes are called 'letters'. | |
| Learning to recognise:<br>• one's name when it is called out. | • During attendance, call out the names of the children in class. When the child hears their name, they should stand up and say 'Present' or 'Yes, I am here.'<br>• After this, hand each child a card with their name written on it. This is done to show each child the 'shape' of their name. | • soft board<br>• set of cards (large, preferably 6 by 3 inches), prepared by the teacher, |

| Content | Method | Teaching materials |
|---|---|---|
| (continued)<br>• the written form of one's name. | • Help the children read their names out loud. Do this by holding up a name card and reading out the name slowly, clearly and loudly. Ask the children to pay special attention to the shape of each name.<br>• Later, pin the name cards to a soft board and ask the children to identify their names. | with the names of all the children in the class<br>• board pins |
| Matching name cards (individual learning) | • Shuffle the set of name cards and choose a card. Share this card with the class and ask them whose name is on the card.<br>• If the child recognises their name, they should say 'Mine'. If the child does not recognise their name, then read the name out loud.<br>• Now ask the child to take the name card and match it with their name card pinned to the soft board.<br>• All the children in class should have the opportunity to do this with their name cards.<br>• Collect the smaller set of name cards and place them in a transparent cover. Pin the cover to the soft board, under the larger set of name cards.<br>• Organise an activity in which the children pick a card from the cover and match the name on that card with its corresponding name card on the soft board. This way they learn to recognise not just their names but their friends' names as well. | • A set of cards (small, preferably 3 by 2 inches), prepared by the teacher, with the names of all the children in the class. |

| Content | Method | Teaching materials |
|---|---|---|
| Matching name cards (group learning) | • Encourage the children to match name cards during their free time. They may do this in groups or with their friends. They may even ask each other for help.<br>• Mix two sets of name cards in a bowl on a table. Let the children pick a name card from one bowl and try to match it with one of the name cards from the other bowl.<br>• Once the children understand how to play this game, have them pick a leader. The leader supervises the other children as they play the game. All the children get a chance to be leader. | • a bowl<br>• a second set of cards (small), prepared by the teacher, with the names of all the children in the class |
| Learning how to:<br>• recognise the sound of the first letter in a name.<br>• recognise the shape of the sound of the first letter in a name. | • Pick a card and read the name written on it. In this example, let us use the name 'Sapna'.<br>• Show the name card to the class and ask them to describe the first sound they hear when you say the name 'Sapna'.<br>• The children should answer by saying 'es'. Mimic the movement of a snake with your arm when they make the sound of the letter 's' and explain that the sound of the letter 's' is like the hissing of a snake.<br>• Encourage the children to hiss the letter 's' and mimic the movement of a snake with their arms.<br>• Next, draw the shape of the sound on the blackboard. If possible, try to draw 's' so that it looks like a snake. | • name cards<br>• sandpit<br>• paper<br>• pencil |

| Content | Method | Teaching materials |
|---|---|---|
| (continued)<br>• draw the shape of the sound of the first letter in a name. | • If you ask the children what 's' looks like, they should be able to answer by mimicking a snake or drawing the shape of the letter 's' in the air.<br>• During outdoor play, encourage the children to draw the letter 's' in sand. After some time, they can move on to practicing writing this letter on paper. | |
| Naming letters | • Teach the children that the sound and shape of the letter they have been learning has a name, and the name is 's', pronounced 'es'.<br>• Pin the letter card 'S' to the soft board, under the name 'Sapna'.<br>• Ask the children: 'What is the name of this letter? What is the sound of this letter?' | • two sets of cards (2 by 2 inches), prepared by the teacher, with the letters of the alphabet |
| Learning how to:<br>a. recognise the sound and shape of the first letter in other children's names.<br>b. draw these new letters. | • Once the children know the first letter of Sapna's name, repeat the process with the other children's names.<br>• Read out the names of the children, one by one, and for each name ask the children to make the sound of the first letter. Draw the sound on the board (for example, for 'Manoj', the children can make the sound for the letter 'M' while you draw the letter 'M'). Name the letter and teach the children how to pronounce it (for example, the letter 'M' is pronounced \|m\|.)<br>• Pin each letter card to the soft board, under a name which starts with its letter. | • set of letter cards |

| Content | Method | Teaching materials |
|---|---|---|
| Recapping letters | • An example of a recap could include saying: 'Children, you have learnt that your names are made up of sounds. Like you, these sounds have names. These names can be drawn, and we can therefore read them. You have learnt the name, sound and shape of the first letter of your name. Now, tell me, what is the name of the first letter in "Sapna"? What is the sound of this letter? Write this letter in your exercise book.'<br>• Take care to cover the names of all the children in class when recapping the topic.<br>• Have the children practice speaking and writing the letters, either individually or in groups. They should copy the letters into their exercise books. | |
| Recapping names and letters using matching cards (group learning) | • Before class, rearrange the order of the name cards on the soft board.<br>• After the children arrive, hold a name card up and asks the children to read out loud the name.<br>• The child whose name is read out loud should collect their name card and match it with the name card pinned to the soft board (now in a new position to better test the child). | • name cards<br>• letter cards |

| Content | Method | Teaching materials |
|---|---|---|
| (continued) | • After this is done for each child, hold up a letter card for the class to see and ask: 'What is the name of this letter? What is the sound of this letter? What is the shape of this letter? Please match this letter card with a name on the wall which begins with this letter.' | |
| Recapping letters using matching cards (individual learning) | • Repeat the previous activity, only, this time it should not be a group activity. Call each child to the front of the class, one by one, and ask them to answer the questions and complete the tasks.<br>• Make sure the children have enough time to understand what they are learning. | |
| Recapping letters through activities | • Organise other activities to help with the learning process. These activities may include games, outdoor play, storybooks and conversations which are related to this topic (for example, drawing the letter 's' in sand). | |

Testing is done to find out if the children have understood what has been taught and whether they are able to use their newfound knowledge to learn more. It is also done to find out if any children need help with the topic.

Tests are not meant to be competitive. They are meant to gauge each child's performance. They should help the children learn with interest and enthusiasm, not fill them with fear. Tests are meant to be healthy challenges. For a teacher, tests are an important part of her observation records.

| Content | Method | Teaching materials |
|---|---|---|
| Testing the children on the subject matter they have learnt | Types of tests:<br>• Matching names: children must match their names and the names of other children with the corresponding name cards.<br>• Reading: children must show they are capable of reading names.<br>• Matching letters: children must match the first letters of names with the corresponding letter cards.<br>• Dictation: children must write down letters which you call out. | A fresh set of name cards, used only for tests. |
| Recording test results | The names of the children, the tests they completed and their results should be recorded in a notebook. A chart should be prepared with the results on display. This chart should be pinned to a soft board in the classroom. The marking provided at the end of this section is an example of such record-keeping. | • notebook<br>• chart paper<br>• soft board<br>• board pins |

| Content | Method | Teaching materials |
|---|---|---|
| Helping slow learners | If we were to look at the sample test record below we would see that two children (Manoj and Sapna) have understood the concepts which were taught, while two children (Hema and Rohit) struggled and require help. One way to help Hema and Rohit is by asking the other two if they are willing to help their friends. Normally the children are generous when it comes to helping each other and will do so willingly and sincerely. Some children are more comfortable learning from their friends, not from adults, as the situation is more relaxed. | |

Sample test record:

| Name | can match own name | can read own name | can match others' names | can read others' names | first letters | | | |
|---|---|---|---|---|---|---|---|---|
| | | | | | name | sound | match | write |
| Hema | ✓ | ✓ | ✓ | 2 | 3 | 2 | 3 | 4 |
| Manoj | ✓ | ✓ | ✓ | ✓ | 4 | 4 | 4 | 4 |
| Rohit | ✓ | ✓ | 2 | 1 | 2 | 1 | 2 | 4 |
| Sapna | ✓ | ✓ | ✓ | ✓ | 4 | 4 | 4 | 4* |

* In this sample, the children were marked out of 4.

# Names of Objects

| Content | Method | Teaching materials |
|---|---|---|
| Introducing the names of objects which share the same first letter of a child's name | • Recap the topic of names, how they can be written and read, how they are made up of letters and how these letters have their own names and sounds.<br>• Allow time for the children to discuss their thoughts and feelings on learning names.<br>• Introduce the idea that not only do people have names but so too do objects, animals, plants, colours, etc. Everything has a name.<br>• Hold up a name card for the class to read out loud. In this example, let us use the name 'Rohit'. Ask the children to identify the first letter of the name.<br>• Once they do so, write the letter 'R' on the blackboard.<br>• Ask the children to name a few objects, animals, colours, etc. which begin with the letter 'R' (such as 'run', 'rabbit', 'rat', 'red' and 'radish').<br>• Write each word on the blackboard and slowly and deliberately repeat it out loud, stressing the first letter for emphasis. | • set of name cards<br>• blackboard<br>• chalk<br>• drawing paper |
| Introducing the names of objects which share the | • If capable, draw (or ask the children to draw) simple sketches of the words. This brings life to the class, and the children enjoy drawing their own pictures. | • pencils<br>• papers |

| Content | Method | Teaching materials |
|---|---|---|
| (continued)<br>same first letter of a child's name | • Allow the children to have a brief conversation on the words on the blackboard. They may draw or act out the meanings of the words. They are allowed to have fun, though this need not go on for very long. | |
| Introducing object cards | • Share the object cards, one by one, with the children. These object cards must carry pictures and names of the words previously discussed in class.<br>• Let the children recognise and identify what is on each object card. | • set of object cards (with pictures depicting words previously discussed in class) |
| Naming objects | • Hold the object cards up for the class to see. This time, when identifying what is on the object card, point at the name to help the children match the picture with its written name.<br>• Share the object cards with the children and let them have a group discussion.<br>• Pin the object cards to the soft board, under the letter they begin with. ('Run', 'rabbit', 'rat', 'red' and 'radish' all come under the letter 'R'.)<br>• Encourage the children to read the object cards in their free time. This will help them match the picture of the object with its name. | • set of object cards<br>• soft board<br>• board pins |

| Content | Method | Teaching materials |
|---|---|---|
| Matching object cards (group learning) | • Place a set of objects cards in a bowl.<br>• As was done with the name cards, encourage the children to practice matching objects cards in the dish with the object cards pinned to the soft board. | • bowl<br>• set of object cards |
| Matching name cards with object cards (group learning) | • Once the children are familiar with the object cards, replace the object cards in the dish with name cards which do not carry any pictures.<br>• The children must practice matching these name cards with the object cards on the soft board.<br>• Encourage the children to perform this activity when they are free or show an interest to learn. | • bowl<br>• name cards to match the object cards pinned to the soft board |
| Names of objects which share the same first letter of a different child's name. | • Repeat the above steps, this time using another child's name. 'Hema' may lead to the children discussing the letter 'H' and coming up with words like 'hut', 'hat', 'hip' and 'horse'.<br>• Gradually take this forward until all the children's names are covered.<br>• After enough practice the children should be able to read the name cards and picture the words. They will no longer need an object card to know what a word means, thus developing their reading skills. | |

In this environment of learning the children have the opportunity not only to discuss what they are learning but also to explore other related topics like colours, animals, plants, actions, parts of the body, etc. The teacher should gauge what the children find meaningful and interesting and attempt to teach them through those topics. For example, if the children show an interest in colours, then the teacher need not rigidly follow the lesson plan on names but can instead teach the same topic through drawing, painting and other activities which make use of colour.

In my experience, children do not spend all their time on activities. Once they have satisfied their urges, they are keen to return to a more formal type of learning which involves reading and writing.

| Content | Method | Teaching materials |
|---|---|---|
| Creative activities | • The children may want to draw, paint, trace outlines or make cutouts of pictures. They must be given the time and space to do this, or else they may find the lesson very boring.<br>• Children may wish to sit by themselves in the library corner and quietly read books. Or they may go through books together, discussing the material and sharing their own experiences. | • sheets of paper<br>• crayons<br>• paints<br>• paintbrushes<br>• glue<br>• scissors<br>• pencils<br>• bowls<br>• picture books<br>• storybooks<br>• charts (for animals, birds, etc.) |

| Content | Method | Teaching materials |
|---|---|---|
| Drawing activity | • Ask the children to think of something. It could be anything—an animal, a bird, a flower, etc. It should be something they connect with or like.<br>• Let them close their eyes and imagine something. When they are ready, they should draw a picture of what they were thinking of.<br>• Have them colour their pictures.<br>• Afterwards, let the children share and discuss their drawings. (Some interesting conversations may follow as a child may have chosen to draw a dog because they believe they are, like dogs, loyal. Whether or not they mean it, there will exist some similarities between themselves and what they draw.)<br>• Pin their drawings next to their name cards on the soft board. | • sheets of paper<br>• pencils<br>• crayons<br>• pins |
| Guessing game #1 | • Place a set of name cards face down on a table or the floor. Pick a random card and ask the children to guess the name.<br>• If they have guessed incorrectly, offer clues by saying things like 'This person's name begins with the same letter as the action "run".'<br>• The children guess again based on this information. Once they understand how to play the game, ley them split into groups and play by themselves. | • name cards |
| Guessing game #2 | • Hold up a letter card and tell the children you are thinking of someone in class whose name begins with the same letter. Ask the children to guess who you are thinking of. | • letter cards |

| Content | Method | Teaching materials |
|---|---|---|
| | • Using the same letter, tell the children you are thinking of an animal whose name begins with the same letter. Ask them to guess the animal.<br>• This game may be repeated so that the children can guess the names of plants, objects, etc., which begin with the same letter.<br>• Once the children understand how to play the game, let them split into groups and play by themselves. | |
| Guessing game #3 | • This game is similar to Bingo. Hand each child a name board and a packet of name cards. The boards are not identical—each one has a different set of names.<br>• Call out a name. The children have to go through their packet of name cards, identify the name called out, and then see if they can match it with the names on their board.<br>• Continue to call out names until a child is able to match all the names on their board. The child who does this first is the winner.<br>• The more names on each board, the longer the game lasts and the more interesting it becomes.<br>• This game need not be restricted to the names of children but could be used to teach them the names of letters, objects, animals, etc. | • boards (12 by 8 inches) for each child, prepared by the teacher, with the names of 3 or more children; the boards are not identical and each board has a different set of names<br>• a packet of cards for each child, prepared by the teacher, with all of the names on the boards |

| Content | Method | Teaching materials |
|---|---|---|
| Testing the children on the subject matter they have learnt. | At the end of the lesson the children must be tested on the following items:<br>• Being able to provide examples of objects which share the same first letter of a name.<br>• Recognising the meaning of a word on an object card.<br>• Matching name cards with object cards.<br>• Recognising the meaning of a word on a name card (without needing to look at the picture on the corresponding object card).<br>Record all results in your notebook and on the chart pinned to the soft board (as done before). | • notebook<br>• chart paper<br>• soft board<br>• board pins<br>• fresh set of name cards (with words discussed in class) used only for tests<br>• fresh set of object cards (with pictures of words discussed in class) used only for tests |

# Worksheets

Below are sample exercises for the children to complete. Teachers should feel free to modify these exercises to suit their needs. As I have mentioned before, these are only for reference.

1. Match the names in column A with the names in column B.

| A | B |
|---|---|
| Sapna | Manoj |
| Rohit | Hema |
| Manoj | Sapna |
| Hema | Rohit |

2. Match each letter in column A with the names which begin with that letter in column B.

| A | B |
|---|---|
| R | Sapna |
| H | Rohit |
| M | Manoj |
| S | Hema |

3. Multiple choice: Match the name in bold with one of the choices.

| **Manoj** | Hema / Rohit / Manoj |
|---|---|

4. Multiple choice: Match the name in bold with its first letter.

| **Manoj** | R / H / M |
|---|---|

5. Multiple choice: match the letter in bold with the name which begins with that letter.

| **S** | Hema / Sapna / Rohit |
|---|---|

6. Match each name in column A with a word in column B which begins with the same first letter.

| A | B |
|---|---|
| Sapna | sun |
| Rohit | horse |
| Manoj | rat |
| Hema | mango |

7. Fill in the blanks.
   a. R _ _ _ t
   b. M_ _ o _
   c. S _ p _ _
   d. H _ _ a
8. Strike out the word which does not belong.
   a. Rohit / star / Manoj / Sapna
   b. Rat / run / rabbit / snake
9. Match each name card with an object card.

| | |
|---|---|
| run |  |
| snake |  |
| car |  |
| dog |  |

10. Match the name cards in column A with the name cards in column B.

| A | B |
|---|---|
| rat | snake |
| horse | mango |
| snake | rat |
| mango | horse |

11. Write the names of the objects, animals, actions, etc. on the picture cards.

| | |
|---|---|
|  | |
|  | |
|  | |
|  | |

# 22

# Colours

| Content | Method | Teaching materials |
|---|---|---|
| Nature walk (to collect colourful objects) | • The best way to introduce colours to children is by taking them on a nature walk or a walk in the park. During such outings the children collect stones, feathers, leaves, flowers, etc.<br>• On such an outing, let the children collect objects which they find colourful. They must remember to return to class with everything they have collected. | |
| Organising objects by colour | • After returning to class, ask the children to organise the objects in their collections by colour.<br>• Provide the children with trays. Each tray represents a colour (this can be made clear to the children by using trays of different colours or by using coloured glazed paper as labels).<br>• Encourage the children to place the objects in their respective trays. For example, if a child has collected green leaves, they should be placed in the 'green' tray. | • trays<br>• coloured glazed paper<br>• scissors and glue (to stick labels to the trays) |
| Names of colours | • An ideal time to discuss the names of colours is after the children have organised their collections. This can be done by recapping how important names are and how even colours have names. If the children learn these names then they will be able to talk about colours and the objects they have collected. | |

| Content | Method | Teaching materials |
|---|---|---|
| Introducing the name of a colour by:<br>• sharing objects which are all the same colour.<br>• naming the colour.<br>• emphasising the colour. | • Share with the class a number of objects which the children are familiar with. These objects should all be the same colour. For this example, let us use the colour red.<br>• Place these objects in the 'red' tray.<br>• Show each object to the class. Ask them to identify each object. The children are allowed to take objects from the tray and each child gets a chance to name an object.<br>• Once they have returned the objects, emphasise they are all red. This can be done by saying: 'This is a pen. It is red. This is a ball. It is red. This is a bangle. It is red.'<br>• Have the class identify objects and their colour. Remember to only use objects which are the colour red (or whichever colour is being introduced to the children).<br>• Have each child identify an object and its colour.<br>• Now ask for a volunteer to hold up objects from the tray so that the class can identify the object and its colour. | • objects which the children are familiar with (pens, pencils, bangles, ribbons, dishes, balls, etc.) and which are all the same colour |
| Matching a colour with an object | • Pin a red card to the soft board. Ask the children to name the colour of the card.<br>• Pin a packet containing a set of matching cards under the red card. This is for the children to practice with during their free time. | • colour card<br>• soft board<br>• pins |

| Content | Method | Teaching materials |
|---|---|---|
| (continued) | • Encourage the children to recognise the colour red in objects inside and outside of their classroom, on their clothes, or on their belongings. They should place these objects in the 'red' tray.<br>• Have the children discuss other red objects like tomatoes, buses, blood, roses, etc. They should draw and colour the objects they think of, and stick these drawings in their books. | • set of matching cards which contain different shapes for the children to match |
| Teaching colours through songs | • The children enjoy singing or chanting songs. Share with them a song about a particular colour. For example:<br><br>*What is red?*<br><br>*My ribbon is red.*<br>*Rani's bangles are red*<br>*Arun's kite is red.*<br><br>*Amma's sari is red.*<br>*Appa's shirt is red.*<br><br>*What else is red?*<br>*A rose is red.*<br>*An apple is red.*<br><br>*Yes, of course!*<br>*A tomato is also red.*<br>*Why?* | • chart paper with illustrations to match the content of the song<br>• soft board<br>• board pins/tape |

| Content | Method | Teaching materials |
|---|---|---|
| (continued) | *Even our blood is red.*<br>*Red, red, red,*<br>*A red rose, a red apple, a red tomato*<br>• Tape to the wall or pin to a soft board a chart which lists the words of the song and contains illustrations for the children to match. | |
| Teaching colours through games | The game provided below helps children observe things in class and extends their classroom experiences into the real world.<br>• Allow the children some time to observe the objects in the classroom. Then tell them you are thinking of a red object in the classroom and ask them to guess the object.<br>• The children are allowed to ask questions like 'Is it in the dolls' corner?' or 'Is it round?'<br>• Another version of this game is to think of something which is red and then offer clues to help the children guess. For example, you could say, 'I am thinking of something red. It is round and something you can eat.' The children can use this clue and other clues you offer to guess 'a tomato'. | |

| Content | Method | Teaching materials |
|---|---|---|
| Writing the name of a colour | • Remind the children that the letters in their names have shapes. This is also the case for the letters in the names of colours.<br>• Show the class the letter card 'R'.<br>• If the lesson plan on colours is connected with the lesson plan on names, then you can discuss the letter 'r' and connect it with the colour 'red'.<br>• On a blackboard, write the letter 'r' and connect it with the word 'red'. Spell out and pronounce the word slowly and carefully.<br>• As done in the lesson plan on names, the children should practice saying the word and writing the letters which make the word. They may do this by using their fingers to draw letters in mid-air, or by drawing letters in sand.<br>• Gradually, the children should be able to write letters on paper. | • letter cards<br>• blackboard<br>• chalk<br>• sandpit<br>• sheets of paper<br>• pencils |
| Matching a colour with its name | • At this point the children should be familiar with the primary colours of red, yellow, blue (and the colour green).<br>• Once the children are familiar with the written names of these colours, share a set of colour cards with them. Each card has a colour and its name printed below.<br>• Also share a set of name cards.<br>• The children must try to match the name cards with the colour cards. | • set of colour cards (each card has a colour and its name printed below)<br>• set of name cards to match with the colour cards |

Since children are used to connecting one experience with various other experiences. They may discuss multiple topics which overlap. For example, names might overlap with colours, leading to a discussion of objects which are the same colour and which begin with the same letter. It is good to encourage such discussions and to write down the words the children mention on the blackboard to help build their vocabulary.

Once all the primary colours are introduced to the children, the games and activities become more interesting and meaningful. As you develop each lesson you will notice that the number of learning activities, materials, games, arts-and-crafts activities increase. The children gain a wider variety of ways to develop their skills. They have the freedom to choose which materials and activities will best help them, and they learn with interest, concentration and discipline.

| Content | Method | Teaching materials |
|---|---|---|
| Colouring, cutting and gluing #1 | • Prepare the outlines of objects like leaves, flowers, pots, boxes, buckets, fruits and vegetables. Place them in a tray.<br>• Prepare the colouring material. Note: use only four colours (red, yellow, blue and green), as too many colours will confuse the children. Fill a bowl with red, yellow, blue and green crayons.<br>• When the class is ready, pick an outline from the tray and give it to a child. Ask the child to colour in the outline.<br>• The child should select a crayon from the dish, show the crayon to the class and name the colour of the crayon. The class should help the child if he is incorrect. | • outlines of simple objects the children are familiar with<br>• a tray<br>• crayons<br>• a bowl<br>• scissors<br>• notebooks<br>• glue |

| Content | Method | Teaching materials |
|---|---|---|
| (continued) | • Now the child gets to colour in the outline. Repeat this activity with the rest of the children so that they all get a chance to identify a colour and colour in the outlines.<br>• Once done, the children may cut out and glue the pictures in their notebooks. | |
| Colouring, cutting and gluing #2 | • This time, choose a colour for the children and tell them the name of the colour.<br>• The children must select the right crayon from the bowl.<br>• If they do this correctly, they may select an outline from the tray and colour it in. If they do this incorrectly, the class may help them. | • outlines<br>• a tray<br>• crayons<br>• a bowl |
| Colouring, cutting and gluing #3 | • Write the name of a colour on the blackboard.<br>• The children should pick a crayon of that colour from the bowl.<br>• Help those who make a mistake. Note: do not give them the correct answer but ask them to match cards to try and arrive at the correct answer.<br>• Once the children have selected the right crayon from the bowl, let them colour in their outlines.<br>• Guide the children when they cut out the outlines and glue them into their notebooks. | • outlines<br>• a tray<br>• blackboard<br>• chalk<br>• crayons<br>• a bowl<br>• scissors<br>• notebooks<br>• glue |

| Content | Method | Teaching materials |
| --- | --- | --- |
| Colouring, cutting and gluing #4 | • Provide the children with sheets of paper on which are drawn the outlines of different shapes of different sizes. For example, there could be a large circle, a small square, a small triangle, etc.<br>• Help the children recognise and name all the shapes.<br>• After this, call out the name of a shape and colour. For example, 'Colour the large circle blue'.<br>• The children must choose the right crayon and colour in the right shape. | • sheets of paper on which are drawn the outlines of different shapes of different sizes<br>• a bowl<br>• crayons |
| Colouring, cutting and gluing #5 | • Similar to the previous exercise, provide the children with sheets of paper on which are drawn the outlines of objects they are familiar with.<br>• Repeat the same steps as the previous exercise, only this time call out the names of objects which have to be coloured in. For example, a red box, or a green leaf, or a yellow lemon, or a blue kite. | • sheets of paper on which are drawn the outlines of objects they are familiar with<br>• a bowl<br>• crayons |
| Colouring, cutting and gluing #6 | • Provide each child with a sheet of paper on which is the drawing of a man holding several balloons by their strings.<br>• Allow time for the children to discuss the drawing. Questions could include: 'Who is this man? What is he doing? What is he holding in his hand? How many balloons does he have?' | • sheets of paper on which are the drawings of a man holding several balloons by their strings |

| Content | Method | Teaching materials |
|---|---|---|
| (continued) | • After this, ask the children to colour a certain number of balloons a certain colour. For example, 'colour 3 balloons red', or 'colour 2 balloons yellow.' | • a bowl<br>• crayons |
| Tracing and scribbling | • Children enjoy tracing objects. Show the children how to trace by taking a flat object like a coin or leaf and placing it under a white sheet of paper. Scribble, shade or trace over the object.<br>• Once the children are comfortable doing this by themselves, encourage them to experiment with different objects.<br>• The children should carefully cut out their drawings and glue them in their exercise books. | • white paper<br>• colouring pencils or crayons<br>• sample flat objects like a coin, leaf, etc.<br>• scissors<br>• exercise books<br>• glue |
| Outdoor game | • Discussed in Chapter 11, the children could play the game 'Colour, colour, what colour?'<br>• Have the children select a leader. The leader faces a wall.<br>• The rest of the children stand far away from the leader and together choose a colour. Then they ask, 'Colour, colour, what colour?'<br>• The leader guesses a colour. If it is not the colour the group has chosen then the group says 'No', and takes a step towards the leader and asks the question again. If it is the colour the group has chosen, then the group says 'Yes' and runs. The leader tries to catch them.<br>• The first child to be caught becomes the new leader. | |

| Content | Method | Teaching materials |
|---|---|---|
| Guessing game | • Using colour cards, cover the printed name and hold up a card. Ask a child to identify the colour.<br>• If they answer correctly then ask the next child and continue till all the children have had a chance to play.<br>• If they do answer incorrectly then ask the class to identify the colour and help the child. | • colour cards |
| Storybooks and picture books #1 | • Encourage the children to read books on colours. They may read individually, in groups or with their friends.<br>• These books should include pictures for the children to easily follow along.<br>• While reading, the children should look at the pictures and identify what they see and what colours are being used.<br>• After reading, allow them time to discuss the books. | • books on colours |
| Storybooks and picture books #2 | • Drawing on conversations from class, recreate a story the children can all follow. For example, in one of my classes a boy called Rohit spoke about his experience flying a kite. The children enjoyed this conversation and the teacher, along with the children, created a picture book. The picture book told a very simple story about a boy trying to fly his yellow kite.<br>• Make sure to incorporate colour into the picture book so that the children learn while playing. | • sheets of paper<br>• pencils<br>• crayons or paints<br>• a bowl |

| Content | Method | Teaching materials |
|---|---|---|
| Worksheets | Children also enjoy completing worksheets or workbooks. Examples of exercises may include:<br>• Matching: match the colours in column A with the colours in column B.<br>• Matching: match the colours in column A with their names in column B.<br>• Multiple choice: select the correct name of the colour provided below. | |
| Recapping colours | Recap the following points:<br>• Collecting objects and organising them by colour<br>• Naming colours (one at a time till the four major colours of red, yellow, blue and green are taught)<br>• Writing the names of colours<br>• Reading the names of colours<br>• Practice reading<br>• Other activities including making picture books and storybooks<br>• Worksheets | |

These activities are not new. The important thing is to help the child connect these activities and experiences to form a solid foundation of concepts. This, in turn, will make their learning more meaningful and rich, further developing their ability to think critically and creatively.

| Content | Method | Teaching materials |
|---|---|---|
| Testing the children on subject matter they have learnt | Types of tests:<br>• Recognising all four colours (using different objects of different colours)<br>• Reading the names of colours (matching and reading exercises)<br>• Recognising the starting letter of a colour's name (for all four colours).<br>• Knowing the name and sound of the starting letter of a colour's name.<br>• Copying these letters and words into exercise books. | |

# 23

# Actions

Children are active by nature, and it is during outdoor play that they engage in various activities and expend a lot of energy. A teacher can make use of this time to teach children about actions.

| Content | Method | Teaching materials |
| --- | --- | --- |
| Imitating animals (this game familiarises children with actions and their names) | • During outdoor play, organise a game where you call out the name of an animal and the children act like that animal. For example, you could say 'Fly like a crow', and the children might flap their arms and caw.<br>• Take care to cover a range of actions/verbs. For example, 'hop like a frog' or 'walk like an elephant' or 'swim like a fish' or 'slither like a snake'.<br>• Help the children, if necessary, by mimicking the action of the animal you call out. | |
| Action game (this game helps children understand and remember actions by performing them) | • During outdoor play, ask the children to practice the actions of skipping, running, walking, jumping, hopping, standing, sitting, climbing, crawling, clapping and turning. They may also practice pretending to swim. | |

| Content | Method | Teaching materials |
|---|---|---|
| (continued) | • Once they are comfortable with these actions and recognise them by name, organise another game. This time, the children should perform the actions you call out.<br>• The actions you call out should be easy to perform. For example, 'Skip to the tree, walk around the tree, then run back' or 'Climb the jungle gym'.<br>• Repeat this game on a daily basis until the children are familiar with the names of the actions and recognise them immediately when they are called out. | |
| Action song #1 | • An action song is a song for children which involves the children singing and performing certain actions.<br>• Ask the children to stand in pairs and hold hands.<br>• Sing the following song:<br>*Walk and walk*<br>*and*<br>*Walk and walk*<br>*and*<br>*Turn around*<br>• The children should sing the song and walk until the final line, when they turn around. | |

| Content | Method | Teaching materials |
|---|---|---|
| (continued) | • The verbs for this action song can change so that the children continue to learn new actions. For example, 'walk' could be replaced with 'run', and 'turn around' with 'sit down'. | |
| Action song #2 | • Have the children stand in a circle. One child is chosen as the leader. She must pass in and out of the circle as she sings the song below:<br><br>*In and out*<br>*The sparkling blue bells*<br>*I am the leader.*<br><br>*Rap-a tap-a tap*<br>*On my shoulder*<br>*You are the leader.*<br><br>• After singing the second-last line, she must tap the shoulder of the child closest to her and sing, 'You are the leader.' That child is the new leader.<br>• The new leader must pass in and out of the circle and the old leader must follow the new leader.<br>• One by one the children become leaders and the chain grows until everyone has had the chance to be leader once. | |

| Content | Method | Teaching materials |
|---|---|---|
| Action song charts | • Prepare charts which have the lyrics to action songs as well as illustrations depicting what the children should do as they sing.<br>• Pin these charts to the soft board so that the children, in their free time, can read and learn about actions. | • chart paper<br>• pencils<br>• soft board<br>• board pins |
| Matching lines from action songs | • On strips of cardboard paper, write down the lines from an action song.<br>• Mix these strips of paper in a plastic bag and pin the bag under the song's chart.<br>• Encourage the children to pull out strips from the plastic bag and match them with the lines on the chart, or organise the lines in the same order as the song.<br>• Though the children may not know how to read the sentences, they register the shapes of the words as they read or sing them. Gradually, they will be able to read without hesitation. When this happens, cut the strips of sentences into words.<br>• The children must now match and arrange the words from the packet. | • cardboard paper with the lines from an action song<br>• scissors<br>• plastic bag<br>• pins |

At this point the children should be familiar with hearing and performing actions. They are now ready to learn to write and read the names of actions. The method by which they learn the names of actions is the same method used in the lesson plans for names and colours.

| Content | Method | Teaching materials |
|---|---|---|
| Writing the names of actions | • Remind the children that the letters in their names have shapes. This is also the case for the letters in the names of actions.<br>• Show the class the letter card 'R'.<br>• If the lesson plan on actions is connected with the lesson plan on names, then you can discuss the letter 'r' and connect it with the verb 'run'.<br>• On a blackboard, write the letter 'r' and connect it with the word 'run'. Spell out and pronounce the word slowly and carefully.<br>• As done in the lesson plan on names, the children should practice saying the word and writing the letters which make the word. They may do this by using their fingers to draw the letters in mid-air, or by drawing the letters in sand.<br>• Gradually, the children should be able to write the letters on paper. | • letter cards<br>• blackboard<br>• chalk<br>• sandpit<br>• sheets of paper<br>• pencils |
| Reading the names of actions | • Explain to the children that you have a pack of name cards with the names of verbs written on them. Call out the name of a verb and show them the name card of the verb as well.<br>• The children must pay attention to the written form of the verb.<br>• Practice this activity until the children are able to read and recognise the names of actions. | • name cards with the names of verbs written on them |

Just as object cards were used in the lesson plan on names to help teach children how to read and write the names of objects, action cards (cards which have the written form of a verb as well as a picture illustrating the verb) should be used to help teach children how to read and write the names of actions. The children should also complete matching activities like matching action cards with name cards to better understand the topic.

| Content | Method | Teaching materials |
|---|---|---|
| Action cards | • Share an action card with the class. Let us say, for this example, that the action card is for the verb 'hop'.<br>• Ask the children to read the word on the action card and identify the first letter of the word.<br>• Ask the class if there are any children whose names begin with the same letter. Are there any objects which begin with the same letter? Doing this will help them connect actions with objects, names and letters. | • action cards |

Once the children are comfortable reading and writing the names of common actions, teachers can introduce a number of activities which test and improve their understanding of the topic. A few examples have been provided below.

| Content | Method | Teaching materials |
|---|---|---|
| Action game #2 | • This game may be played inside the classroom. Stick labels to the door, window, blackboard, table and wall. | • labels with the names of objects written on them |

| Content | Method | Teaching materials |
|---|---|---|
| (continued) | • Ask the children to stand in a group. When they are ready, tell them that you will hold up a few cards and that they will have to read the cards and complete the actions. For example, if the cards are 'walk', 'door', 'touch' and 'table', then the children have to walk to the door, touch the door, then walk to the table.<br>• Make sure to help those children who struggle with the rules of the game. | • name cards with the names of the objects that are labelled<br>• name cards with the names of verbs written on them |
| Writing practice | • Encourage the children to try and write about actions. They may use their experiences playing games or completing activities to do this.<br>• Examples of sentences the children could write include:<br>*That is a crow. It is flying.*<br>*Look at the frog. It is hopping. It says wog, wog. It is green.*<br>*Look at the cat. It is drinking milk. It is my cat. I like my cat.*<br>*This is a dog. Its name is rocky. It is Karthik's dog. It is barking.* | |

<table>
<tr><th>Content</th><th>Method</th><th>Teaching materials</th></tr>
<tr><td>Rhyming (to informally teach the sounds of vowels and the names and sounds of letters)</td><td>
<ul>
<li>Ask the children to name an action. Let us say, for this example, they name ‘hop’. Write ‘hop’ on the blackboard.</li>
<li>Ask the children to think of words which rhyme with ‘hop’.</li>
<li>Repeat the above steps with different verbs, then prepare a chart with all these words for the children to read. An example of how the chart might look is provided below:
<table>
<tr><td>hop<br>top<br>shop<br>crop</td><td>skip<br>dip<br>hip<br>lip<br>tip<br>trip</td><td>run<br>fun<br>bun<br>gun<br>sun</td><td>tap<br>gap<br>lap<br>map<br>rap<br>clap</td></tr>
</table>
</li>
<li>This activity prepares the children for formal reading and writing when they turn six.</li>
</ul>
</td><td></td></tr>
</table>

# 24
# Animals

That which takes place in a nursery—a visit, conversation, story, incident, etc.—is not trivial. An observant and attentive teacher will take advantage of these events in her classroom to creatively increase the children's knowledge, interest and curiosity about the world around them. This will give the children a good foundation for developing their skills in reading, writing and mathematics, which are all vital life skills.

This lesson should be taught simultaneously with the lessons on names, colours and actions, as all four topics are interrelated. As I have mentioned before, the lesson plans are not definitive and are instead meant to be used as a source of reference. The sample rhymes and activities I have provided here are to help teachers develop their own creative lessons on the topic.

| Content | Method | Teaching materials |
|---|---|---|
| Rhymes, songs and poems (to teach the children about animals) | • Cut out the illustration of a giraffe and glue it to a piece of cardboard. Cut the carboard along the outline of the giraffe. Glue the stick to the back of the cardboard giraffe so that it is now a puppet you can move.<br>• Arrange a type of stage where the curtain hides the cardboard giraffe from the children. | • illustration of a giraffe<br>• cardboard<br>• stick (the size and length of a straw)<br>• scissors |

| Content | Method | Teaching materials |
|---|---|---|
| (continued) | • Recite the following poem to the children.<br><br>*I am a giraffe*<br>*My name is So-so.*<br>*My neck is so, so so, so so, so so, so long!*<br><br>• As you read the lines, slowly reveal the giraffe. For every 'so', stick its neck farther and farther out from behind the curtain.<br>• Variations of the above poem include:<br><br>*I am a monkey*<br>*My name is Lo-lo*<br>*I have a very long, long, long, long, tail!*<br><br>*I sit on a tree*<br>*And dangle my tail!*<br><br>And:<br><br>*I am a fish*<br>*My name is Go-go*<br>*I swim in water*<br>*I go this way*<br>*I go that way* | • cloth which could be used as a curtain |

Naturally, illustrations and puppets would change based on the animal. These poems proved to be wildly popular in our classes. Children pretended to be giraffes, monkeys and fish. Some were fierce tigers or roaring lions. They used their belts as tails and prowled about. The children pretending to be monkeys climbed the jungle gym and sat comfortably at the top, dangling their tails.

During conversation class the children held excited discussions about animals. Their fantasies about animals were all expressed. Time and space was given for this activity. The children need this.

| Content | Method | Teaching materials |
|---|---|---|
| Classifying animals | • Encourage the children to have a conversation on animals. During the discussion, steer the topic towards classification.<br>• Differentiate between birds and other animals.<br>• Birds have two legs, wings, feathers, and a beak for a mouth. They lay eggs. Most can fly.<br>• Animals (mammals—though this term is too advanced for the children to learn at this age) walk on four legs, have a tail, and some are covered in fur. They give birth and feed milk to their young ones.<br>• After discussing their differences, ask the children to think about the similarities between birds and animals. This should lead to a discussion about how both groups eat, move, make noise, are born and die. In short, they are living things. | |

Depending on the children's interest and enthusiasm, the teacher must now decide where to steer the conversation next. A discussion on animals can cover many topics, as can be seen below:

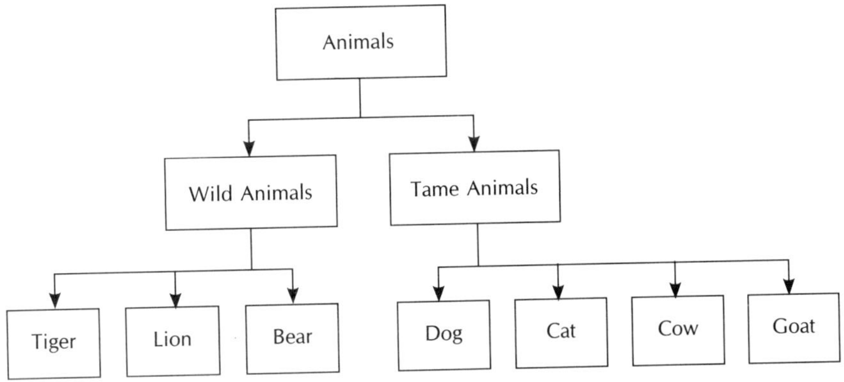


Questions that could be asked include: What are wild animals? Where do they live? What do they eat? What are tame animals? Why are they called 'tame'? What do they eat? Discussing these topics can result in a more specific form of classification:

1. Animals the children know and recognise: dogs, cats, rabbits, horses, donkeys, cows, goats and sheep.
2. Different kinds of dogs.

3. Animals which eat meat (carnivores) and animals which eat grass, vegetables, leaves, etc. (herbivores).
4. Animals which help or are useful to humans.

| Content | Method | Teaching materials |
|---|---|---|
| Visiting a zoo, aquarium, bird sanctuary or museum | • Nowadays there are plenty of DVDs on nature, but children truly benefit from a trip to a zoo, aquarium, bird sanctuary or museum.<br>• On such a trip, encourage the children to be as observant and attentive as possible.<br>• Topics of interest should be further discussed in class. | |

# 25

# Shapes

Children at this age are interested in shapes and parts of the body. A detailed lesson plan is not necessary for these topics, though I would like to share some of my observations. Children, no matter their background, tend to enjoy drawing the outlines of their hands or feet. They do this with chalk on a floor, or with pencils in their drawing books. They often fill their books with drawing after drawing of the outlines of hands. They also enjoy drawing the outlines of their friends' hands and feet. After some time, they move on to drawing the outlines of their belongings, like their pencil boxes, or books or play materials, etc. Over time, they are able to progress to drawing flowers, houses, people and vehicles.

| Content | Method | Teaching materials |
|---|---|---|
| Introducing shapes (circles and squares) | • Encourage the children to observe the shapes of objects in the classroom.<br>• Ask the children to bring objects of different shapes and sizes to the classroom for comparison.<br>• After the children share these objects with one another, try to organise the objects by shape (square-shaped or circular).<br>• At this stage, the children need only learn about squares and circles. | • trays with the labels 'square' and 'circle' |

| Content | Method | Teaching materials |
|---|---|---|
| Object cards | • Share the object cards with the children and teach them the names of the shapes.<br>• Pin the object cards to the soft board and encourage the children to learn to recognise the shapes and read their names. | • object cards for the following shapes: circle, square and triangle<br>• soft board<br>• pins |
| Colouring, cutting and pasting the outlines of shapes | • Share the sheets of paper with the outlines of shapes on them with the children.<br>• Leave a bowl filled with crayons of different colours for the children.<br>• Call out the name of a shape and a colour. The children must fill in that shape's outline with the colour you have called out.<br>• After colouring the shapes, the children should cut out the shapes and glue them into their books. | • sheets of paper with the outlines of circles, squares and triangles<br>• crayons<br>• bowl<br>• scissors<br>• glue |
| Colouring, cutting and pasting the outlines of objects | • Share the sheets of paper with the outlines of objects on them with the children.<br>• Leave a bowl filled with crayons of different colours for the children. | • sheets of paper with the outlines of leaves, flowers, houses, boxes, buckets, etc. |

| Content | Method | Teaching materials |
|---|---|---|
| (continued) | • Call out the name of an object and a colour. The children must fill in that object's outline with the colour you have called out.<br>• After colouring the outlines, the children should cut out the outlines and glue them into their books. | • crayons<br>• bowl<br>• scissors<br>• glue |

There are other activities children can perform to learn about shapes. These include:

- Using matchsticks and broken bangles to make new and different shapes.
- Folding paper to create different shapes or objects. This requires teaching the children how to fold paper to create paper fans, caps, boats, windmills, rockets, etc.
- Collecting objects such as stones, coins, shells, etc. during a trip and organising them by shape.
- Drawing and creating patterns using the paper cutouts of geometrical shapes.
- Playing with clay. Encourage the children to create different shapes using clay. After the lesson, the clay shapes are left to dry. The children can then paint their clay shapes.
- Outdoor play involving instructing the children to stand in a straight line, or form a triangle, or stand in a circle or square.

# 26

# Parts of the Body

Children of this age group are already aware of the names of certain parts of the body: arms, hands, fingers, head, face, eyes, ears, nose, mouth, teeth, legs, feet and toes. For this lesson, they require plenty of sensory and motor experiences which introduce concepts related to the body.

| Content | Method | Teaching materials |
|---|---|---|
| Activity #1 (identifying parts of the body) | • Ask the children to identify parts of the body. This can be done by asking, 'Children, show me your legs (or hands, etc.).'<br>• The children must point at or show you the body part you mentioned.<br>• Once they are capable of correctly doing this, ask the children some easy-to-answer questions about the body part. For example, 'How many legs do you have? What do you do with your legs?' | |
| Games and songs | Build on the children's answers from activity #1 to encourage them to participate in creative activities. For example:<br>• while discussing legs and how you use them to walk, you could have the children sing an action song involving the action of 'walking'.<br>• while discussing hands and how you use them to clap, you could have the children sing an action song and clap along. | |

| Content | Method | Teaching materials |
| --- | --- | --- |
| (continued) | • while discussing eyes and how you use them to see, you could have the children close their eyes and try to guess objects in your hand. After a few guesses they are allowed to open their eyes and correctly identify the object. | |
| Discussing compassion | • Children should learn to appreciate their body. They should also show compassion towards those who are physically disabled.<br>• Discuss physical disabilities like being blind, deaf or unable to speak, and encourage the children to have a conversation on such a topic. | |
| Outings | • Visit a school for the blind (or the deaf, or for those unable to speak). Such an outing teaches children to value their ability to see, hear and speak. It also encourages children to be more compassionate towards those who are physically disabled. | |
| Chart | • Prepare a chart which has a labelled illustration of the human body. Parts of the body which are important to know about at this age (these are mentioned at the beginning of this chapter) should be labelled.<br>• Pin the chart to the soft board.<br>• Encourage the children to read the chart in their free time. | • chart paper<br>• pencils<br>• soft board<br>• pins |

| Content | Method | Teaching materials |
|---|---|---|
| Action song #1 | • This is a song which can be used to teach the children about parts of the body.<br>*I can see with my eyes*<br>*I can hear with my ears*<br>*I can smell with my nose*<br>*I can walk with my legs*<br>*I can touch with my hands*<br>*I can talk with my mouth*<br>• Encourage the children to point at the parts of the body which they are singing about while they sing. | |

Songs which could be used to help teach the children parts of the body include 'Where is Thumbkin?' and 'Five Little Fingers'. Once the children are able to confidently identify various parts of the body, introduce the activities of reading and writing the names of parts of the body the same way as has been outlined in the lesson plans on colours and actions.

# 27

# Trees and Plants

This is a very interesting and lively topic for children as it is connected with nature. In addition to learning about nature, the children cultivate values such as loving, protecting and caring for nature through this lesson.

| Content | Method | Teaching materials |
|---|---|---|
| Visit a garden, field or park | • The best way to introduce children to trees and plants is by taking them on a trip to a garden, field or park.<br>• There, surrounded by nature, the children can observe trees or plants or birds and animals in their natural environment. | |
| Bringing seeds to class | • Often, while visiting the garden, field or park, the children might collect sticks, stones and seeds. If they do not collect any seeds, request each child to bring the seed of a plant to class. The seed could be from any plant. The idea is to try and grow the plant.<br>• Discuss how plants grow (what they require, etc.) and what their function is. Mention the importance of soil, water and sunlight.<br>• Encourage the children to have a discussion on plants. | |

| Content | Method | Teaching materials |
|---|---|---|
| Gardening | • This is an activity the children truly enjoy. Gardening helps them work hard and keeps them alert and active. They develop patience by watching the plants slowly grow. Above all, they learn to work together and experience a sense of community and peace from being so close to nature.<br>• Some children might prefer to plant their seeds in a pot, other might prefer to plant their seeds in a plot. The children are free to choose.<br>• The plot should be prepared. This means weeds and stones must be removed and the soil needs to be dug up. Manure should be mixed with the soil to help the plants grow. The children should learn this as they prepare the plot.<br>• Have the children plant their seeds. | • outdoor plot where the children can plant their seeds<br>• pots |
| Reading | • Provide the children with illustrated and easy-to-read books on trees and plants.<br>• During class they should try to read and discuss the points covered in the books. | • illustrated and easy-to-read books on trees and plants |

While this lesson plan suggests the teacher should prepare the children for gardening plants, I have often found the children, in time, express a desire to understand how plants grow. This is a more organic way and, with their curiosity raised, a more impactful way by which they can learn.

# 28

# Numbers (for 3-year-olds)

The content in this lesson plan has been designed for three-year-old children and focuses on the concepts of 'a few' vs 'many'. Children of this age group are only vaguely familiar with these terms, which may have occasionally come up in class.

| Content | Method | Teaching materials |
|---|---|---|
| Introducing the concepts of 'a few' and 'many' (through pictures) | • Select two pictures which clearly illustrate the concepts of 'a few' and 'many'. For example, one could be of a market or railway station or wedding where there are 'many' people, and one could be of an apartment or garden or a forest where there are only 'a few' people.<br>• Sharing the pictures with the class, ask the children to describe how many people they see in each picture. Encourage them to have a discussion on numbers (for example, there may be only a few people in the forest, but there may be many trees).<br>• Have the children compare the pictures. Introduce the concepts 'a few' and 'many'.<br>• Pin the pictures to a soft board so that the children can talk about the pictures whenever they are free. | • pictures which illustrate the concepts of 'a few' and 'many'<br>• soft board<br>• board pins |

| Content | Method | Teaching materials |
|---|---|---|
| Introducing the concepts of 'a few' and 'many' (through objects) | • Ask the children to collect a type of object in the classroom. This could include pencils, pens, crayons, beads, etc.<br>• Split the collection into two groups. One group should be larger in number, to represent 'many', and one group should be smaller in number, to represent 'a few'.<br>• Ask the children to identify which is which. This could be done by asking: 'Which group has only a few pencils? And which group has many pencils?'<br>• Repeat the activity with different types of objects so that the children do not associate 'a few' and 'many' with only one object. | |
| Groupwork (using objects) | • After completing the above activity, encourage the children to split into groups and, within their groups, repeat the above activity.<br>• Encourage the children to bring objects from outside of the classroom. They could collect stones, flowers, leaves, seeds, etc.<br>• One child should split the collected objects into two groups. One group should be larger in number, to represent 'many', and one group should be smaller in number, to represent 'a few'.<br>• The rest of the children have to decide which group represents 'a few', and which represents 'many'.<br>• Observe the children as they play. They are free to discuss the material. | |

| Content | Method | Teaching materials |
|---|---|---|
| Discussing 'a few' and 'many' during play activities | • Children often converse amongst themselves during play activities. Encourage them to try and use 'a few' and 'many' when discussing their play materials. For example, while threading beads the children could say 'Kartik has threaded only a few beads. Ambika threaded many beads. His chain is short. Her chain is long.'<br>• There are plenty of opportunities during doll play, kitchen play, block play and other activities for the children to compare their work and make use of the concepts of 'a few' and 'many'.<br>• In a nursery, the children frequently compare quantities by using words like 'a few and many' or 'more and less' or 'big and small' or 'long and short' or 'fat and thin'. An observant teacher should make the children aware of these concepts whenever they use them. | |
| Activity #1 (comparing quantities) | • Fill one bowl with only a few beads, and one bowl with many beads.<br>• Ask the children to identify which bowl has only a few beads, and which has many beads.<br>• Children may answer as a group or individually.<br>• To ensure the children do not relate this concept only with beads, use other materials and objects. | • two bowls<br>• beads |

| Content | Method | Teaching materials |
|---|---|---|
| Activity #2 (comparing quantities) | • Split the children into two groups.<br>• One group fills the bowls with beads. One bowl should have only a few beads, the other bowl should have many beads.<br>• The other group must now identify which bowl has only a few beads, and which bowl has many beads. | • two bowls<br>• beads |
| Activity #3 (comparing quantities) | • Ask the girls to form a group, and the boys to form a group.<br>• Ask the children to identify which group is larger and which is smaller. | |
| Activity #4 (outing) | • On an outing, ask the children to observe all the things around them.<br>• Encourage them to try and name the things they see.<br>• Encourage them to use the words 'a few' and 'many' to describe what they see and collect. For example, they may see many cars on the road, but only a few cyclists. | |
| Game #1 | • Place the beads, tamarind seeds, stones and crayons in the centre of the classroom.<br>• Place the two bowls next to the objects.<br>• Split the class into two groups—group A and group B. | • beads<br>• tamarind seeds<br>• stones<br>• crayons |

| Content | Method | Teaching materials |
|---|---|---|
| (continued) | • A child from group A must issue instructions which test the children's knowledge of 'a few' and 'many' to a child from group B. For example, Sangeetha from group A could instruct Sunil from group B to fill bowl 1 with many tamarind seeds and bowl 2 with only a few tamarind seeds.<br>• The children check to see if the child has completed the task correctly. If so, that group wins a point. If not, the group can help the child.<br>• Now the child from group B can call out the name of a child from group A and ask them to fill the bowls with 'a few' or 'many' beads, etc.<br>• Continue the activity till the children lose interest. | • two bowls (labelled 'bowl 1' and 'bowl 2' |
| Game #2 | • Split the children into two groups.<br>• One group is given two bowls and the beads.<br>• They must fill one bowl with many beads and one bowl with only a few beads.<br>• They ask the other group to identify which bowl has 'many' beads and which only has a 'few'. If the other group answers correctly, they score a point and it is their turn to fill the bowls with beads.<br>• Points are for enjoyment and not for competition. | • two bowls<br>• beads |
| Game #3 (object cards) | • Each child is dealt an object card. Some of the cards illustrate many of the same object, and some of the cards illustrate a few of the same object. For example, one card might illustrate ten flowers, while another might illustrate two birds. | • object cards (illustrating either a few or many objccts) for each child |

| Content | Method | Teaching materials |
| --- | --- | --- |
| (continued) | • Select a child, and that child must place their card on the ground for everyone to see.<br>• The child must state whether their card illustrates many objects, or only a few.<br>• If the child says 'a few', then the other children who believe their cards illustrate only a few objects should place their cards on the ground. If the child says 'many', then the other children who believe their cards illustrate many objects should place their cards on the ground.<br>• The children can classify and order their cards depending on the number of objects illustrated. | |
| Game #4 (matching object cards with 'a few' and 'many' labels) | • Pin the card with many dots on the soft board, and place the bowl labelled 'many' under it.<br>• Pin the card with a few dots on the soft board, and place the bowl labelled 'a few' under it.<br>• Mix the objects cards and leave them in the large bowl.<br>• Split the children into groups of three or four.<br>• A child from each group must collect a card from the large bowl and share it with their group.<br>• Each group must hold a discussion and decide if their object card illustrates many objects or only a few. They must then place their card in either the bowl labelled 'many' or the bowl labelled 'a few'. | • two bowls (labelled 'a few' and 'many')<br>• large bowl<br>• object cards<br>• soft board<br>• board pins<br>• two cards (one with many dots, one with a few dots) |

# 29

# Numbers (for 4-year-olds)

The content in this lesson plan has been designed for four-year-old children. It focuses on naming number concepts from 1 to 5 and draws on material covered in Chapter 20, under the section 'Number Concepts and Number Names'.

After learning about 'a few' and 'many', children are often taught the numerals 1, 2, 3, 4 and 5. The common belief is that they now have enough experience with numbers to be taught numerals. But we have to remember to 'begin where the child is'. Children have to be led, step by step, so that intelligent learning takes place and their minds remain active and curious. So what is the next step? The next step is naming numbers.

| Content | Method | Teaching materials |
|---|---|---|
| Comparing quantities using the concepts 'a few' and 'many' (and illustrating the idea that 'a few' and 'many' are imprecise terms) | • Have the children sit in a semicircle and place four bowls in the centre.<br>• Explain that the bowls are empty and marked 'A', 'B', 'C' and 'D'.<br>• Pour some beads into bowl A and more beads into bowl B. Ask the children to identify which bowl contains a few beads, and which contains many.<br>• After the children correctly answer the question, pour beads into bowl C. There should be more beads in bowl C than in bowl B.<br>• Ask the children to focus on bowls B and C and identify which bowl contains a few beads, and which contains many. | • four bowls (labelled 'A', 'B', 'C' and 'D')<br>• beads |

| Content | Method | Teaching materials |
|---|---|---|
| (continued)<br>Note: This activity is discussed in some detail in Chapter 20. | • After the children correctly answer the question, draw attention to the fact that earlier they had said bowl B contained many beads, but now they say bowl B contains a few beads.<br>• Ask them: 'How is it possible that the same number of beads is sometimes 'a few' and sometimes 'many'?<br>• Some of the children may be confused while some may answer that the reason for this is because bowl C contains more beads than bowl B.<br>• Now pour beads into bowl D. There should be more beads in bowl D than in bowl C.<br>• Ask the children to concentrate on bowls C and D and identify which bowl contains a few beads, and which contains many.<br>• After the children correctly answer the question, draw attention to the fact that earlier they had said bowl C contained many beads, but now they say bowl C contains a few beads.<br>• Explain that the concepts 'a few' and 'many' are not fixed and can change depending on the situation.<br>• Now ask the children whether bowl B contains a few beads or many.<br>• It is likely some children will saw a few, some will say many and some will say they do not know.<br>• Explain that unless they give a name to the quantity in each bowl, it will be difficult to say whether bowl B contains 'a few' or 'many' beads. | |

| Content | Method | Teaching materials |
|---|---|---|
| Introducing the smallest quantity of 'a few' | • It might be useful at this stage to remind the children of the lesson on names, and how they use names to avoid confusion when talking about people.<br>• Returning to bowls A and B, remove a bead from bowl A. Ask the children to explain what happened.<br>• The children should be able to state that the quantity in bowl A has reduced.<br>• Remove another bead from bowl A.<br>• The children at this point should still be stating that bowl A contains a few beads.<br>• Continue to remove beads from bowl A until only one bead remains. Explain that if you were to remove the last bead then bowl A would not have any beads in it. One bead is the smallest possible quantity of 'a few'. | |
| Using the smallest quantity of 'a few' | • Draw the following concept on a blackboard: ⊙<br>• Explain to the children that this concept represents the one bead in bowl A. It therefore represents the smallest possible quantity of 'a few'.<br>• Encourage the children to try and identify parts of the body which are equal to ⊙. Examples could include the nose or mouth.<br>• Draw the children's answers on the blackboard and connect them with the concept ⊙. | • blackboard<br>• chalk |

| Content | Method | Teaching materials |
| --- | --- | --- |
| Activity #1 (using the smallest quantity of 'a few' to count objects) | • Place the bowls with the pencils, crayons, beads, stones, seeds and buttons at the front of the classroom.<br>• Draw the concept of the smallest quantity of 'a few' (⊙) on the blackboard.<br>• Ask the children to select an object from any of the bowls and match it with the concept on the blackboard.<br>• If a child takes more than one object, allow the other children to help the child. | • pencils<br>• crayons<br>• beads<br>• stones<br>• seeds<br>• buttons<br>• bowls for the above objects<br>• blackboard<br>• chalk |
| Activity #2 (using the smallest quantity of 'a few' to count collected objects) | • Encourage children to collect objects from outside of class. They may collect leaves, flowers, sticks, etc.<br>• When they bring these objects to class, they should try to match the objects with the concept ⊙.<br>• The idea in doing this is to allow the children time to understand that the concept ⊙ is a standard which can be used to compare different objects of the same quantity (the smallest quantity of 'a few'). | • blackboard<br>• chalk |

| Content | Method | Teaching materials |
|---|---|---|
| Giving a symbol and name to the concept ⊙ | • Remind the children that the concept ⊙ represents the smallest quantity of 'a few'. This concept has a name.<br>• Draw the concept ⊙ on the blackboard, and beside it write the word 'one' and the numeral '1'.<br>• Explain to the children that the concept ⊙ has a name and a symbol. The word 'one' is the concept's name, and the number '1' is the concept's symbol.<br>• Point at the name and symbol as you explain the above point.<br>• Ask each child to come up to the blackboard and say the word 'one'. As they do so they should point at the concept ⊙, then point at the word 'one' and the symbol '1'.<br>• Over time the children should be able to instantly associate the name 'one' and the numeral '1' with the concept ⊙. | • blackboard<br>• chalk |
| Activity #3 (using 'one') | • Ask the children to look for objects in the class which are equal to one.<br>• The children should touch the object and say its name and quantity. For example, 'one blackboard', or 'one duster', or 'one door'. | |

| Content | Method | Teaching materials |
|---|---|---|
| Activity #4 (tracing, colouring, cutting and pasting) | • Provide the children with a sheet of paper containing the outlines of objects like a flower, a leaf, a box, etc.<br>• Using colour pencils, the children must fill in the outlines.<br>• After filling in the outlines, the children must cut out the pictures and glue them inside their picture books.<br>• Under each picture they must write the name of the object and its quantity. For example, 'one flower', 'one leaf', 'one box', etc. | • a sheet of paper containing the outlines of objects<br>• colour pencils<br>• scissors<br>• glue |
| Activity #5 (threading beads) | Note: the following activity should be completed only after the children have learnt about colours.<br>• Ask the children to thread beads, one at a time, based on their colour. Remember to prioritise the number 'one'. For example, you could say, 'Children, thread one red bead. Now thread one blue bead. Now thread one green bead.'<br>• The children should repeat the number and the colour of the bead as they thread it. | • beads of different colours<br>• threads |
| Game #1 | • This is a guessing game which involves telling the children that you can see something in the classroom which is equal in quantity to 'one'. | |

| Content | Method | Teaching materials |
|---|---|---|
| (continued) | • Ask them to guess what you are looking at. This could be done by saying, 'Children, I can see something that is equal to one in the dolls' corner. Can you guess what I'm looking at?'<br>• Once the children are comfortable with the rules of the game, divide the class into groups and allow them to play amongst themselves. | |
| Singing a song about 'one' | • Prepare an illustrated chart which has the lines to a song about 'one'. A sample song has been provided below:<br>*My head is 1*<br>*My nose is 1*<br>*The sun is 1*<br>*The moon is 1*<br>*What else is 1?*<br>*I am 1*<br>*You are 1*<br>*This dot ⊙ is 1*<br>*This is 1*<br>The above is a simple song written by the children and the teacher in our nursery school.<br>• Pin the chart to the soft board.<br>• The children enjoy the illustrations and are free to sing the song when they want. | • chart paper<br>• pencils<br>• soft board<br>• board pins |

| Content | Method | Teaching materials |
|---|---|---|
| Introducing the next number concept (by using 'one' as a standard) | • Have the children sit in a semicircle. Fill the bowl with beads and place the bowl and number card (for 'one/1' on the floor.<br>• Ask a child to match a bead from the bowl with the number card.<br>• The child should take one bead and place it next to the number card.<br>• Now ask another child to match a bead from the bowl with the number card.<br>• The other child should take one bead and place it next to the number card. Now there are two beads next to the number card for 'one/1'.<br>• Ask the children if the beads match with the number card. They should answer 'No'.<br>• Take the concept cards which have the concept • and explain that each card represents one bead. But when you have two beads, they make ••.<br>• Place the concept card •• beside the two beads and ask the children if they match. They should answer, 'Yes'.<br>• Explain that the concept •• has a name. It is called 'two'. It has a symbol, '2'. As you explain this, write the name and symbol on the concept card.<br>• Ask the children to name the concept ••. They should answer 'two'. Ask the children to write the symbol of the concept. They may draw it in the air with their fingers or try to draw it in their books. | • Number card (with the name 'one' and symbol '1')<br>• Concept cards (two cards with the concept •, and one card with the concept ••. |

As was done with the number concept '1', the teacher will have to provide the children with the activities, games and songs listed above to help them learn the number concept '2' and, in time, the number concepts '3', '4' and '5'.

Once the children are capable of reading and writing the number concepts '1', '2', '3', '4' and '5', the teacher can prepare the following charts, activities and games.

| Content | Method | Teaching materials |
|---|---|---|
| Charts | Create illustrated number charts and pin them to the soft boards in the classroom. This way the children can read and learn about numbers in their free time. A sample chart has been provided below. | • chart paper<br>• pencils<br>• soft board<br>• board pins |

| • | •• | ••• | ••<br>•• | ••<br>••• |
|---|---|---|---|---|
| 1 | 2 | 3 | 4 | 5 |

At this point it is worth creating object cards to help the children learn numbers. Ideally, you should try to prepare the following:

1. Object cards: A sample set can be seen below:

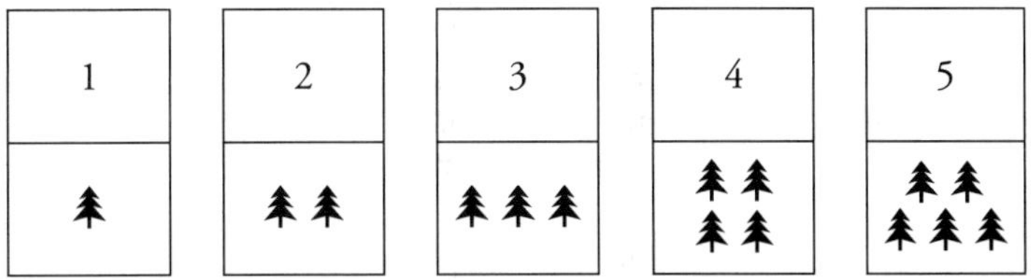


   Each card has a picture on one side and a numeral on the other side. The numeral matches the number of objects in the picture. Create five sets, each set of a different object.
2. Dot cards: A set of five, with dots on one side and a numeral on the other side. The numeral matches the number of dots. Create five sets.

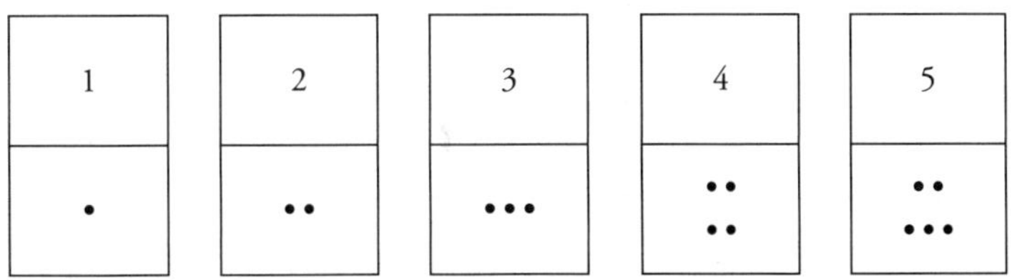

3. Dot/object cards: A set of five, with dots on one side and a picture on the other side. The dots match the number of objects in the picture. Create five sets, each of a different object.

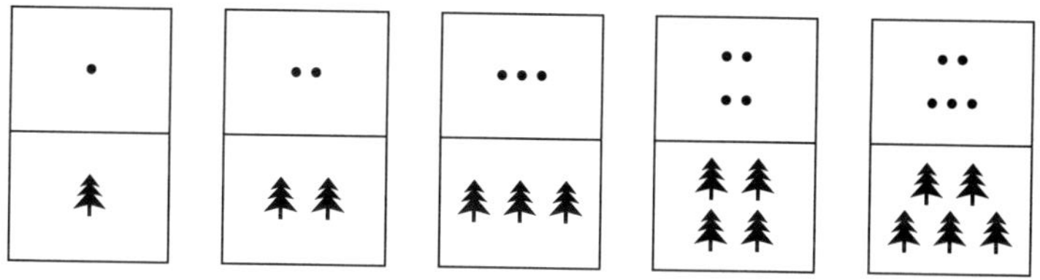

| Content | Method | Teaching materials |
|---|---|---|
| Matching numbers (using object cards, dot cards and number cards) | • Allow the children time and space to go through the object cards, dot cards and number cards.<br>• This is a useful quiet activity. | • object cards<br>• dot cards<br>• number cards |
| Group work (object cards) | • Distribute the 25 object cards among a group of five children. Each child gets a set of five cards.<br>• Have one child begin by placing a card on the floor with the picture facing up. The child must state what is on the card. For example, if the picture is of two flowers, she must say, 'Two flowers'.<br>• The other children must now match a card from their set with the card on the floor. If, for example, the card on the floor is of two flowers, then the other children must place on the floor an object card with a picture of two objects (two trees, two cats, etc.). | • object cards |

| Content | Method | Teaching materials |
|---|---|---|
| (continued) | • After each child has put down the correct card, the next round begins and another child places a card on the floor.<br>• They each get a turn to state the name and number of the object cards on the floor. 'Two flowers, two mangoes, two trees, two cups, two chairs.' As they do this, they should turn the cards and look at the numeral printed on the back.<br>• The game continues until the children finish placing all five of their cards or lose interest. | |
| Group work<br>(dot cards, number cards) | The above activity may be repeated with dot cards or number cards. The idea is to expose the children to the numerals and to have them practicing saying the names of numbers. | |

Children also enjoy playing with domino cards. A set of domino cards for two children may look something like this:

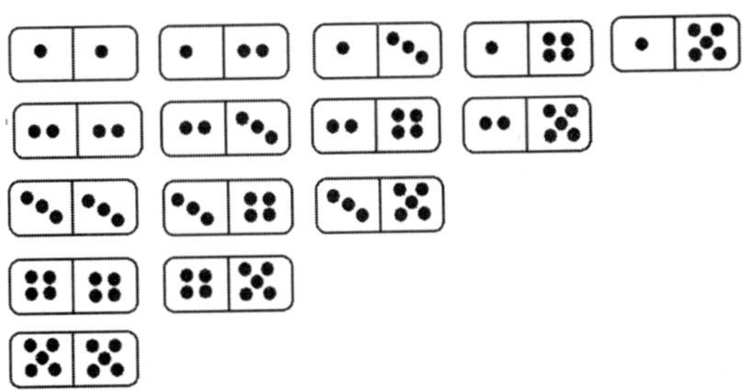

| Content | Method | Teaching materials |
|---|---|---|
| Playing with domino cards | • Distribute domino cards between two children. One child gets eight cards, the other gets seven.<br>• The child with eight cards places one of her cards on the floor.<br>• The other child must now use one of their cards to match with the card on the floor. An illustration of how cards are matched has been provided below.<br>• The game continues till the children use all their cards. | • domino cards |

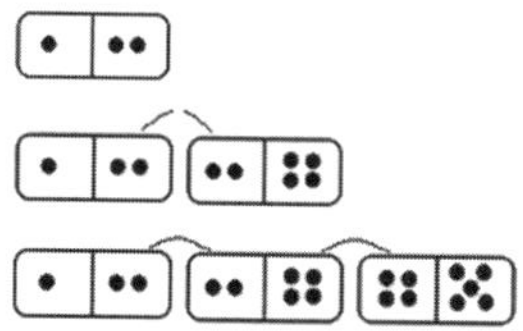

Children also enjoy playing Housie. This game requires the following:

1. A set of five large cards, six by six inches in size, with numbers printed on them in the following arrangement:

**A**

| 1 | 2 |
|---|---|
| 3 | 4 |

**B**

| 1 | 3 |
|---|---|
| 2 | 5 |

**C**

| 2 | 4 |
|---|---|
| 5 | 3 |

**D**

| 3 | 5 |
|---|---|
| 4 | 1 |

**E**

| 1 | 2 |
|---|---|
| 5 | 4 |

2. A set of five small cards with the numerals '1', '2', '3', '4' and '5' printed on them.
3. Twenty small cards. These should be split into 5 sets. Each set should match one of the large cards above. Set A should therefore have the letter A printed on the back of four cards, and the four cards should have the numerals '1', '2', '3' and '4' printed on the front. Set B should have the letter B printed on the back of the four cards, and the four cards should have the numerals '1', '3', '2' and '5'.

| Content | Method | Teaching materials |
|---|---|---|
| Playing Housie | The rules of Housie are as follows:<br>• Children are split into groups of five.<br>• One of the children is chosen as the leader. He is given a set of number cards.<br>• The other children are given (a) a large card with four numbers written on it and (b) number cards with numerals which match the numerals on their large card.<br>• The leader selects a card at random from his set and calls out the number. The other children must go through their number cards to see if they have that number. If they do, they must match the small number card with the numeral on their large card.<br>• The game continues until one of the children is able to match all their number cards with their large card. | • large cards (6 by 6 inches)<br>• number cards with numerals which match the numerals on the large card<br>• set of number cards with numerals ranging from 1 to 5 |

| Content | Method | Teaching materials |
|---|---|---|
| Outdoor play | • Have the children form a large circle in the playground.<br>• Stand in the centre of the circle and sing the following line:<br>*Fire on the mountain, run, run, run!*<br>• Continue to sing as the children run around and expend their energy. When you stop, call out a number.<br>• The children must form groups that are the size of that number. If, for example, you call out '4', then they must form groups of four.<br>• If, after the groups have formed, there are one or two remaining children unable to form the right number, then they must sit down as they are out.<br>• The game continues until the children lose interest or there are two or three children left. | |
| Activity #6 (colouring) | • Provide each child with a sheet of paper which has the outlines of five circles.<br>• Provide crayons or colour pencils to the class.<br>• Call out a colour and a number (which is below 5). The children must fill in that many circles with that colour. For example, you could say, 'Colour two circles red.' | • sheet of paper with the outlines of five circles<br>• crayons or colour pencils |

| Content | Method | Teaching materials |
|---|---|---|
| (continued) | • Now ask the children how many circles are left. After they answer, ask them which colour they'd like to use. The children are free to fill in the remaining circles with a colour of their choice.<br>• This activity could be repeated with the outlines of different shapes and objects. | |
| Activity #7 (colouring) | A variation of the above activity is to provide the children with paper and crayons or colour pencils, and to ask them to draw a certain number of objects in a certain colour. For example, you could say, 'Draw three squares in red.' | • paper<br>• crayons or colour pencils |
| Activity #8 (gluing) | • Prepare cutouts of objects the children can easily recognise. Place these cutouts in a bowl for the children to use.<br>• Ask the children to glue a certain number of objects in their exercise books. For example, you could say, 'Children, glue 2 leaves and 1 box in your books'.<br>• The children must carefully listen and carry out your instructions. | • cutouts of objects the children are familiar with<br>• a bowl<br>• glue |
| Activity #9 (threading) | • A variation of the above activity is to provide the children with a bowl filled with beads of different colours. Also provide each child with string for threading beads.<br>• Ask the children to thread a certain number of beads of a certain colour. For example, you could say, 'Thread two blue beads. Then three red beads.' | • bowl<br>• beads of different colours (that the children recognise and know)<br>• string |

| Content | Method | Teaching materials |
|---|---|---|
| Counting numbers through illustrations | • Draw a picture of a house on the blackboard.<br>• Ask the children questions about the picture, especially questions which require they count. For example, 'How many windows are there?'<br>• The picture need not be only of a house but could also be of a garden, classroom, playground, etc. | • blackboard<br>• chalk |
| Counting numbers through objects | A variation of the above activity is to ask the children questions about objects they are familiar with. Questions could include:<br>• How many legs does a dog/cat/monkey have?<br>• How many eyes does a donkey/crow/baby have? | |

# Worksheets

Children of this age group also enjoy completing worksheets. In our nursery, the worksheets on numbers which we provided contained three types of questions:

1. Matching
2. Multiple choice
3. Fill in the blanks

Matching questions could include any of the following:

- Matching dots with dots
- Matching dots with objects
- Matching dots with numerals
- Matching objects with objects
- Matching objects with numerals
- Matching numerals with numerals

Some sample exercises have been provided below:

*Match the dots in column A with the dots in column B. The first one has already been done for you.*

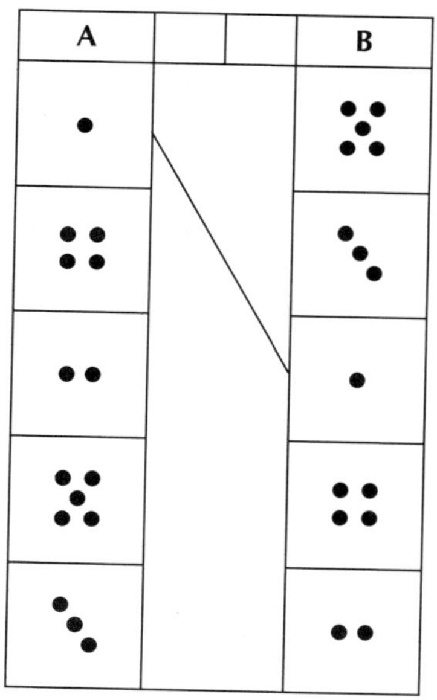

*Which of the following matches the number of dots in the first square?*

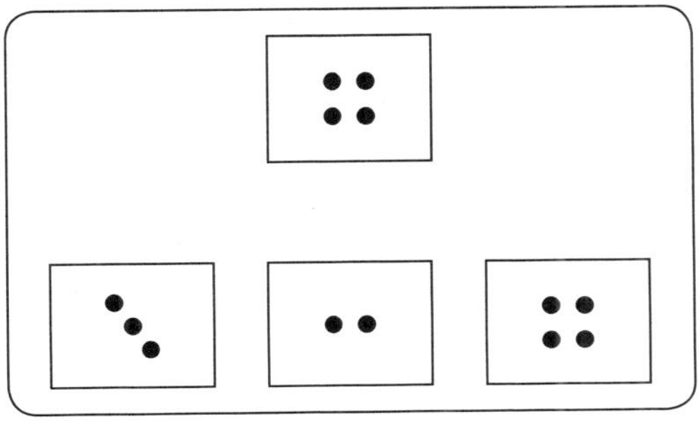

**Note:** Provide the children with clear instructions on how to answer the questions. The children must understand what they are doing and not mechanically answer the questions.

*Fill in the blanks with the correct numeral, or number of dots, or number of objects.*

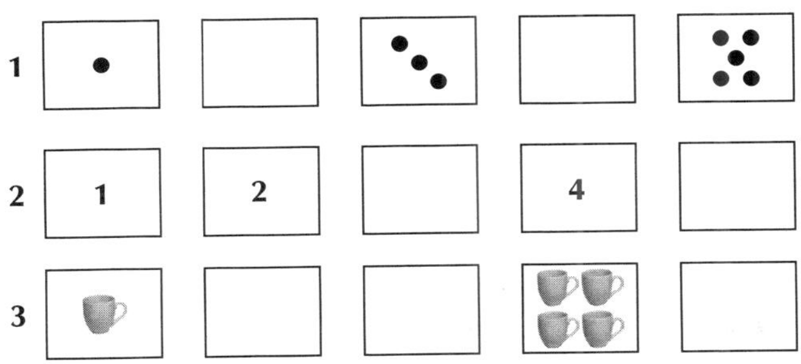


**Note:** Care must be taken to show the children how to answer such questions. It is important they be given enough time to understand what is expected of them.

# 30

# Numbers (for 5-year-olds)

The children are by now familiar with the names of the numbers one, two, three, four and five. They know how to count them and are able to recognise their written and numeral forms. The next concept which should be introduced is the idea that a big number is made of smaller numbers.

| Content | Method | Teaching materials |
|---|---|---|
| Recapping numbers and introducing the concept of a big number being made of smaller numbers | • Remind the children that they have learnt the names of a few numbers. Ask them to use their fingers to count up to five.<br>• As the children count up to five, write the numerals on the blackboard.<br>• Ask the children to identify the smallest number (1) and the largest number (5). Explain that 4 is smaller than 5, 3 is also smaller than 5, 2 is also smaller than 5, and that 1 is the smallest number.<br>• In order to help the children better understand the concept of a big number being made of smaller numbers, compare the concept of numbers with family. This could be done by saying: 'Just as you belong to a family where you have little brothers and little sisters, and big brothers and big sisters, numbers also belong to a family. This family of numbers is made up of the smallest, which is 1, and the largest, which is 5.' | • blackboard<br>• chalk |

| Content | Method | Teaching materials |
|---|---|---|
| Using objects to learn about how big numbers are made of smaller numbers (1) | • Have the children form a semicircle and sit down. Place a bowl in the centre of the semicircle and fill the bowl with five beads.<br>• Ask the children to count the number of beads in the bowl. Once the children correctly answer the question, use the chalk to draw a circle on the floor. Place the five beads in the circle and write '5 beads' under the circle.<br>• Ask the children: 'What is the smallest number of beads in this circle?'<br>• The children should answer 'one'. Once they do, have a child remove a bead from the circle and place it on the floor. Draw another circle around this bead. There should now be two circles—one containing four beads, the other containing one bead:<br>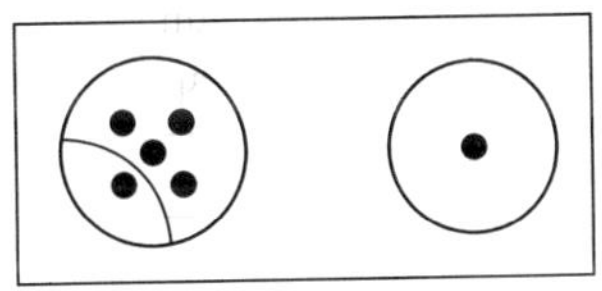<br>• Point at the circle containing one bead and ask the children: 'Where did this bead come from?' | • bowl<br>• chalk<br>• beads |

| Content | Method | Teaching materials |
|---|---|---|
| (continued) | • Once the children correctly answer the question, emphasise that the bead came from the circle which contained '5 beads'. Using the comparison of family, you could say: 'This one bead belongs to the family of 5 beads. In that family, it is the smallest number.'<br>• Ask the child to return the bead to the circle called '5 beads'. | |
| Using objects to learn about how big numbers are made of smaller numbers (2) | • Following the above activity, ask the children to name the number which is slightly larger than 1.<br>• Once the children answer with the number 'two', ask them if 'two' is in the circle of 5 beads.<br>• Have a child remove two beads from the circle of 5 beads and place them in the empty circle. Now ask them: 'How many beads are in the new circle?' The children should answer 'two'.<br>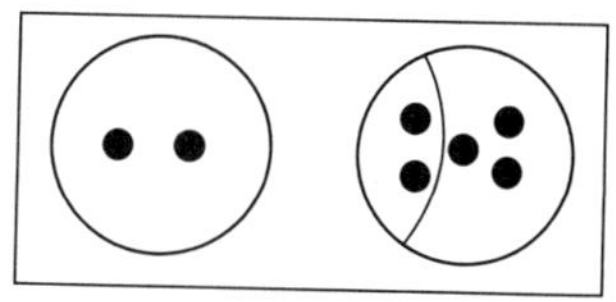<br>• Point at the circle containing two beads and ask the children: 'Where did the two beads come from?' | • bowl<br>• chalk<br>• beads |

| Content | Method | Teaching materials |
|---|---|---|
| (continued) | • Once the children correctly answer the question, emphasise that the beads came from the circle which contained '5 beads'. Using the comparison of family, you could say: 'The two beads also belong to the family of 5 beads.'<br>• Ask the child to return the beads to the circle called '5 beads'. | |
| Using objects to learn about how big numbers are made of smaller numbers (3 and 4) | • Repeat the above activity, only this time increase the numbers from two to three, and after that, three to four.<br>• The children must understand that in addition to '1' and '2', '3' and '4' also belong to the family of '5'.<br>• The children must also understand that the big number of '5' is made of the smaller numbers '1', '2', '3' and '4'. This can be explained by drawing the following on a blackboard:<br>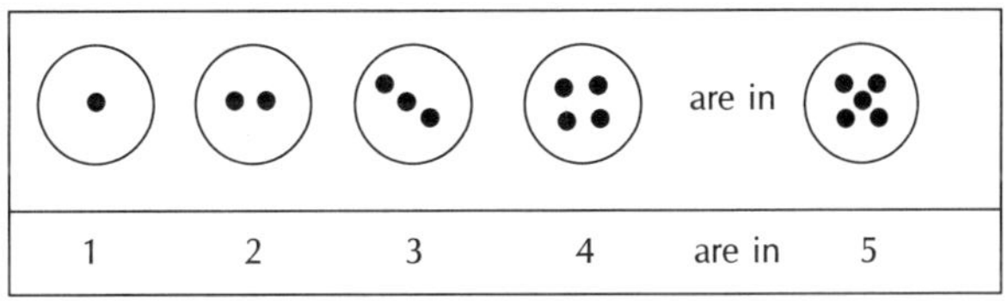 | • bowl<br>• chalk<br>• beads<br>• blackboard |

| Content | Method | Teaching materials |
|---|---|---|
| Chart on numbers | Prepare a chart which illustrates the information the children have learnt. The chart could look like this:<br>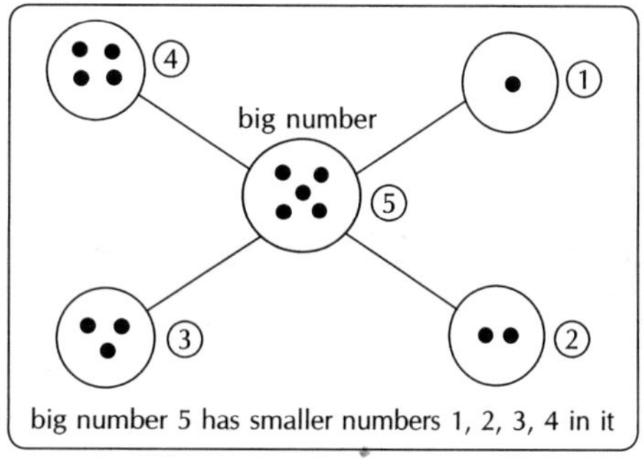<br> | • chart paper<br>• pencils<br>• soft board<br>• board pins |
| Groupwork #1 (using objects to learn about how big numbers are made of smaller numbers) | • Divide the class into groups of five.<br>• Each group gets five objects in a bowl. The objects should vary from group to group. For example:<br>Group 1: 5 seeds<br>Group 2: 5 stones<br>Group 3: 5 beads<br>Group 4: 5 buttons<br>Group 5: 5 shells<br>• Allow the children time to count the number of objects they have. | • bowls<br>• seeds<br>• stones<br>• beads<br>• buttons<br>• shells<br>• other objects of your choice |

| Content | Method | Teaching materials |
|---|---|---|
| (continued) | • Ask the children to remove objects from their group, beginning with the smallest number (1). As they remove an object, remind them that one comes from the larger number of five. Let them place the object back inside the bowl.<br>• Have them repeat the above step, this time removing two objects from the group of five. They should acknowledge that two comes from the larger number of five.<br>• Have them repeat the above step, this time removing three objects, then four objects.<br>• After completing the activity, each child gets the opportunity to tell the class that the small numbers '1', '2', '3' and '4' are in the big number '5'. | |
| Groupwork #2 (using objects to learn about how big numbers are made of smaller numbers) | • If their interest levels remain high, have the children repeat the above activity, only this time, reduce the number of objects in the group to 4.<br>• The children learn that the small numbers '1', '2', and '3' are in the big number '4'.<br>• Repeat the activity with the number of objects in the group reduced to 3. The children learn that the small numbers '1' and '2' are in the big number '3'.<br>• Repeat the activity with the number of objects in the group reduced to 2. The children learn that the smallest number '1' is in the big number '2'. | • bowls<br>• seeds<br>• stones<br>• beads<br>• buttons<br>• shells<br>• other objects of your choice |

<table>
<tr><th>Content</th><th>Method</th><th>Teaching materials</th></tr>
<tr><td>Charts on numbers</td><td>Prepare charts which illustrate the information the children have learnt. The chart could look like the following samples:<br>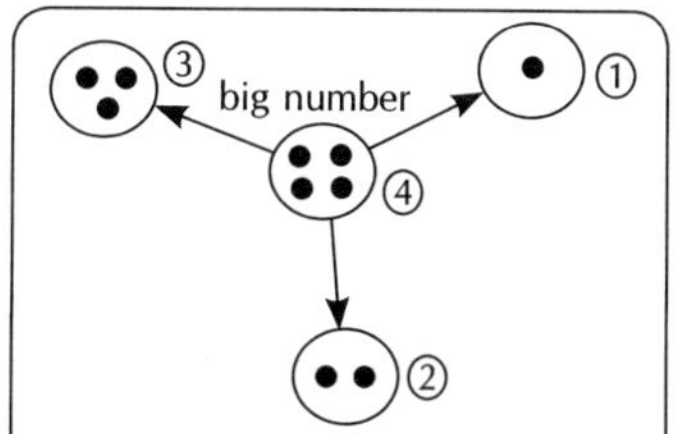<br><br>The big number 4 has small numbers 1, 2, 3 in it<br>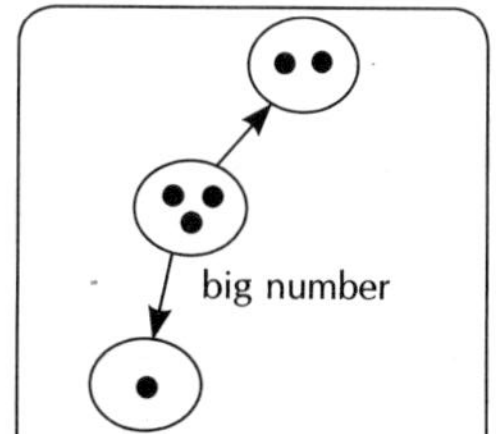<br><br>The big number 3 has small numbers 1, and 2 in it<br>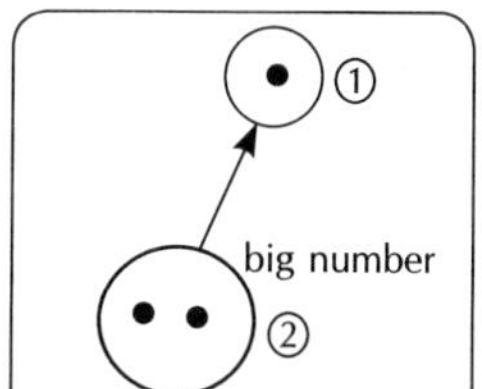<br><br>The big number 2 has small number 1 in it<br>Using the charts as a reference, the children can repeat the above activity using objects of their own choice. This way they learn that the concept is not limited to certain objects.</td><td>• chart paper<br>• pencils<br>• soft board<br>• board pins</td></tr>
</table>

| Content | Method | Teaching materials |
|---|---|---|
| Game | • Divide the class into groups of five. Each group should stand in a circle.<br>• One of the children becomes the leader. She must call out a number between 1 to 5. If she calls out '4', then the other four children must step outside the circle and say, 'We are 4. We are from the group of 5.'<br>• The game continues with the leader calling out different numbers.<br>• The game can be changed so that the size of the group is reduced to 4, 3 or 2 children. | |
| Revision | • At this stage it is a good idea to cover the material the children have learnt. This can be done by discussing how small numbers are in big numbers.<br>• Ask the children questions which have already been covered in this lesson. For example, 'Children, what are the small numbers in the number 5?' and 'What are the small numbers in the number 4?' | |
| Splitting a big number into smaller numbers | • Distribute the chalk and tamarind seeds among the children. Make sure each child has a piece of chalk and 5 seeds.<br>• Ask the children how many seeds they each have. They should answer 'five'. | • bowl<br>• tamarind seeds (or beads)<br>• chalk |

<table>
<tr><th>Content</th><th>Method</th><th>Teaching materials</th></tr>
<tr><td>(continued)</td><td>

- Now ask the children to draw two circles on the floor and label them 'Circle A' and 'Circle B'.
- The children must now take their seeds and divide them into two groups. One group goes into Circle A, and the other group into Circle B.
- It is possible the children may find it difficult to understand the instructions and may be confused. Take care to help them understand what they need to do.
- Once the children have completed the task, go round the classroom and ask each child what they have done. The children should explain how many seeds they have put in Circle A, and how many seeds they put in Circle B.

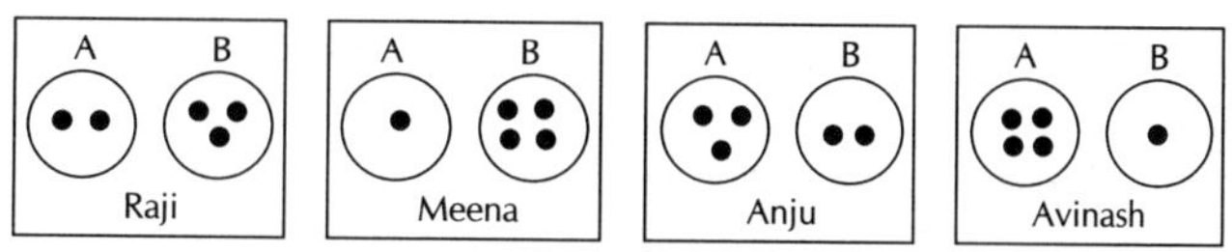


- In the above example, Raji should say 'From the 5 seeds I have put 2 in A and 3 in B.' Meena should say, 'From the 5 seeds I have put 1 in A and 4 in B.' Anju should say, 'I have put 3 in A and 2 in B.' And Avinash should say 'I have put 4 in A and 1 in B.'

</td><td></td></tr>
</table>

| Content | Method | Teaching materials |
|---|---|---|
| Combining small numbers to form a big number | • After completing the above activity, write down the results on a blackboard. If we use the example already provided, then the following should be on the blackboard: 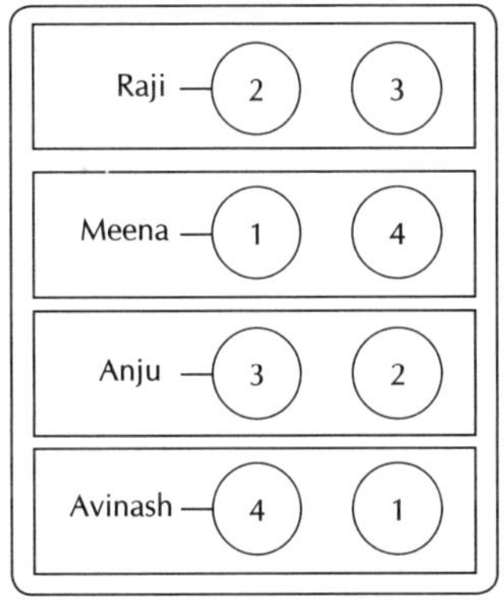  • Now ask the children to combine their numbers. This can be done by asking them, 'Where did you get these two numbers from?' The children should answer, 'From the bowl of 5 seeds.' • Have the children collect the seeds from their two circles and place the seeds back inside the bowl. Now ask them 'How many seeds do you have in the bowl?' | • blackboard<br>• chalk |

| Content | Method | Teaching materials |
|---|---|---|
| (continued) | • Explain that when you put together the seeds from Circle A and Circle B, you get the number 5. It is important to explain that no matter the combination (2 and 3, 1 and 4, 3 and 2, 4 and 1), when the seeds from circles A and B are put together you get 5. | |
| Splitting a big number into smaller numbers and combining small numbers into big numbers | • Allow the children the time and space to repeat the above activities, this time using different types of objects.<br>• As they grow familiar with the concepts they are learning, reduce the number of objects in the bowl to 4 and 3.<br>• While teaching these lessons, remember to not make them very formal. The children should enjoy themselves. Let it be a game without diluting the concepts that are being taught. | • bowl<br>• objects (the children may choose their own objects)<br>• blackboard<br>• chalk |

It was interesting to observe how much the children enjoyed this process of splitting a group into smaller groups, then combining these smaller groups to reform the original group. Once, a girl in our nursery woke her mother in the middle of the night and asked, 'Mama, 4 and 1 put together is 5?' Her mother said, 'Yes'. After some time she woke her mother again and asked, 'Mama, 3 and 2 put together is also 5?' Her mother said, 'Yes'. After some time she once again woke her mother and said, 'Mama, 2 and 2 and 1 put together is also 5?' Her mother, tired of being woken up so many times, said, 'Yes, now go to sleep.' The girl said, 'But 1 and 1 and 1 and 2 put together is also 5?' Her mother told her to go to sleep, and when she next met me told me that her child kept on disturbing her sleep. 'What a pest!' she said. 'She kept waking me up to make sure the numbers added up to 5. What did you teach her?'

# 31
# Addition

| Content | Method | Teaching materials |
|---|---|---|
| Introducing the concept of addition through the word 'join' | • Recap material covered in the previous lesson so that the children remember small numbers put together make a big number.<br>• Have the children sit in a semicircle. Place the bowl in the centre of the semicircle and pour 5 beads into the bowl.<br>• Ask a child to take the beads from the bowl and split them into two groups. Once this is done, ask another child to count the number of beads in each group.<br>• If, for example, there are 4 in one group and 1 in the other, explain that 4 and 1 are the small numbers from the big number 5.<br>• Take all the beads and place them back in the bowl. Explain that if you 'join' 4 and 1, then you get 5. Write this on the board.<br>• Ask another child to take the beads from the bowl and split them into two groups.<br>• If, for example, there are 3 in one group and 2 in the other, explain that 3 and 2 are the small numbers from the big number 5.<br>• Take all the beads and place them back in the bowl. Explain that if you 'join' 3 and 2, then your get 5. Write this on the board. | • 5 beads<br>• bowl<br>• blackboard<br>• chalk |

| Content | Method | Teaching materials |
|---|---|---|
| Using the word 'join' | • At the end of the previous activity, the results should be written on the blackboard. They may look like this:'If you join 4 with 1, you get 5', or '3 joined with 2 is 5'.<br>• The children should read these lines together and by themselves. It is important they grow familiar with the word 'join' and what it means. | |
| Introducing the mathematical word and symbol for 'joining' numbers (plus/+) | • Recap the concept of numbers having names and symbols. This could be done by recapping how the word 'one' and numeral '1' represent one object, just as 'two' and '2' represent two objects, and so on.<br>• Building on that point, explain how there is a name and a symbol for 'joining' numbers. The symbol for joining numbers is '+', and the name of the symbol is 'plus'.<br>• Under the lines on the blackboard which explained how 'If you join 4 with 1, you get 5' and '3 joined with 2 is 5', write '4 + 1 is 5' and '3 + 2 is 5'.<br>• Have the children practice saying the lines out loud. They should understand that '+' means 'plus' and that both the symbol and word mean 'to join'. This could be done by asking 'What does "plus" mean?' and 'What is the symbol for plus?' | • blackboard<br>• chalk |

| Content | Method | Teaching materials |
|---|---|---|
| Practicing reading and writing the symbol '+' and saying the word 'plus' | • Have the children write down the lines on the blackboard: 4 + 1 is 5, 3 + 2 is 5.<br>• They should read out the lines. Each time they say the word 'plus', they should touch the symbol '+' in their exercise books. This will help them associate the word with the symbol. | • exercise books<br>• pencils |
| Activity #1 | • Each child should be given 5 beads.<br>• Ask them to split their 5 beads into two groups.<br>• They must then write down how the two groups, when joined equal 5. This may be written as follows:<br>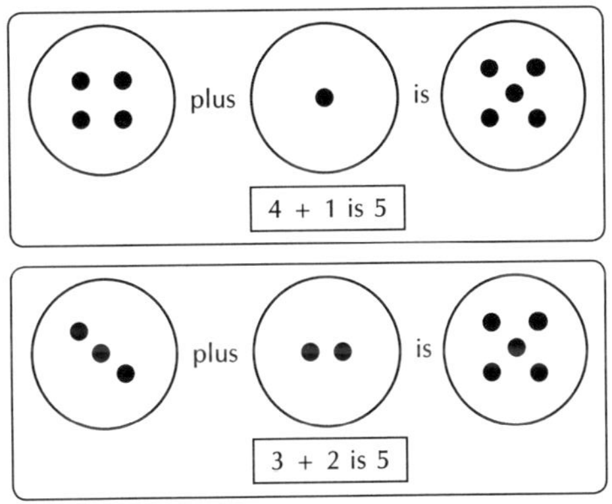<br><br>• The children must use the symbol '+' to show how the two groups, when added together, form the number 5. | • beads<br>• exercise books<br>• pencils |

| Content | Method | Teaching materials |
|---|---|---|
| Chart | • Create a chart which displays the following information:<br><u>What is 5?</u><br>*4 + 1 is 5*<br>*4 plus 1 is 5*<br>*3 + 2 is 5*<br>*3 plus 2 is 5*<br>*2 + 3 is 5*<br>*2 plus 3 is 5*<br>*1 + 4 is 5*<br>*1 plus 4 is 5*<br>• Pin the chart to a soft board in the classroom.<br>• Encourage the children to read the chart in their free time. | • chart paper<br>• pencils<br>• soft board<br>• board pins |
| Repeating Activity #1 (but reducing the number of beads so the children learn about the numbers 4, 3 and 2) | • Now that the children understand 5 is made up of 4 + 1, or 3 + 2, or 2 + 3, or 1 + 4, have the children repeat Activity #1, but this time reduce the number of beads each child receives to 4.<br>• Just as they learnt that 5 is made up of a combination of smaller numbers added together, they should learn that 4 is made up of 3 + 1, or 2 + 2, or 1 + 3. | • beads<br>• exercise books<br>• pencils<br>• chart paper<br>• soft board<br>• board pins |

| Content | Method | Teaching materials |
| --- | --- | --- |
| (continued) | • Have the children Repeat Activity #1 but this time reduce the number of beads each child receives to 3, then 2.<br>• As was done for the number 5, prepare charts for the numbers 4, 3, and 2. These charts should display the following information:<br><u>What is 4?</u><br>*3 + 1 is 4*<br>*2 plus 2 is 4*<br>*1 + 3 is 4*<br>and<br><u>What is 3?</u><br>*2 plus 1 is 3*<br>*1 + 2 is 3*<br>and<br><u>What is 2?</u><br>*1 plus 1 is 2*<br>• Pin the charts to a soft board in the classroom.<br>• Encourage the children to read the lines in their free time. | |

| Content | Method | Teaching materials |
|---|---|---|
| Recapping material covered | • Recap all the material discussed so far in the lesson.<br>• It is important the children learn with understanding and do not mechanically learn things by heart. Repeat activities where necessary and use different objects or smaller groups to help the children fully grasp the concepts. | |
| Using learning cards to understand addition | • Prepare learning cards. The front of each card should have a sum printed on it, like '4+1' or '2+2'. The back of each card should have the answer to the sum.<br>• Have the children sit in groups. Select a leader and provide the leader with the learning cards.<br>• The leader must show the sum on the front of the card to the other children, and the other children must try to solve the sum.<br>• If the children are unable to correctly solve the sum, the leader must show them the back of the card.<br>• At the end of the activity, the children should go through the learning cards, paying special attention to those sums they incorrectly answered.<br>• Though this is a group activity, children can use the learning cards to practice solving sums by themselves. | • set of learning cards (the front should have a sum, like 4+1, and the back should have the answer) |

| Content | Method | Teaching materials |
| --- | --- | --- |
| Adding more than two numbers | • At this point some of the children realise they can add more than two groups of numbers to form a big number.<br>• Use beads to demonstrate the following:<br>*1+2+2 is 5*<br>*1+1+1+2 is 5*<br>*3+1+1 is 5*<br>• Encourage the children to explore the ways in which small numbers can be added to form a big number.<br>• Encourage the children to use different types of objects, like seeds, beads, buttons, bottle lids, erasers, shells, objects cards, etc. when they learn to add. | • beads |
| Activity #2 (Using the phrase 'same-same' and introducing the mathematical word and symbol for 'same-same' (equals/=) | • Children are familiar with the phrase 'same-same'. They usually say it when matching objects.<br>• Use chalk to draw two large circles on the floor. Name the circles 'A' and 'B'.<br>• Have 5 children stand in circle A. Have the other children count the number of children in circle A.<br>• Have 3 children stand in circle B. Have the other children count the number of children in circle B. | • chalk<br>• blackboard |

| Content | Method | Teaching materials |
|---|---|---|
| (continued) | • Ask the children whether there are the same number of children in both circles.<br>• After the children answer the question (no), explain that circle A has 5 children and circle B has 3 children. How many children should 'join' B to make A and B 'same-same'?<br>• After the children answer the question (2), draw another large circle and name it 'C'. Ask two children to stand in circle C.<br>• Now ask the other children whether the number of children in B and C are the 'same' as A.<br>• Explain that when you use numbers, the word you use to say 'same' is 'equals', and the symbol you use for 'equals' is '='.<br>• Write the word and its symbol on the blackboard. | |
| Understanding the concept of 'equals' and the equals sign | • Have the children sit in a semicircle. Place the two bowls in the centre of the semicircle. Name one 'A' and one 'B'.<br>• Pour four beads into A and three beads into B. Ask the children if A and B are 'equal'.<br>• Help those who answer incorrectly. Then change the number of beads in A and B. For example, A could now contain 5 beads and B could contain 1. Ask them once again if A and B are equal. | • 2 bowls<br>• beads<br>• blackboard<br>• chalk |

| Content | Method | Teaching materials |
|---|---|---|
| (continued) | • Repeat this activity. Encourage the children to change the number of beads in A and B. They can try this in groups or by themselves. Do not be afraid to use other objects.<br>• Write on the blackboard the results of the activity (2 = 2, 3 = 3, 4 = 4, 5 = 5). | |
| Understanding the concept of 'equals' using wooden building blocks | • Stack 5 blocks one on top of the other.<br>• Stack 3 blocks next to the stack of 5.<br>• Ask the children to count the number of blocks in both stacks. Ask them if the two are equal. Ask them how many blocks need to be added to the smaller stack to make the two stacks equal.<br>• The children should answer '2'. Help those who answer incorrectly.<br>• Ask the children: 'What is the name for joining numbers?' (The children should answer 'plus')<br>• Ask the children: 'What is the sign for plus?' (The children should write in their exercise books '+')<br>• Summarise that 2 blocks need to join the stack of 3 blocks to be the same as the stack of 5 blocks. Therefore, 3 plus 2 is equal to 5, or 3 + 2 = 5.<br>• Allow the children to play with the wooden building blocks. Encourage them to repeat the activity and change the number of blocks in each stack. | • wooden building blocks<br>• exercise books<br>• pencils |

| Content | Method | Teaching materials |
| --- | --- | --- |
| Understanding the concept of 'equals' using a balance | • Have the children sit in a semicircle and place, in the centre of the semicircle, a balance. Explain how a balance is used to weigh objects.<br>• Take five 1kg weights and place them on one scale.<br>• Take four 1kg weights and place them on the other scale.<br>• Ask the children if the two weights are equal. Ask them how many kilograms need to be added to make them equal.<br>• Once the children understand how to use the scale, allow them to play with it and try to balance weights.<br>• The benefit of using a balance is that the children can see the concept of 'equals'. | • a simple balance for weighing objects<br>• weights |
| Charts | • To help the children understand the concept of 'equals', create charts—similar to those used when teaching the children 'plus/+'—which use the equals sign. For example:<br><u>What is 5?</u><br>*4* + *1* = *5*<br>*3* + *2* = *5*<br>*2* + *3* = *5*<br>*1* + *4* = *5*<br>• Pin the charts to a soft board and encourage the children to read them when they can. | • chart paper<br>• pencils<br>• soft board<br>• board pins |

| Content | Method | Teaching materials |
|---|---|---|
| Using learning cards to understand 'equals' and the arrangement of sums | • Provide the children with learning cards which they can use to individually practice addition.<br>• The learning cards should come in two types: one where the sum is horizontally arranged and one where the sum is vertically arranged.<br>$4 + 1 = 5$ and $\begin{array}{r} 4 \\ +\ 1 \\ \hline 5 \\ \hline \end{array}$<br>• The children might be confused by this new and unfamiliar arrangement of numbers. It is important to explain to them how to read the sums.<br>• Have the children use the learning cards to practice solving sums by themselves.<br>• If a child is struggling with the concepts, encourage the other children to help him understand. Monitor their progress, and if the child continues to struggle with the concepts, repeat the activities using different objects. | • set of learning cards (the front should have a sum, like 4+1, and the back should have the answer) |
| Tests | • Use the fresh set of learning cards to test the children's understanding of the concepts of addition and equals.<br>• In addition to the learning cards, ask other questions like: What is 5? What is 4? What is 3? What is 2?<br>• Record the results of the tests in your book of observations. These records are important as they will allow you to keep track of the each child's progress. | • learning cards (a fresh set used only for tests) |

## Worksheets

To strengthen their understanding of the concepts discussed in this lesson, the children should practice solving plenty of sums. Sums should be written in both horizontal and vertical arrangement. With enough practice, the children should be able to solve these types of questions with ease.

It is also important to have the children practice solving questions without counting or using objects. This can be done by calling out a sum ('How much does 4 + 1 equal?') and asking a child to answer the question.

Sample questions from a worksheet have been provided below:

Solve the following:

<table>
<tr><td rowspan="3">2 +</td><td>3 =</td></tr>
<tr><td>1 =</td></tr>
<tr><td>2 =</td></tr>
</table>

Matching: *Match the sums in column A with the answers in column B.*

| A | B |
|---|---|
| 2 + 1 | 5 |
| 3 + 2 | 4 |
| 2 + 2 | 3 |
| 1 + 1 | 2 |

Multiple-choice questions: *Which of the sums equals 5?*

a. 3 + 1
b. 2 + 2
c. 1 + 2
d. 1 + 4

Statement sums: Read out statement sums and ask the children to write down the answers in their books. Examples include:

1. *I have 3 marbles. My sister gave me 2 more. How many marbles do I now have?*
2. *There are 3 boys in our group. 1 new boy joined our group. How many boys are now in our group?*
1. *Our score was 1 point. Then Rahul scored 2 more points. What is our score now?*

# 32

# Subtraction

| Content | Method | Teaching materials |
|---|---|---|
| Recapping addition | Before beginning the lesson on subtraction, it is a good idea to quickly recap the material covered in the previous lesson. This could be done by asking the following set of questions:<br>• What is the name of the word used for 'joining' numbers?<br>• Write the symbol used for the plus sign.<br>• What is the name of the word used to say two numbers are 'same-same'?<br>• Write the symbol used for the equals sign.<br>• Provide examples of numbers which are equal.<br>• Are 5 and 3 equal? (use other numbers as well for practice)<br>• How do you make 5 and 3 equal?<br>• Write down how you would make 5 and 3 equal. | |
| Introducing the term 'take away' | • Using the chalk, draw a circle on the floor. Place 5 beads in the circle.<br>• Ask the children to count the number of beads in the circle. | • chalk<br>• beads<br>• blackboard |

| Content | Method | Teaching materials |
|---|---|---|
| (continued) | • Explain to the children that you will now 'take away' two beads from the circle. Remove two beads from the circle.<br>• Ask the children to count the number of beads remaining in the circle.<br>• After the children correctly answer the question, write on the blackboard: 'If you take away 3 from 5, you get 2' or '3 taken away from 5 is 2'. | |
| Game #1 (playing 'take away' with 5 beads) | • Provide each child with a stick of chalk and 5 beads.<br>• Encourage the children to repeat the above activity.<br>• Every time they remove beads from the circle, they should say what they have done, using the term 'take away'. For example, 'I take away 2 beads from 5.' | • chalk<br>• beads |
| Game #2 (playing 'take away' with 4, 3 and 2 beads | • Have the children repeat the above game, only this time provide each child with 4 beads, then 3 beads, then 2 beads. | • chalk<br>• beads |
| Introducing the mathematical name and symbol for the term 'take away' (minus/-) | • The children already know that there is a name and symbol for 'joining' numbers (plus/+), and that there is a name and symbol for numbers that are the 'same-same' (equals/=).<br>• Building on that point, explain that there is a name and symbol for 'taking away' numbers. The name is 'minus' and the symbol is '-'. This can be done by drawing the plus sign on a blackboard and comparing it to a cross. | • blackboard<br>• chalk |

| Content | Method | Teaching materials |
| --- | --- | --- |
| (continued) | Explain that there are two lines—a 'standing' line and a 'sleeping' line. Ask the children to draw the cross without the 'standing' line. The 'sleeping' line which they draw is the minus sign. Explain that the minus sign means 'to take away'. | |
| Using the word 'minus' and the minus sign | • Draw a circle on the floor and place 5 beads inside the circle.<br>• Remove 2 beads from the circle. Ask the children what happens if you 'take away' 2 beads from the 5 beads in the circle. How many beads are left in the circle?<br>• After the children have correctly answered the question, write on the blackboard: 'If you take away 2 from 5, you get 3' or '2 taken away from 5 is 3'.<br>• Under that line, write the sum: $5 - 2 = 3$.<br>• It is important that the children understand the minus sign means 'take away'.<br>• Place the beads back inside the circle and allow the children time to 'take away' beads. Write the results of their activity on the blackboard.<br>• Have the children practice saying the lines out loud. They should understand that '-' means 'minus' and that both the symbol and word mean 'to take away'. This could be done by asking 'What does "minus" mean?' and 'What is the symbol for minus?' | • chalk<br>• beads<br>• blackboard |

| Content | Method | Teaching materials |
|---|---|---|
| Practicing reading and writing the symbol '-' and saying the word 'minus' | • After the above activities, have the children write down the lines on the blackboard.<br>• They should read out the lines. Each time they say the word 'minus', they should touch the symbol '-' in their exercise books. This will help them associate the word with the symbol. | • exercise books<br>• pencils |
| Chart | • Create a chart which displays the following information:<br>*If you take away 4 from 5, you get 1*<br>*5 – 4 = 1*<br>*If you take away 3 from 5, you get 2*<br>*5 – 3 = 2*<br>*If you take away 2 from 5, you get 3*<br>*5 – 2 = 3*<br>*If you take away 1 from 5, you get 4*<br>*5 – 1 = 4*<br>• Pin the chart to a soft board in the classroom.<br>• Encourage the children to read the charts in their free time. | • chart paper<br>• pencils<br>• soft board<br>• board pins |
| Charts | • As was done for the number 5, prepare charts which show what happens when you subtract numbers from 4, 3, and 2.<br>• Pin the charts to a soft board in the classroom.<br>• Encourage the children to read the charts in their free time. | • chart paper<br>• pencils<br>• soft board<br>• board pins |

| Content | Method | Teaching materials |
|---|---|---|
| Activity #1 (using learning cards to understand subtraction) | • Prepare learning cards. The front of each card should have a sum printed on it, like '5-1' or '3-2'. The back of each card should have the answer to the sum.<br>• Have the children sit in groups. Select a leader and provide the leader with the learning cards.<br>• The leader must show the sum on the front of the card to the other children, and the other children must try to solve the sum.<br>• If the children are unable to correctly solve the sum, the leader must show them the back of the card.<br>• At the end of the activity, the children should go through the learning cards, paying special attention to those sums they incorrectly answered.<br>• Though this is a group activity, children can use the learning cards to practice solving sums by themselves. | • set of learning cards (the front should have a sum, like 5-1, and the back should have the answer) |
| Game #3 (playing Sit/Stand to understand subtraction) | • Have 5 children stand in a circle. The other children must watch to learn how to play.<br>• Explain that when you say 'sit', the children must sit, and when you say 'stand', the children must stand. If a child stands when they are supposed to sit, then that child is out. Practice playing the game until the children are comfortable with the rules. | |

| Content | Method | Teaching materials |
|---|---|---|
| (continued) | • Play the game, saying 'sit' or 'stand' in no particular order. You could say 'Sit, sit, sit, sit, stand.' When the children make a mistake, ask the other children to count the total number of children in the group, and the number being 'taken away' from the group. So, for example, if 2 children make a mistake, the other children should say '5 are in the group. 2 are taken away. 3 are left.'<br>• The children should write down these sums:<br>$5 - 2 = 3$.<br>• Once the children understand how to play the game, split the class into groups of 6, with 5 standing in a circle and 1 as the leader. | |
| Activity #2 (matching problem and answer cards) | • Have the children sit in a circle and give half the children the problem cards.<br>• Explain that the problem cards have sums on one side, but no answers on the other side.<br>• Give the remaining half of the children the answer cards.<br>• Explain that the answer cards have the answers to the problem cards.<br>• A child who has a problem card should begin the game by placing the problem card face up in the centre of the circle. | • set of problem cards (each card has a sum on one side, but no answer)<br>• matching set of answer cards (each card has an answer on one side, but no sum) |

| Content | Method | Teaching materials |
|---|---|---|
| | • Now the children with the answer cards must see if the number on their card holds the answer to the problem card. So, for example, if the problem card is '5 – 1', then the child with the answer card '4' must place the answer card next to the problem card.<br>• The game continues until all the cards are matched.<br>5 – 4   5 – 1   4 – 2   4 – 1<br>= 1   = 4   = 2   = 3 | |
| Songs | • Prepare illustrated charts which show the lines to a song about subtraction.<br>• Pin the charts to the soft board so that the children can read the lines and sing the song.<br>• Examples of songs which could be used to teach the children about subtraction include '5 Little Ducks' and '5 Green Bottles'. | • chart paper<br>• pencils<br>• soft board<br>• board pins |
| Recapping material covered | • Recap all the material discussed so far in the lesson.<br>• It is important the children learn with understanding and do not mechanically learn things by heart. Repeat activities where necessary and use different objects or smaller groups to help the children fully grasp the concepts. | |

# Worksheets

To strengthen their understanding of the concepts discussed in this lesson, the children should practice solving plenty of sums. Sums should be written in both horizontal and vertical arrangement. With enough practice, the children should be able to solve these types of questions with ease.

It is also important to have the children practice solving questions without counting or using objects. This can be done by calling out a sum ('How much does 4–1 equal?') and asking a child to answer the question.

Sample questions from a worksheet have been provided below:

Solve the following:

| | |
|---|---|
| 5 – | 3 = |
| | 1 = |
| | 2 = |

Matching: *Match the sums in column A with the answers in column B.*

| A | B |
|---|---|
| 3 – 1 | 1 |
| 5 – 2 | 4 |
| 5 – 1 | 3 |
| 3 – 2 | 2 |

Multiple-choice questions: *Which of the sums equals 1?*

a. 3–1
b. 4–2
c. 2–1
d. 5–3

Statement sums: Read out statement sums and ask the children to write down the answers in their books. Examples include:

1. *I have 5 pencils. I give 2 to Sunil. How many pencils do I have now?*
2. *I have 3 sweets. I gave away 1 to my friend. How many sweets do I have now?*
3. *There were 4 eggs in a basket. Two eggs had gone bad. How many eggs were good?*

# 33

# Conclusion

Teaching is a creative art. As is learning. Words cannot accurately describe the sense of joy, contentment and achievement a teacher experiences when she succeeds in providing the right environment for the children in her care, thereby allowing them to gradually develop their own bright and unique personalities.

Still, teaching is no bed of roses. There are plenty of hardships, seemingly impossible obstacles, disappointments and failures to overcome. When I speak with teachers, they often share with me frustrating or depressing stories about the difficulties they face in the classroom. They worry that important educational values all seem to be at stake. It is impossible to brush away the reality of such problems.

In the early years of my teaching I too faced many exasperating situations because I did not understand the children and their motivations. One thing I learnt was, as a teacher, I should not be quick to judge. It is easy yet irresponsible to dismiss a child as lazy, selfish, jealous, aggressive, intelligent, etc. Instead of passing judgment, I learnt to ask myself questions like: Why is the child behaving like this? What is he trying to tell me through his behaviour? How should I respond?

Remember, all children have the intention and willingness to shape themselves into good human beings. They are searching for guidance.

We teachers must act with intent. We must try to understand the children in our care and generously give them the love, security, compassion and firmness they require to grow into positive, loving, contributing members of society.

This is the ideal I believed in as a teacher, and it is what I have tried to share in this book.

# Nadya's Outline

**"Outline"**

**Plan Used for Observing and Recording Certain Aspects of Growth in Children from 3–5 years.**

**A Tentative Hypothesis.**

Nadya Ornstein,
65 W. 68th St.,
New York City,
(Formerly of the Walden School)

Growth in relation to the Freudian conception of the libido during childhood (through 5th year).

What indications are given in the child's behaviour to bear out this Freudian hypothesis?

<u>Thesis</u> (Tentative)—Impressions gathered from observation

1. That personality growth is dependent on emotional liberation (If one first eliminates organic hindrances which obviously retard the growth of the human organism.)
2. The correlated manifestations of this growth may be observed in all activities in which the child engages. They give a clear indication of the developmental phase at which he is. Be these activities in relation to people, big or little, or in relation to the content of his play, or the things he fashions for play purposes out of raw materials.
3. That growth through these first five or six years of life should carry the child successfully to a more complete feeling of self, find him ready

to wean himself further from the family ties, and to find love objects in friends among his contemporaries. His sense of independence from the adult becomes marked at the close of this period.

During this period there are three distinct phases of emotional development, and characteristic expressions of them, as outlined by Freud, that is, Oral, Anal, Genital.

At each phase these is an experience of pleasure. This pleasure is incorporated into an accumulating feeling of self, depending upon the success of outgrowing each phase. The deprivation suffered as a result of relinquishing the pleasure of each stage should not be so great as to block the natural strivings of the organism to reach the next pleasurable phase.

(It is at these points that the work of education is essential.)

Nor should there be uncompensated deprivation of frustration. Growth experiences that are successful are accompanied by and lead to pleasure.

4. That definite signs mark the successful growth at the close of each phase and of this whole period. And that these same signs usher in a period of adolescence, marked with the same intensity of emotion experienced at this early period, which it so closely resembles. These are:
   a. A sense of the body and ease in handling it, with a correspondingly greater mastery of the outer world and a sense of greater safety in it.
   b. Active inquiry into the workings of this outer world and the beginning of a sense of the inter-relationships of activity in it. A grasp of cause and effect.
   c. A sense of I-Myself, and a sense of the other fellow. Via the earlier attachments to parents, the teacher as parent substitute, and finally another child as a "best friend". At this time children begin to forego

personal gratification because, "I love you, you're my best friend."

5. That definite phantasies, or myth-like fabrications, show the strivings of the individual during the three phases at this period. These phases are not clearly marked as beginning here and ending there, but tend to overlap and shade into each other, until the preceding phase is somewhat resolved, and the newer phase entered upon. There are carry-overs from earlier experiences in an attempt to explain the nature of the newer awareness in terms of previous gratification. This overlapping tends to express itself in what often looks like a pull-back to an earlier, more infantile phase, whenever a new spurt forward takes place. It gives the effect in behaviour of a rather pendulum-like movement in progression; or to use another figure—"two steps forward and one step backward". This, I believe, often accounts for repetitions of pattern in the things children create, other than the verbal phantasies—in clay, paints, wood, blocks—and in the relationship plays and games with other children.
6. That there are definite worries, anxieties and fears accompanying each phase and definite hurdles to be taken on the way to growth. That when the psychic energy has been successfully spent in overcoming them, this energy is then freed for active inquiry into the world of people and things. He becomes concerned with the aspects of objective reality. The personal and subjective is on the wane. He begins to be an active "social" creature.

Plan Used for Observation and Recording with 3- to 5-year-olds

1. Play Content
   a. How much is concerned with:
      i. Reproduction of family situations. (These plays give a rather clear

picture of the child in relation to his home group.)

ii. Reproduction of workday situations.

iii. Sexual curiosity (Interest in genitals. Castration games and magic.)

iv. Functions of eating and elimination.

b. Element of identification and projection in play.

i. With adults at home and at school.

ii. With other children.

iii. With animals (elephants, dogs, cats, etc.)

iv. Symbolic figures (soldiers, firemen, robbers, doctor, engines, boats, etc.)

v. Symbolism of the body and parts of the body.

vi. With toys and hugables (teddies, dolls, etc.)

c. Relationship plays and games.

i. Note the children involved at different periods, and the shifts in relationships.

NOTE: The subjective content: Is there an indication of an emotional level? When does the content which seems factual and concerned with things real, actually become stripped of subjective instinctual content under which it originally manifested itself? Can this chart a sublimating process which is normal to all children? That is, from subjective instinctual reality to objective factual reality. Can one find parallels at each phase of growth, i.e., mouth, excretory, genital? Then what are the common symbols and the usual end sublimations?

2. Materials

a. How they are used.

b. The child's motives and drives in the use of them.

i. Is there a sequence in development in the use of materials; i.e., from random movement, to experimentation, to conscious plan or definite patterns?

ii. Are certain materials used more frequently at two years and then tend to be supplanted by others; that is, liquids to semi-solids to solids? Or, to phrase it differently, from water and urine games to "mushing" with mixtures of water, paint and clay, to manual activity requiring mastery and skill.

iii. And does this shift in interest parallel the emotional phases of growth? Can the emotional phase be traced through this medium?

c. What is the child's standard?

d. What is the teacher's function?

NOTE: List the major activities with materials in the nursery groups, and questions which have arisen in my mind over the years.

A. *Water and Pipes*

This interest seems to centre around oral, anal and urethral activity. It seems to indicate the child's attitude toward wetting and soiling, toward training in habits of cleanliness, toward penis and lack of penis.

B. *Clay*

a. Note the development of forms at the different periods. Are there usual forms which one might call typical or common?

b. Development of individual patterns. The use of individual symbols. Do these change or become elaborated?

c. What is the meaning of the symbols for the child?

d. Smearing and "design" and "decorations".

C. *Paints and Drawings*

a. Has color a symbolic meaning for children?

b. Development of forms—(typical to all children.)

c. Development of individual patterns (elaborations and displacements.)
d. The meaning of pattern for the child (symbolism).
e. Are there usual forms which one might call typical or common?
f. When does objective reality, interest in things real, take the place of the deeper subjective reality in this medium?

D. *Woodwork*
a. Tools at different ages
b. Type of wood at different ages
c. Type of activity in relation to tools and wood
d. Type of things produced
e. The use of the thing produced. What light does this throw on the emotional phase, if any?
f. Are there typical forms?
g. When does the desire for accuracy in measurement and nailing appear? For things "real" vs. "pretend"? Manual dexterity in relation to masturbation.

E. *Blocks—Indoors and Roof*
a. Record the forms and content for subjective implications.
b. What are the problems in construction and thinking with which the child copes at each phase in this medium? (Harriet M Johnson used to ask this question, and the fruit of her observations were published in 1933, in "The Art of Block Buildings", #1 of the Co-operating School Pamphlets.)
c. Follow through relationships with other children. When shifts in relationships occur, is there any corresponding change in play or construction?
d. Follow the shift in content, from the deeper subjective reality to objective reality interests, although the content seems the same in both cases.

e. Beginnings of social sciences. Reproducing the workday world about him in this medium. His interest in the inter-relationship of peoples' work. (This seems to appear at a time when he is able to work in larger groups and when portions of a job are handled by individual members of the group; when a small group can work with relatively little friction on a common job over a fairly long stretch of time.)

F. *The Nature Study Experience*
   a. Types of animals which arouse love or fear
   b. Birthing experiences
   c. Planting and growing
   d. Things dying
   e. Cycles of growth
   f. Identifications

G. *Experiences with Fire, Steam, Electricity*
   a. Shift from subjective interest to a more "scientific" observation of the phenomena

H. *Musical experience and equipment*
   a. Release through body and sense of power.
   b. Pleasure of rhythm
   c. Children's chants, improvisations and patterned manifestations in <u>all</u> of a little child's activity

I. *Cooking*
   a. Phases of pretend and real
   b. Origins in mushing, "poisons", and devouring
   c. Anal and oral gratifications

3. <u>Fantasy</u>
   a. Manifestation in play (typical)
   b. Verbal:
      i. Conversations; note setting
      ii. Stories told by children (Adaptations of story material to their own use.)
      iii. Monologues at bed-time and eating-time

c. Dreams:
    i. Spontaneously given
    ii. Terror situations at home
    iii. Terror situations at school-time rest
d. Content of drawings, clay, wood, etc. (typical)
e. Songs and chants; note setting
f. Hugables: pet toys brought from home and used as bed-time comforts. "Something to hold."

NOTE: Is there a personal, individual myth which each child creates for himself, with himself as the central figure? What is its origin? Does this change with successive phases of development? Are these individual myths typical of all children at these phases? What are they?

NOTE: Meaning of symbols used by children. Do they parallel the symbolism of the adult unconscious? What relation do they bear to the myths and symbolism of primitive peoples? Let the material prove itself, if it can. Examine all products of the child from these angles as well.

4. <u>Curiosities and Interests Common to this Period</u>
    a. "So big". "so strong", "the biggest", "the first".
    b. Experimentation with parts of the body and the body as a whole. (symbolism of body and its parts.)
    c. Exploration of the immediate environment: things and people.
    d. Sexual differences.
        i. The wonder of "why" girls are without a penis.
        ii. The wonder of "why" the difference. (relation of penis to "hole"—and birth.)
        iii. The fears expressed both directly and in fantasy regarding this difference.

iv. The gradual change in attitude in the boy and the girl. (It seems to take the little girl longer to get over the pain of her lack.)

v. How children attempt to overcome their fears in this regard.

vi. Boys want to be girls and girls want to be boys.

e. Birth

i. "Where did I come from?"

ii. "Where did the <u>first</u> person come from?"

iii. Where do other things come from?" (This is the time when the thrust is into the world of objective reality. Seems to come after the mystery of birthing and differences of sexes is somewhat clarified.)

iv. How do things work? How are they made? How do they grow?

f. Death

NOTE: This interest seems to arise almost spontaneously with interest in birth and seems to be directly connected with point g below.)

i. The wish to never die.

ii. The wish to grow "big, big, big up to da sky—big as daddy", alongside the fear of daddy.

iii. Where things go to when they're dead or discarded. (Beginning of concern with more objective phenomena stripped of the personal, comes at the end of this period?)

g. Magic (interest in cause and effect)

i. Relation to masturbation (genital sensations, phallic symbolism for magical expression). The feelings of power and inadequacy.

ii. The relation to castration: Things off and things on again—"Now you see it, now you don't". (games)

iii. The use of the body substances for magical purposes—"spit", "pee", "bowel movement".

iv. The part of the body anointed with substance or the part of the body threatened with annihilation by contact with substance. (Games of dying and coming alive again.)

v. The attempt to control natural phenomena through magical power.

h. Animals

i. (See Nature Study)

ii. Element of identification—for what purposes

i. Origins (seems to usher in the reality phase at the close of this period.)

i. The relation to interest in scientific and factual concepts

ii. Relation to emotional phase—sublimations

j. Natural Phenomena

i. Wind, rain, evaporation, hail, snow, fog, fire, steam, smoke: and relation to an earlier subjective level of inquiry

NOTE: Setting in which these interests appear. The episode which seems to stimulate the activity or interest. The children or adults connected with experience, when it is a common enterprise. The backgrounds of those involves. The conversations and play material involved.

5. <u>Interests (individual)</u>

a. Types of activity engaged in

b. Preferences marked (relation to emotional phase?)

c. Shifts in interest (relation to emotional phase?)

d. Sensory and motor (include here development of "tricks" and games of skill; note periods in which this interest arises.)

6. <u>Experimentation with (group)</u>
    a. Materials
    b. Each other and adults
    c. Language—distortions and foreign languages Patterns (motive?)
    d. Music and rhythm (see Music)
        i. When this accompanies activity
        ii. When engaged in for sheer sensory pleasure it yields
        iii. Songs and chants (content—note setting)
        iv. Bed-time
7. <u>Friendships</u>
    a. Identifications among children and with adults
    b. Boy and girl relationships
        i. When they seem to separate and show antagonism
        ii. When positive
        iii. Standards which boys set for girls. Why?
    c. Shifts in relationships
        i. Relation to identifications and their resolution
        ii. As indication of emotional growth or bloc
        iii. Ambivalence
    d. The statement—"I love you, you're my best friend."

NOTE: The function of the teacher as parent substitute during this period in helping child to gradually wean himself from the adult ties of dependency. To seek other objects of love among his contemporaries. The ability of children to <u>begin</u> to accept deprivation for the sake of a loved person and a "best friend".

8. <u>Relationships to:</u>
    a. Family group
        i. From parents
        ii. From content of play

iii. From relation to children and adults at school

b. Teachers and children
   i. Love and hate(positive and negative behaviour.)
   ii. Aggression or lack of
   iii. Bids for attention and affection of inability to do so
   iv. Bids for punishment
   v. Expressions of love and hate
      - Gifts
      - Stealing
      - Terms of opprobrium: "vagina", "penis", "pee-pee", "bowels", "duty", etc.

NOTE: For teachers and children, time of occurrence and check with the home where possible.

9. <u>"Habits"</u>

a. Eating
   i. Special food dislikes
   ii. Are there common food dislikes and preferences?

NOTE: Food often is a symbol for something deeply subjective. Not always a simple conditioning. Often connected with the first oral weaning, the mother's sexual development—oral, anal and genital anxieties and confusions.

b. Defecation (is there a physical anal type?)
   i. Effects of too early training and its relationship to child's attitude towards messiness and cleanliness.
   ii. Anxieties in relation to bowel movements.
   iii. Confusions usual to little children between anal substance and male genital.
   iv. Confusions expressed in fantasy material regarding oral-anal birth theories.

v. Anal talk at meal time.

NOTE: Periods at which children begin to move bowels freely at school and its relation to child's emotional attachment to teacher. "Bowels" as gifts. "Bowels" as poisonous substance for hate expression—colour, brown, "bowel movement colour". (Brown, green, purple, grey.)

c. Urination
   i. Methods employed by girls in imitation of boys.
   ii. Bed-wetting and anxieties. Fear "to touch".
   iii. Water plays—play with urine. Tasting urine.
   iv. The colour of urine and the association to letter P. Relation to eating—yellow food, peas, etc.

d. Masturbation
   i. Substitutes (hugables, bed toy and fantasies)
   ii. Relation to handedness (manual skills)
   iii. Relation to castration anxieties and threats.
   iv. Relation to security.
   v. Relation to magic.

e. Thumb-sucking (physical type)
   i. Substitutes
   ii. Relation to security

f. Sleeping
   i. Terrors
   ii. Bad fantasies
   iii. Bed toys (hugables, etc.)
   iv. Why some children "can't close my eyes"
   v. The irregularity of mid-day rest
   vi. Gradual shortening of the rest span
   vii. The folly of insisting on "habit" for routine's sake

g. Dressing
   i. The breakdown of this habit (also eating, etc.) in "well-trained", "thoroughly independent" children.
   ii. The urge to be big and independent and little and dependent, side by side in the child as it grows. Its relationship to emotional status of the child.
   iii. Fatigue and off-days

NOTE: Difficulties, time of appearance, duration, disappearance for all "habits" listed. Bear in mind that a "good habit" or a "bad habit" may only be a symptom of a more fundamental disturbance. That it takes <u>time</u> to establish <u>sound</u> habits which make for emotional health. It is sometimes the wiser course to consciously side-track routine. It need not be harmful to a child to slip up on routine. It is the <u>emotional tone of the adult</u> in the situation which bears upon the child's psyche with deep impress.

10. <u>Individual difficulties and traits</u>
11. <u>Physique</u>
    a. Muscle tone
    b. Skin (colour, texture)
    c. Quality of the expression in the eyes
    d. Colour
    e. Posture
    f. Voice
    g. Co-ordination
    h. Gay or silent
12. <u>Accidents</u>
    a. Note the setting (people involved, the situation, etc.)
    b. Note the kinds
    c. Note the part of the body
    d. Note frequency in any given child and to any given part of body
    e. Possible relation to anxieties—self-punishment guilt

<u>List and Date if possible</u>

1. Stories told to the children
   a. Choices made by them
   b. Modifications made by them on those themes
2. Introduction of materials
   a. When, why, response of children
3. Introduction of information
   a. Books, pictures, facts
   b. When, why, response of children
4. Trips
   a. When, why, response of children
   b. How long after experience is the observation reproduced in play and speech?
   c. Is it reproduced as objective reality, or does it still show signs of a relation to subjective life?
5. Discussions
6. Appearance of interest—use of number
   a. Written symbol (clay and paintings)
   b. Weight, balance, measuring
7. Inventions
8. Group rules

# Bibliography


Axline, M. Virginia. *Play Therapy*. 1969. Ballantine Books, 1980.

Biber, Barbara. "A Dream for the Nursery Years." *69 Bank Street*, vol. 1, no. 3. Bank Street Publications, 1934.

---. "Nursery School as the Beginning of Education." *69 Bank Street*, vol. 2, no. 8. Bank Street Publications, 1936.

Black, Irma Simonton. *Off to a Good Start*. 1941. Harcourt, Brace & Company, 1946.

Cane, Florence. *The Artist in Each of Us*. Pantheon Books, 1951.

Freud, Sigmund. *Case Histories 1: Dora and Little Hans*. Translated by Alix and James Strachery. The Pelican Freud Library, vol. 8. Penguin Books, 1977.

Isaacs, Susan. *Intellectual Growth in Young Children*. 1930. Routledge & Kegan Paul, 1970.

Johnson, Harriet Merrill. *The Art of Block Building*. The John Day Company, 1933.

Margaret, K. T. *The Open Classroom*. Orient Blackswan Private Limited, 2012.

Mitchell, Gregory. "Sigmund Freud and Freudian Psychoanalysis." *Mind Development,* http://www.mind-development.eu/freud.html. Accessed 24 August 2017.

*Montessori in Perspective*. Edited by the National Association for the Education of Young Children (USA). *NAEYC Publication*, no. 406. National Association for the Education of Young Children, 1966.

Neill, A. S. *Summerhill*. 1960. Pelican Books, 1980.

Ornstein, Nadya. *"Outline" Plan Used for Observing and Recording Certain Aspects of Growth in Children from 3–5 Years: A Tentative Hypothesis.*

Skemp, Richard. *The Psychology of Learning Mathematics*. 1971. Penguin Books, 1977.

Skinner, Charles E. *Educational Psychology*. 1959. Prentice Hall of India Private Limited, 1974.

Spitalny, Terry. "Meeting Reality." *69 Bank Street*, vol. 3, no. 5., Bank Street Publications, 1937.